100 YEARS OF STANFORD MEN'S BASKETBALL

100 Years of Stanford Men's Basketball

Book and jacket design: Iain R. Morris
Editor: Mark Burstein
Copy editors: J. Matthew Huculak, Jan Hughes

All images courtesy of Stanford Athletics, except page seven of the color section: © Getty images

ISBN: 978-1-93735-88-1

Printed in the United States of America
10 9 8 7 6 5 4 3 2 1

Roundtree Press
6 Petaluma Blvd. North, Suite B-6
Petaluma, CA 94952

(707) 769 1617
www.roundtreepress.com

100 YEARS OF STANFORD MEN'S BASKETBALL

JOHN PLATZ

Roundtree Press

Contents

Introduction

One hundred years of doing *anything* is a big deal.

Making it to the century mark is not easy. Many governments, most corporations, and virtually all human beings fall short of reaching a hundredth birthday. So when something has lasted one hundred years, it is perfectly proper to pause for a moment to reflect upon and acknowledge the milestone.

Sometimes, however, a moment is not enough. When something—whether a person, organization or activity—has not only existed for a century but also has distinguished itself with a multitude of achievements during those hundred years, mere acknowledgment of the milestone seems insufficient. Commemorating should be added to the acknowledging.

Stanford University's men's basketball program—which, for convenience, we will reference with the phrase Stanford Basketball in these pages—completed its 100th season in 2014-15. That in itself is not a unique accomplishment; several college basketball programs had already crossed the century mark as of 2015. Is Stanford Basketball's 100 years of squeaking sneakers, smart screens, sweet jump shots, and solid stick-backs so special that a book should commemorate it?

The answer, in this author's mind, is yes.

Every school with a century-old college basketball program has a history. Some college basketball histories are more interesting than others, but every school's history has its high points—its great players, its special seasons, its memorable games. At most schools with 100 years of history or more, these special people and events are dutifully noted on the team's website or within the team's yearbook or other informational materials, but typically without much more fanfare than that.

But merely reciting or acknowledging history, in Stanford's case, is not enough. Stanford Basketball's achievements in its first century are many and span the full ten decades. No, Stanford is not one of those dozen or so schools that can boast of multiple NCAA Tournament championships. But Stanford does have an NCAA title, won in 1941-42. And in the period that precedes the birth of the NCAA Tournament in the late 1930s—that is, when there was no end-of-season event to determine the collegiate champion—Stanford was voted national champion one season and finished second in the voting another year. Three other times in its history, a Stanford Basketball team won the National Invitation Tournament (NIT) title. The school definitely is not wanting for basketball championships, if the full century and both the NIT and NCAA postseason tournaments are taken into account.

Championships, however, are only a part of the century-long Stanford Basketball story. Whether one's standard for a college basketball program's excellence is the whole of the 100-year period or just the most recent quarter century—the television-driven "March Madness" era in which the sport's popularity has reached unimaginable heights—Stanford Basketball has stood alongside, or at times even above, the very best. That is why this commemorative book is worthy of being written.

Examples? During the first half-century of the sport's existence, arguably the best player yet to play the sport—the Michael Jordan of the 1900-1950 period, if you will—was a Stanford Basketball player named Hank Luisetti, who led Stanford to landmark wins at places like Madison Square Garden in the 1930s. From the 1920s through the 1950s, Stanford's basketball rosters were dotted with nationally known athletes including Pro Football Hall of Famer Ernie Nevers, world-record-setting shot putter Harlow Rothert, NBA pioneer George Yardley, and 1956 U.S. Olympic Basketball team members Ron Tomsic and Jim Walsh, who played on the gold-medal-winning U.S. team. This book tells their stories and those of many other remarkable Stanford Basketball players through the decades.

As far as college basketball programs whose stars have shone most brightly during the March Madness era, Stanford Basketball surely stands among that group as well. Stanford was the nation's #1-ranked team for parts of three different seasons during the three decades that preceded the program's 100th anniversary. Stanford reached the Final Four once during that 1985-2015 period—in the magical 1997-98 season. Nine different Stanford players were named to All-America teams during that 30-year period: Brevin Knight, Adam Keefe, Mark Madsen, Todd Lichti, Casey Jacobsen, Jason Collins, Jarron Collins, Josh Childress, and Brook

Lopez, each of whom went on to play several seasons in the NBA. Even a Stanford coach during that period, Mike Montgomery, won a national Coach of the Year award. This book recounts these historically significant personalities and seasons.

I have had a better-than-a-bay-window seat to Stanford Basketball's history. Thanks to a Stanford head coach named Dr. Tom Davis, who chose to have a streak-shooting but mediocre-defending guard on his roster, I was a member of Stanford Basketball teams in the early 1980s. In part because of that experience, I became a member of Stanford's radio broadcast team in 1988, and by the 100th season in 2014-15, I had broadcast 26 seasons and nearly 800 games' worth of Stanford Basketball. Given the skewing of this book's coverage toward the latter one-third of Stanford's hundred-year history, most of this book's contents reflect my firsthand observations.

Thanks also to relationships developed with current and former Stanford players, coaches, broadcasters, and administrators, along with extensive access to historical periodicals that the Internet provides, I have been able to fill in the gaps and otherwise complete this book with an accuracy and spirit worthy of the Stanford Basketball program. I would like to call out a few of these helpful individuals in the next few paragraphs.

Former teammates of mine on the early 1980s Stanford teams—Keith Jones, Earl Koberlein, Dave Patzwald, and Kent Seymour—as well as successive Stanford radio colleagues—Bob Murphy, Dave Flemming, Drew Shiller, and Scott Reiss—are certainly a big reason my Stanford Basketball journey has been a rich one. I have been helped and educated, both as a player and broadcaster, by a number of prior Stanford Basketball coaches, including my own head coach Tom Davis, Montgomery–era assistant coaches Doug Oliver, Jeff Jackson, Eric Reveno, and Russell Turner, and finally the Johnny Dawkins–era assistant coaches Tim O'Toole, Charles Payne, and Mike Schrage, each of whose unique talents and passion for coaching college basketball are a delight to watch.

Stanford Athletics officials past and present have made my three-decade Stanford Basketball ride, including this book project, both enriching and a lot easier than it would have been without them. Special thanks, in this regard, go to Jeff LaMere, Bob Vazquez, Gary Migdol, Brian Risso, Alan George, and David Kiefer—the latter two of whom played a large role in facilitating provision of the many fine photographs contained herein. Among Stanford graduates or game-attenders (or both) who have recently or in the past provided inspiration, encouragement, or other form of enabling support for a book on this subject, the following deserve mention: Margaret Bang, Bryan Cameron, the late Greg Cox, Mel Froli, Doug Gamble, Bill Garrett, the late Sam Goldman, Professor William Gould, Ken and Karen Imatani, Tony Joseph, Doug Marty, Pete Ross, Steve and Karen Ross, and Jed Solomon. Finally, this book would not have been published without the insights and intervention of Stanford Senior Associate Athletic Director Kevin Blue, for whose efforts I am grateful, and the vision, talent, and efforts of the Cameron + Company team—specifically Chris Gruener, J. Matthew Huculak, Mark Burstein, and Iain R. Morris—to each of whom I hereby express my appreciation.

Three Stanford head coaches have provided the proper backdrop to enable me to put together this book. Former coach Mike Montgomery, whose 393 victories in 18 seasons remains Stanford Basketball's high-water mark, afforded me exceptional access to the program during his tenure on the Farm. Current TCU coach Trent Johnson, whose contributions as a Stanford head coach went far beyond his 20-wins-per-season average, shared many insights with me during his time on the Farm and remains a good friend. He reminds me of current Stanford football coach David Shaw in how much he loved pitching a high-level college education to recruits as well as in how zealous he was that his players always do the right thing, whether inside or outside the lines. Finally, Stanford's current head coach, Johnny Dawkins, has been the embodiment of what Stanford Basketball has always sought in its coaches: a fierce competitor, a terrific leader and teacher, an exemplar of focused effort and discipline, and—as many in the basketball world and elsewhere have long known—a consummate gentleman away from the court.

A high school teacher and basketball coach of mine, David Crist, once told me I could make it as a writer. A prominent Stanford baseball coach, the late William "Dutch" Fehring, once told me I could make it as a broadcaster. I don't know if I have yet hit lofty levels of accomplishment in either area. But if enjoying the journey counts as much as reaching the goal, then there is no doubt I have "made it" while journeying at Stanford University as an athlete, broadcaster and writer. I hope this book reflects, and passes on to readers, at least some of that joy.

John Platz
Mountain View, California

ABOVE: *The Stanford Pavilion was the home arena for Stanford Basketball for most of the program's first half-century (from 1922-1968);* OPPOSITE TOP: *Arthur Harris, all-conference player of the late 1960s, in a Stanford Pavilion game against rival Cal;* OPPOSITE BOTTOM: *A sold-out Stanford Pavilion in its later years.*

BEARS
31

I. Beginnings

A New Game, a State-of-the-Art Pavilion, and Rosters with Olympians and Rose Bowl MVPs

Just as the great universities of the United States appeared initially in the eastern portion of the country and later spread west, basketball got its start at Stanford University considerably later than at many of its East Coast college counterparts. Basketball at Stanford was first recognized as a sport during the 1913-14 academic year, a bit more than two decades after Dr. James Naismith gave birth to the sport by hanging a peach basket at the institution now known as Springfield College in Springfield, MA.

Stanford was organized as a university in 1891, the same year Dr. Naismith hoisted his famous hoop. Football was the sporting king on the Stanford campus in those days. Games were played in the big nearby city, San Francisco, rather than in Palo Alto. Large numbers of people attended the games. A popular student and a future President, Herbert Hoover, served as a Stanford Football student manager for a time during that era. The jocks on campus, in the years prior to and following the turn of the century in 1900, had no time for a new and relatively unknown sport known then as *roundball*.

But basketball—which eventually replaced roundball as the game's name—was too new and too cool a sport to be ignored for long. The first young men on campus to take up the game were not the varsity athletes, however. Instead, the first hoopsters consisted of a smattering of male students who played the game on dirt courts beginning in about 1905.[1] From these modest beginnings, basketball's evolution on the Farm—the nickname for Stanford's campus then as now—began. That evolution culminated nearly a decade later with the establishing of men's basketball as an official sport at Stanford.

To borrow a Silicon Valley phrase, the 1913-14 academic year was the "start-up phase" of organized basketball at Stanford. Sixty students turned out for the first Stanford men's basketball team. There is no record of how many young men were cut from that first team, which was coached by Harry Maloney. Opponents that first season included California, St. Mary's, Nevada, St. Ignatius (predecessor of the present-day University of San Francisco), and College of the Pacific (predecessor of the present-day University of the Pacific). The first game was played on December 3, 1913, a home game against St. Ignatius, and Stanford won by two points.

Most of the games that 1913-14 year were played on campus or within 100 miles of campus. The start-up edition of Stanford Basketball did schedule one ambitious road trip that season: a five-game excursion to the Los Angeles–area during spring break. Stanford Basketball's foes on that road trip were the Long Beach YMCA, Whittier College, Huntington Beach High School, the Orange Athletic Club, and the Los Angeles Athletic Club.

What was the mode of transportation of that first-ever Stanford Basketball road trip? No, it was not by plane—aviation was little more than Wright Brothers–type propelled gliders in those days. It was not by train. It wasn't even by car. The team traveled—get this—by steamship on the Pacific Ocean! Thus ended, via a return voyage up the California coast, the first-ever season of Stanford Basketball. For the record, Stanford won three and lost two on that season-ending road trip.

The 1913-14 Stanford Basketball team finished its inaugural season with a won-loss record of 7-5. Extending the start-up analogy a bit further, the first year—indeed, the first decade—of Stanford Basketball reflected the growing pains of a new intercollegiate sport being played at a relatively new and growing university. But one by one, milestones of progress came for Stanford Basketball.

In year three, the 1915-16 season, home basketball games were played indoors for the first time. The home arena was Encina Gymnasium, which no longer stands but was located on land situated behind the current (2015) site of Stanford's Admissions Office. Yet even with a World War I–era expansion, no more than 1,000 spectators could fit inside Encina Gymnasium to watch games—in time, seating shortages would become a problem. A new coach oversaw the team that third season, as Harry Maloney had given way to E. C. "Squire" Behrens in 1915-16.

In the fourth year of the program's existence, Stanford joined a league—the new Pacific Coast Conference (PCC), which then comprised of Cal, Washington, and Oregon State, in addition to Stanford. Stanford's debut season in the PCC was not an auspicious one. The team lost all six of its PCC games.

Coaches came and went during that first decade of Stanford Basketball. Six men in all served as head coach during the first nine seasons. In addition to Maloney and Behrens, the head coaches were Russell Wilson, M. C. (Bob) Evans, Walter Powell, and C. E. Van Gent. Most of these men coached one or more additional sports on the Farm besides basketball. But perhaps in a sign of the good coaching to come in the decades ahead, each of those first-decade Stanford Basketball coaches—except Behrens—had a career coaching won-loss record that exceeded the .500 mark.

Two of those coaches deserve special mention. Russell Wilson, in the program's fifth year (1917-18), has the distinction of being the coach of the first Stanford Basketball team—after eight consecutive losses spanning the prior four seasons—to defeat the Cal basketball team. The win, by a score of 22-18, happened on February 14, 1918. Wilson was succeeded as head coach by Bob Evans, whose only season as Stanford Basketball's head coach was the 1919-20 campaign. He and his Stanford players made the most of it, going 12-3 and finishing in first place in the PCC with a 9-1 record.

A top player during that first Stanford Basketball decade was Cornelius Erwin "Swede" Righter, a center from 1917-21. Righter, despite missing the 1917-18 season along with several teammates due to World War I service obligations, upon his return became the first-ever All-Conference honoree in Stanford Basketball history. He repeated the feat as a senior in 1920-21, a 15-3 Stanford Basketball season that included a second consecutive season of winning or sharing the PCC championship. Righter, while a Stanford student, also found time to play rugby, a sport he mastered well enough to earn a spot on the United States Olympic Rugby team that won the gold medal at the 1920 Summer Olympic Games in Antwerp, Belgium.

Righter was joined on the 1920-21 All-Pacific-Coast-Conference team by teammate Fred Adams, a second prominent Stanford Basketball player during the mid-1910s-to-mid-1920s era. Adams, team captain in 1920-21, was a forward who won a total of seven letters in four sports during his time as a student-athlete on the Farm.

Basketball was becoming a big deal on campus by 1920-21. In that year, Stanford took the PCC championship for a second consecutive season by defeating California in back-to-back games to end the season—the second game of which was played on March 5, 1921, in front of 10,000 fans at the Oakland Auditorium. Writing in the *Stanford Illustrated Review*, Shelly Pierce, from the Stanford Class of 1922, commented on the surge of interest in basketball during that 1920-21 season and, in particular, the first of those two season-ending games against Cal—the home finale at Encina Gymnasium:

> *Never before had such interest been shown in basketball at Stanford. In every conference game played here, there were several hundred people unable to gain admission to Encina Gymnasium and there was a line in front of the building three hours before the California game was scheduled to start.*[2]

The *Stanford Daily* corroborated Pierce's account, reporting that there were several hundred fans in line when the doors opened at 6:30 P.M. and that by 7:00 P.M. every seat and standing-room space had been taken.[3]

Obviously, there was a need, by the end of the 1920-21 season, for a new and bigger building for Stanford Basketball to play in. The good news was that construction of what came to be known as the Stanford Pavilion—or simply the "Pavilion" to the locals—had already commenced and would be completed on January 13, 1922. At the time, and for some years thereafter, it was the largest facility exclusively for basketball in the United States. The building's completion was accompanied by an all-night university dance.

The Pavilion was built across the street from the landmark Encina Hall building on Stanford's campus and was financed in large part by a $1 tax on each Stanford student. In November 1920, the student body had voted 1,089 to 70 to tax its members for this purpose. The total cost to construct the Pavilion was $185,000.

Another interesting aspect of the new building was the floor. It was something quite new—maple laid on a foundation of several layers of wooden supports. Both the uniqueness of the floor and the "maple" identifier were features that would characterize not only the Pavilion but also the building that nearly a half-century later would become the next home of Stanford Basketball—Roscoe Maples Pavilion.

Another notable player during the latter part of the first decade of Stanford Basketball was John "Nip" McHose, a 5′ 10″ playmaking guard who played from 1922–24. McHose could dominate games with his passing, ball-handling, defense, and scoring. In a two-game series against USC at the Pavilion in 1923, McHose scored 37 of Stanford's 52 points. In the fourth Stanford-USC game that season, in Los Angeles, Stanford outlasted the Trojans 24-21, in a game that went four overtime periods. McHose, naturally, scored the game-winning field goal.

Andy Kerr took over as Stanford Basketball head coach in 1922-23, a year in which the Cardinal—for the third time—earned at least a share of the PCC championship. A school-record-tying 11-game winning streak in the beginning portion of the season helped the team achieve a 12-4 season record.

Kerr would coach four seasons in all, never experiencing a losing season and never winning less than 10 games at a time when the total number of games played in a season rarely exceeded 16 games. Perhaps the most famous basketball player of the Kerr coaching era was even better known for his exploits as an All-American Stanford Football player. Ernie Nevers—the great Stanford Football star, Rose Bowl MVP, and member of the Pro and College Football Halls of Fame—played basketball on the 1923-24 and 1924-25 Stanford Basketball teams.

As told in *The Color of Life Is Red*, Don Liebendorfer's comprehensive book on Stanford Athletics history published in 1972, Ernie Nevers was "a fine shooter, an excellent dribbler, tough on defense, and generally a terrifying figure for the opposition."[4] Liebendorfer, who was a longtime Stanford's Sports Information Director and an occasional statistician at basketball games, demonstrated a fine eye for in-game detail in providing this vivid description of Ernie Nevers the hoopster:

> *Nevers took full advantage of the rules of those days, when a man with the ball was king. A charging foul was practically unknown and if the defender challenged the dribbler, it was at his own risk. I [Liebendorfer] shall never forget one game against the Trojans who had their usual rough and rugged team.*
>
> *One of the toughest of their guards was Gordon Campbell, also a football player. Campbell and Ernie had been "trading pleasantries" all evening, and the former had been particularly effective at working "Swens" over while the official was looking the other way (there was only one whistle-tooter in those days). Nevers, who was incapable of dirty play, also never took a backward step from punishment whether he was dealing it out or taking it; he didn't say a word and bided his time.*
>
> *Finally, as Ernie was dribbling the ball down the floor, the Trojan came across the floor and challenged him for possession. This is what he had been waiting for. At the moment of impact, "Swens" turned on a full head of steam and swung that big fanny of his around with the force of a pile drive.*
>
> *Campbell went flying through the air and landed among the*

spectators in the first row behind the scorekeeper's bench with his legs draped around the scorekeeper's neck. Ernie never broke his dribble, continuing down the floor and lofting the ball into the basket. On the way back for the center jump, the big fellow trotted past me [the scorekeeper] with a grin on his face and inquired innocently, "Which way did he go?" [5]

The four-season Andy Kerr coaching era of Stanford Basketball concluded in 1925-26 and yielded to the E. P. "Husky" Hunt era, with Hunt serving as head coach from the 1926-27 through the 1929-30 seasons. *The Color of Life Is Red* describes Hunt as a soft-spoken man who served the Athletic Department for more than three decades in more varied capacities than any other prior employee with the exception of Harry Maloney.[6]

Husky Hunt served, at one time or another, as Stanford's head basketball coach, freshman basketball coach, freshman baseball coach, freshman football coach, assistant varsity football coach, head wrestling coach, and head gymnastics coach. *The Color of Life Is Red* adds further color to Hunt's long and notable Stanford Athletics Department career:

For some time he [Hunt] took all of Stanford's official game movies and filmed some other sports too. Husky found time also to dedicate himself to promotion of the welfare of the real American Indian. By means of photographs and other documentary presentation, he interested the government in stimulating the sale of Indian products, on which he became a recognized authority.[7]

Husky Hunt did not have a winning record his first two seasons, but in his last two Stanford Basketball seasons he produced better-than-.500 won-loss records of 13-6 and 10-9. His best player during those years was also the best player yet to wear a Stanford Basketball uniform, guard Harlow Rothert, who played freshman basketball in 1926-27 and then his three varsity years for Coach Hunt.

Harlow Rothert was another of Stanford Basketball's early era multi-sport stars, winning a total of nine letters in three sports: football, track and field, and basketball. So good was Rothert that he won All-America honors in each sport, and he remains the only Stanford athlete to achieve All-American status in as many as three major sports. In addition to being an All-American in basketball, Rothert won three NCAA shot put titles, set the world shot put record as a senior in 1930, and, two years after graduation, won the silver medal in the shot put at the 1932 Summer Olympic Games in Los Angeles.

Husky Hunt stepped down as head coach following the 1929-30 season. The nation had just endured an epic stock market crash and was heading into a decade of economic uncertainty. Yet on the Stanford campus, Athletic Director Al Masters had no uncertainty about his target for the next Stanford Basketball head coach.

Stanford had outgrown the hire-from-within practice that had characterized the prior eight coaching hires. Stanford University was becoming more and more national in scope. Notable professors from Ivy League and comparable universities and colleges were accepting offers to come west to teach on the Farm. The football team had already played in four Rose Bowls against prominent East Coast and Midwest opponents. Stanford was by now a well-known and well-respected brand in intercollegiate athletics.

In the spring of 1930, accordingly, Masters turned to the University of Kansas and its legendary basketball coach Phog Allen for a head coach recommendation. Allen did not hesitate, recommending John Bunn for the position. Bunn had both played for and served as an assistant coach under Allen at KU.

In contrast to the later-career success he would enjoy, Bunn's first five seasons as Stanford's head coach, from 1930-31 to 1934-35, were unremarkable. In fact, in none of those seasons did the Indians—the nickname for Stanford's athletic teams from 1930 to 1972—have a winning record. Yet, as had been the case in the pre-Bunn era, those first five seasons featured several remarkable Stanford Basketball players.

Phil Moffatt, an All-American Stanford Football player, played basketball from the 1928-29 through 1930-31 seasons and was a team cornerstone at the forward position on Bunn's first team in 1930-31. Another key contributor on that first Bunn-coached squad was guard Vance Fawcett, a classmate of Moffatt's. The 1931-32 Stanford Basketball team, which won only six games, is notable in that a letter-winner on that squad was David Packard, an engineering student who shortly following graduation would become a cofounder and namesake of the iconic Hewlett-Packard corporation.

The 1932-33 Stanford Basketball team won three more games than the 1931-32 squad did, and it had as one of its key players yet another football star in Keith Topping, who lettered seven times in basketball, football, and boxing during his time on the Farm. Topping was a member of the legendary "Vow Boys," a group of Stanford Football classmates who vowed as freshmen to never lose to USC in varsity football. Not only did Keith Topping and his football mates fulfill their vow regarding USC, they also played in three consecutive Rose Bowls from 1934 through 1936, with Topping earning co-MVP honors in Stanford's 7-0 Rose Bowl triumph over SMU in the last of those three Rose Bowl contests.

The 1933-34 and 1934-35 Stanford Basketball teams finished with won-loss records of 8-12 and 10-17, respectively. One positive aspect of the 1934-35 Stanford Basketball campaign was the season-long excellence of guard Bryan "Dinty" Moore, the team's leading scorer and most valuable player who earned All-Conference honors even though he was only a sophomore.

It isn't known whether Moore knew, following his sophomore season, that he would be immediately relinquishing his status as Stanford Basketball's best player in his two upperclassman years to come. What is known is that history-making Stanford Basketball seasons lay just around the corner. While the ill winds of the Great Depression were sweeping the country in 1934-35, a beneficent phenomenon of significant proportion was about to sweep over not only Stanford Athletics but also over the national sporting scene as a whole.

To borrow another Silicon Valley analogy, if the first two decades of Stanford Basketball were the start-up and brand-growing phases of Stanford Basketball, the late 1930s were witness to a wildly enriching event—a "basketball IPO," if you will—that would send Stanford Basketball fortunes soaring. The precipitating event was a new addition to the team. His name was Angelo "Hank" Luisetti.

II. National Prominence

Luisetti's Greatness, East-Coast Showcase Wins, and an NCAA Championship

Of the thousands of Stanford athletes profiled in his book *The Color of Life Is Red*, author and 45-year Stanford Athletics publicist Don Liebendorfer reserved his most glowing words for the late-1930s basketball prodigy Hank Luisetti:

> *If there ever was a perfect athlete this slender, dark, good-looking Italian youngster out of Galileo High School in San Francisco was he. Luisetti had perfect coordination, excellent speed, lightning reactions, a fierce competitive instinct, a "touch" as light as a feather, and an extremely keen eye. He had the power of relaxation and was one of the two most graceful athletes I have ever seen, the other being Hugh Gallerneau, halfback on the famous [Stanford] 1940 Wow Boys football team.*[8]

Hank Luisetti stood 6′ 2″, weighed 180 pounds, and, because of his superior leaping ability, played the forward position. In 1935-36, as a member of Stanford's freshman basketball team—freshmen not being allowed to play on the varsity at the time—Luisetti obliterated all then-existing freshman scoring records and led the frosh to a 13-2 season won-loss record.

As it happened, Luisetti was just 18 months younger than another gifted Italian-American athlete from San Francisco—a baseball phenom named Joe DiMaggio. Just as a twenty-something DiMaggio did in baseball, Hank Luisetti in his early 20s became the best player nationally in *his* sport, basketball. Both men rose to national prominence at about the same time, the late 1930s. Like the New York Yankee superstar DiMaggio, Luisetti gained notoriety not only because he repeatedly performed in large venues before thousands of fans in major U.S. cities, but also because he—like DiMaggio—did things in his sport that had simply never been seen before.

Only Ernie Nevers and Harlow Rothert had scaled the heights of athletic achievement and national notoriety as Stanford athletes that Hank Luisetti would reach during his time on the Farm. And Luisetti would eclipse even those men by the end of his storied Stanford Basketball career. Nevers (football) and Rothert (track and field) were dominant American athletes in their sports, as was Luisetti in his, but they didn't *revolutionize* their sports. Luisetti did.

His coach, John Bunn, did not foresee the revolution that would come during Luisetti's landmark varsity career on the Farm. Bunn was a basketball traditionalist. He had played for legendary Kansas coach Phog Allen, who himself was a student under the game's inventor Dr. James Naismith. He wasn't a radical coach. He believed in deliberate offense and two-handed set shots. But once he saw Luisetti swishing one-handers from all over the court—something neither he nor any other college coach had ever seen before—he embraced the innovative path. And that path would be an exceptionally winning one for the Luisetti-era Stanford teams.

Hank Luisetti had a good supporting cast as his Stanford Basketball varsity career began in the late fall of 1935. In addition to Dinty Moore, the junior guard who had been an All-Conference player the prior season, Luisetti had as a teammate 6′ 4″ center Art Stoefen, whose nickname was "Stork" and who excelled inside on both offense and defense. Rounding out the lineup were 6′ 2″ Howie Turner and 6′ 4″ Jack Calderwood, the latter of whom was a rebounding-fiend whose nickname was Frankenstein owing to his frequently ominous-looking facial expressions.

Luisetti's star was evident early. In his second varsity game, he scored 31 points—an enormous scoring total in those days—in a win over Utah State. A month later, while watching a Stanford home game against a powerful USC team, Liebendorfer in *The Color of Life Is Red* described sophomore Hank Luisetti in these terms:

> *The Trojans were hot and built up a lead of 12 points at halftime. With 11 minutes to go in the second period, they had stretched that margin to 15 and the Indians appeared to be beaten. At this point Luisetti and his teammates caught fire and nearly blew the Southern Californians off the floor. A blistering attack, led by Hank who hit 14 consecutive points at one stage to pull his team even, caused [his team] to score a tremendous victory.*

Luisetti added nine more points toward the end of the contest to bring his total for the evening to 30. He did everything with the ball but eat it in those 11 minutes, stealing the casaba for driving layups, blocking shots, shooting from outside, feeding his teammates and playing superbly on both boards.[9]

Hank Luisetti's competitive fire would also show up in a game against rival Cal later that 1935-36 season. During the early 1930s, Cal almost always had had a better team than Stanford, and that trend had continued in 1935-36, with Cal winning the first three games between the two schools. But in the fourth and final game between the two schools in 1935-36, with Stanford in contention for the conference championship, sophomore Luisetti and his teammates rose up. In a rough and defense-oriented game at the Pavilion, the Indians held Cal to just 26 points and won by 14 points, 40-26. Luisetti led Stanford in scoring with double figures in points.

The PCC by this time had split into two divisions, with Stanford, Cal, USC and UCLA in the Southern Division and Washington, Washington State, Oregon, Oregon State, and Idaho in the Northern Division. Stanford and USC finished tied for first place in the Southern Division standings at the end of the 1935-36 regular season, and the Luisetti-led Indians won the one-game playoff over the Trojans to claim the Southern Division title. Next up were two games against the Northern Division champion Washington Huskies, a team that had beaten Stanford twice in two games earlier in the season. The rematch games were no contest, with Luisetti averaging 26.5 points in two decisive Stanford wins over the Huskies.

Hank Luisetti, the sophomore, scored 416 points in 29 games that 1935-36 season, by far a Stanford single-season scoring record. He also earned first-team All-America honors, becoming just the second Stanford Basketball player to have ever done so. Harlow Rothert had been the first, achieving the honor back in 1928-29.

As for the team, the 1935-36 squad produced a 21-8 won-loss record—the most wins in a season a Stanford Basketball team had ever produced. The previous high was 15 wins in 1920-21. Could there be an even better, higher-level, more-exciting Hank Luisetti year coming in 1936-37? The answer would be a resounding "yes."

The 1936-37 Stanford Basketball schedule began modestly enough in late November of 1936. Stanford began the campaign with decisive home wins over the California Aggies (41-16) and the Olympic Club (60-49), followed by a road win over San Jose State (31-24).

The team then embarked on a road trip east. The first stop was in the state of Kansas, where Stanford polished off a very good Warrensburg State Teacher College squad by a score of 51-31. Six days later, in Philadelphia, the Indians got past a strong Temple team, 45-38, with Hank Luisetti scoring 14 points. And then it was on to New York City. The next Stanford Basketball game would turn out to be one of the most memorable games not only in New York City sports history but also in basketball history.

The date was December 30, 1936. The place was Madison Square Garden in New York City. The matchup: unknown but much whispered-about Stanford and Hank Luisetti versus Clair Bee's nationally celebrated and undefeated Long Island University (LIU) Blackbirds. LIU was the figurative Goliath of the college basketball world, a juggernaut that had won 43 consecutive games, with many of those wins coming against the best teams in the nation. Stanford, by contrast, was the upstart from the West Coast. The national media buzz in the weeks leading up to the game was immense. Going back to the prior season, a steady stream of reports had filtered to the East Coast from California that this Stanford team—led by a mysterious but amazing player named Luisetti—was an extremely talented and highly unconventional basketball team.

The day before the game, the Stanford Basketball team practiced at Madison Square Garden. A horde of writers was on hand to observe and document the Stanford practice session. Don Liebendorfer described it this way in *The Color of Life Is Red*:

> *Naturally, the sportswriters had heard of the famous Luisetti and his teammates, and came out in force to watch the practice session. They were very much impressed with what they saw, except for one thing—Hank's method of shooting with one hand. Nat Holman, the famous coach of the City College of New York teams, told them the one-handed shot never would be popular or adopted generally. At least 90 percent of the players in those days employed both hands in lofting the ball toward the basket; as a matter of fact, Hank shot his free throws with both hands, using the one-hand cast-off only from the floor.*[10]

The Stanford players showed no apprehension about the next evening's game—far from it, in fact. They joked with New York reporters, laughing off recommendations that they would receive their comeuppance from LIU. This amiability earned them the appellation "Laughing Boys," a nickname that would remain with the team during the remainder of Hank Luisetti's time on the Farm.

A crowd of 17,623 jammed the Garden on that December 30, 1936, evening. The East Coast, and New York City in particular, viewed itself as the center of the basketball universe. The best teams and coaches in the nation played there, media interest was the highest there, and basketball fandom was concentrated there. Hordes of media and fans alike were eager to see what the great Hank Luisetti and the upstarts from the Left Coast could do against the mighty Blackbirds, the team with the long winning streak and widely regarded as the best team in the United States.

LIU scored first. Then Stanford scored. Then a Blackbird free throw made the score 3-2 in favor of LIU. The LIU-partisan crowd expected the home team to explode at any time, as the Blackbirds had done so many times on that very Madison Square Garden floor against whatever competition they faced.

The expected LIU breakaway, however, did not happen. Far from it. LIU was befuddled by Stanford's quick defense, its fast-break offense and Hank Luisetti's all-around game. Luisetti seemed to be everywhere on the court, making one-handed shots, executing perfectly timed passes, stealing the ball from LIU guards, and even getting his share of rebounds against the big LIU front line, which included 6′ 8″ center Art Hillhouse.

Hank Luisetti scored again and again in the first half. Said Luisetti: "The first one came after a fake and a pivot near the foul line. It was over one of the big men. He looked at me and said, 'you lucky so-and-so'. He didn't say a word when the next one dropped in."

Stanford closed the first half by outscoring the Blackbirds 11-3 in the final minutes of the half to take a 22-14 lead. The MSG crowd was equal parts stunned by the score and amazed by Stanford's unorthodox style of play. When Hank Luisetti and his teammates left the floor at halftime, the fans gave the squad a standing ovation. LIU continued to be stymied by Stanford as the second half got underway. They had no answer to the Stanford dominance in the second half either. So flustered was LIU by Stanford's unique tempo and effective playmaking on both ends of the court, that at one point during the game the Blackbirds went seven minutes without scoring.

Something way, way different was going on that late-1936 evening on the Madison Square Garden court, a style of basketball that the East Coast nerve center of college basketball had never seen before. Stanford wasn't playing basketball the usual way, with slow, deliberate and patterned offense and the traditional two-handed set shot. Sportswriter Ron Fimrite, in a Hank Luisetti tribute piece that appeared in *Sports Illustrated*, beautifully described the radical contrast between Stanford's brilliantly innovative style of play that night in New York and the then-conventional way basketball was played:

> *The Eastern teams played ball-control offense and man-to-man defense. They shot the ball in the traditional manner, and they rarely shot at all until the ball had been worked in with half a dozen passes or more. Stanford's team was an enigma to the Easterners. On offense, the Stanford players roamed like prairie dogs, switching positions to meet changing situations. Luisetti, the most liberated free-lancer of them all, might play the post, bring the ball downcourt or switch from the left to the right side at will. On defense, switching positions was perfectly acceptable. To Eastern audiences, it all smacked of anarchy.*[11]

Stanford maintained its dominance in the second half and cruised to a 45-31 victory over the Blackbirds, which ended LIU's historic winning streak at 43 games. Hank Luisetti finished with a game-high 15 points and was lauded not only for dribbling, passing, rebounding and playing defense better than anyone on the court but also for doing so with a style as effective as it was unusual.

In watching the unorthodox Luisetti and his Stanford teammates easily dispose of mighty LIU, many basketball fans at Madison Square Garden that evening sensed they were witnessing a revolutionary change within the sport—the faster, more free-flowing and quicker-to-shoot team had won, and had won easily. Media members covering the game were likewise flabbergasted. As Don Liebendorfer chronicled it in *The Color of Life Is Red*: "all of the writers were convinced after that shellacking and climbed on the bandwagon." He added, "seldom has a team received such lavish praise as was heaped on Bunn's team by the Manhattan press."[12]

To borrow from Silicon Valley lingo, coach John Bunn's Stanford hoopsters had "changed the world"—the world of basketball. As compared to innovative college basketball teams that would come along in future decades, watching Stanford Basketball that night was like watching, for the first time, UCLA's suffocating full-court press in the 1960s, or Houston's Phi Slamma Jamma teams in the 1980s, or the quick-shooting, three-point-shot-crazy Hank Gathers &

Bo Kimble Loyola Marymount teams of the early 1990s. Stanford Basketball of the 1930s, however, was the first college team to engineer a truly large evolution of the sport. Ron Fimrite, critiquing the impact of the Stanford-LIU game in *Sports Illustrated*, offered this perceptive assessment of the Stanford-instigated sea change that would soon take hold within the game of basketball:

> *The Stanford-LIU game was no mere intersectional upset. It was a pivotal game in the sport's history, introducing the nation to modern basketball. Players throughout the country began shooting on the run and with one hand. The deliberate style of play gave way to the fast break, the man-to-man would yield to the zone and combination defenses, and the following season the center jump after goals and would be abandoned forever. Scoring suddenly increased, and a game that had served, in many areas, merely to fill the gap between the football and baseball seasons abruptly began to enjoy widespread popularity of its own.*[13]

It has long been said that for something new and significant to happen in American culture, it has to happen in New York City. Clearly, Hank Luisetti and the Stanford Basketball team were a "happening" there on December 30, 1936. It was only the fifth game of the year for Stanford. But in a New York Minute, it suddenly had become apparent that this unorthodox Stanford Basketball team was not only having a revolutionary impact on the sport's development, it was arguably also the best college basketball team in the nation.

One thing was beyond argument. Stanford certainly had the nation's best player. New York City certainly could vouch for that—and in fact did. Hank Luisetti was named the outstanding athlete—not just basketball player, *athlete*—to perform in Madison Square Garden in 1936. Writing in *Sports Illustrated*, Les Woodcock accurately captured how Luisetti was the cornerstone of Stanford's groundbreaking performance that night at Madison Square Garden:

> *The architect was Luisetti. As great a floor man as he was a shot, he set up most of his team's play with electrifying dribbling and passing. But his real contribution was his shooting. Instead of setting himself for the obligatory two-hander, Luisetti pushed the ball softly toward the basket with one hand while on the run.*[14]

Hank Luisetti had come to New York City in late December 1936 as a relative unknown. He left New York City as well known in the Boroughs in basketball as his San Francisco childhood contemporary Joe DiMaggio—a New York Yankee rookie in 1936—was in baseball.

The road trip continued, with the team backtracking westward toward home. Wins followed in Buffalo (over Canisius 39-29); in Cleveland (over Western Reserve 67-27); in St. Paul, Minnesota (over Hamline University 58-26); and in Bozeman, Montana (over Montana State 66-28). The 1936-37 Stanford Basketball team, at that point in the season, had built a won-loss record of 10-0.

Four home wins followed. Then came the first loss of the year, 42-39, at USC. Eight more wins ensued before the second loss occurred, 44-31, at Cal. But by that time Stanford had clinched the PCC Southern Division title. Washington State was the PCC Northern Division champion, but in the playoff series between the two division champions the Cougars were no match for Stanford as Hank Luisetti led the Laughing Boys to two straight wins over WSU to end the 1936-37 season.

There was no NCAA postseason tournament in those days. A college basketball team, at that time, could not win a postseason national championship on the floor. But the Helms Foundation, then a respected authority on amateur sports, later named Stanford as the national champion in college basketball for the 1936-37 season.

And why not? Stanford was certainly deserving of the honor, with a sterling won-loss record of 25-2. To add to Stanford Basketball's laurels, Hank Luisetti was an All-America selection for a second straight year, and he was also named National Player of the Year by the Helms Foundation. He and Dinty Moore were named to the All-PCC team, Moore for the third time and Luisetti for the second.

It was new and heady stuff. In 1936-37, Stanford had been national championship-worthy, had played on the biggest stage (in New York City), had defeated a Goliath (LIU) in the most well-publicized game to date in college basketball history, and, of course, had the best player in the sport on its roster. Of the suddenly nationally prominent Stanford Basketball program, many college basketball observers had this thought going into the 1937-38 season: What could Stanford Basketball do for an encore?

The Stanford schedule in 1937-38 was even more ambitious, travel-wise, than the 1936-37 schedule had been. Road games were scheduled in Arizona, in Philadelphia, in New York City, and in Cleveland. Basketball fans everywhere wanted to see the great Hank Luisetti and the powerful Stanford Basketball team. And they had to do it in person—games typically were not broadcast on radio, and televised college basketball games were not even a dream yet.

Hank Luisetti was elected captain for his senior season in 1937-38, but he had less talent around him than in prior seasons. Dinty Moore and Howie Turner, two three-year starters who for two seasons had played solidly alongside Luisetti, had graduated in June of 1937.

Stanford won its first two games of the 1937-38 season, both home games. Then came the two-week, 6,000-mile road trip. The Indians won at Arizona (44-28), snagged two wins in New York City over City College of New York (45-42) and—once again—Long Island University (49-35), but then lost to Temple in Philadelphia, 35-31, just twenty-four hours after its grueling LIU win.

The next game on the road trip would be in Cleveland, on New Year's Day 1938, against Duquense University. It is hard to imagine Hank Luisetti could find something else to top what he had already accomplished in his Stanford career. He was part of the reigning national championship team, he had won a National Player of the Year award, and he was the toast of not only the college basketball world but indeed the entire sport!

And yet he found something else to top all of that. This is how *The Color of Life Is Red*, described the January 1, 1938, Stanford-Duquense game and the performance of Hank Luisetti that evening in Cleveland:

> *Stanford played a good Duquense University team in Cleveland, Ohio, and defeated the Dukes 92-27. Now in these days of astronomical scores when some teams don't know what defense means and couldn't care less, 92 points doesn't sound like many. However, in 1938 the game of basketball was entirely different and 90 points was thought to be almost impossible. For instance, in three years the Luisetti teams averaged 48.5 points in their 80 games.*
>
> *The most amazing thing about the Duquense slaughter was that Hank scored 50 points, which broke practically every single game record in existence—Stanford, conference, regional, national, etc. Half a hundred points for one individual in one game had the entire country gasping. And the great one's total would have been even higher had not John Bunn removed his star with three minutes to go. Luisetti had 23 field goals and four free throws for the night.*[15]

Hank Luisetti scored 35 points in the first half alone, and his 49th and 50th points late in the game symbolized his otherworldly mastery of the art of scoring the basketball. Having collided with teammate Bill Rapp, Luisetti flung the basketball—one-handed, naturally—toward the basket while tumbling backwards, and the shot splashed perfectly into and through the netting.

When the game was over, a police escort was necessary to escort Hank Luisetti out of the Cleveland arena, so taken were the patrons and media by the Stanford senior's incredible 50-point performance. Those 50 points broke the college single-game record of 41 points then held by Chuck Chikovits of Toledo.

Longtime Duquense coach Chick Davies had this to say after Luisetti's landmark scoring performance: "I had to just sit there and watch the most remarkable exhibition of shooting I had ever seen." And perhaps the greatest testimony about Hank Luisetti's 50-point feat in Cleveland that evening is this: Nearly 80 years later, as of the 100th anniversary of Stanford Basketball in 2014-15, Luisetti's Stanford Basketball single-game scoring record *still* stands.

The remainder of Hank Luisetti's senior season unfolded as one would have expected. Stanford again won the PCC Southern Division, with a 10-2 record, and again won the PCC championship, with two wins over the Northern Division champion, Oregon. Fittingly, Luisetti was dominant in the two Oregon games—his final two as a collegian. He scored 46 points in the two games, 46 of Stanford's 111 total points in the two wins.

Stanford's won-loss record in 1937-38 ended up being 21-3, not quite good enough to be designated national champion by the Helms Foundation, which would have meant two consecutive Helms-designated national crowns for Stanford Basketball. The Helms-voted championship in 1937-38 went to Temple, which had barely defeated Stanford earlier in the season—the 35-31 victory in Philadelphia on December 30. In that game, Temple employed a "box and one" defense on Hank Luisetti and held him to just 11 points, although Stanford nearly pulled out a come-from-behind win when Stanford sophomore Leon Lafaille famously came off the bench to score three baskets in succession late in the second half.

Had Stanford won that Temple game, it likely would have been designated the national champion by Helms instead of Temple, whose final won-loss record of 23-2 was slightly better than Stanford's. As for Stanford individual player honors, Hank Luisetti was named All-American for a third straight season and was named Helms Foundation National

Player of the Year for a second consecutive year. Appropriately, Luisetti's uniform #7 was eventually retired by the University—still the only uniform number in Stanford Basketball history ever to have been retired.

It is not an exaggeration to say that Hank Luisetti was the best basketball player on earth during the first half of the twentieth century—basically, the first five decades of the sport's existence. The only debatable rival would be DePaul and Minneapolis Laker star George Mikan, who came along a bit later than Luisetti. But Mikan's achievements were more as a professional player and more due to his height. Luisetti's accomplishments, on the other hand, were less due to his size and athleticism than to his style of play, which as compared to Mikan's was far more revolutionary, far more entertaining, and far more widespread in its impact on fans and future players.

To say that change would be coming to Stanford Basketball in the year and years following Hank Luisetti's graduation would be an understatement. In the weeks following the 1937-38 season, the change could be summarized in one word—*Dean*. After nine years, John Bunn resigned as Stanford Basketball head coach and accepted a position as *Dean of Men* at Stanford University. And shortly thereafter, Athletic Director Al Masters named a coach with the surname *Dean* to become the new head coach of the Stanford Basketball program.

Forty-year-old Everett Dean was another coach identified and recruited according to the Al Masters playbook: look east, look for a winning track record from a pedigreed program, look for a consummate teacher, and look for a gentleman who would reflect Stanford values. Since 1925, Everett Dean had been both head basketball coach and head baseball coach at Indiana University, and he had won Big Ten championships in both sports. Everett Dean's nickname at IU? "Gentleman."

Despite the graduation-caused departures of four of the five starters off of the 1937-38 team, including the great Hank Luisetti, Everett Dean's first Stanford Basketball team in 1938-39 managed a fine 16-9 record and a third place finish in the PCC Southern Division. A year later came a 14-9 record and a second place conference finish.

It took Everett Dean a couple of years to learn the West Coast recruiting ropes as he sought to acquire talent that, though it might not be Luisetti-level individually, could collectively produce teams that could win at the rate that the Luisetti-era teams did. One early recruiting-target locale was San Francisco, California. Hank Luisetti had played high school basketball at Galileo High School in San Francisco. Everett

Dean's mother lode for talent would not be Galileo, as things turned out, but another San Francisco high school: Lowell High School.

In 1939-40, guards Don Burness and Bill Cowden, both Lowell grads, joined the Stanford Basketball team. The next year Burness and Cowden, together with forwards Forddy Anderson and Don Williams and guard Ken Davidson, formed the starting five of a 21-win Stanford Basketball team in 1940-41 that won the PCC Southern Division with a 10-2 conference record. All five young men were named first-team All-PCC-Southern-Division in 1940-41, the first and only time during the history of the PCC Southern Division that the entire Stanford starting unit made first team.

To close out the 1940-41 season, Stanford went 0-2 in a playoff against the PCC Northern Division champion, Washington State, losing the two games in Pullman, Washington, by the narrow margins of three and four points. But the seeds of future greatness had been planted.

Three starters, Anderson, Williams, and Davidson, were lost to graduation following the 1940-41 season. But three more Bay Area natives stepped in to become the new starters alongside Don Burness and Bill Cowden: junior Ed Voss from Oakland's University High School, sophomore Jim Pollard from Oakland Tech, and sophomore Howie Dallmar from Menlo Junior College and Lowell High School. In 1941-42, Voss was entering his second year as a varsity player, while Pollard and Dallmar would be making their varsity debuts in 1941-42.

On paper, based on the returning talent and what was known about the incoming players, it seemed like Stanford Basketball in 1941-42 would have a good season, but it did not seem like a team that would be in the hunt for a national championship. A few things, however, were certain right from the start: The 1941-42 team was tall, liked to run and move on offense, and above all else, was an exceptionally close-knit group. The team's top eight players had played high-school ball within eight miles of one another!

More importantly, it was a team whose individual on-court skill sets, as coach Everett Dean recognized, seemed to fit. Jim Pollard, with 36-inch vertical jumping ability, played forward and could score both inside and outside. Bill Cowden was a tough, physical defender who typically was assigned to defend the opposing team's high-scoring guard. Ed Voss patrolled the paint at center and was a reliable-rebounding big man. Don Burness, like Cowden, was a veteran at the guard position and was the floor general. Howie Dallmar played forward and was the "x" factor, not huge as a statistics-generator but always capable of coming up with a clutch play or providing, when necessary, significant scoring in a big game. Said Dallmar years later: "We were the first big team that could run. With our success, people began to realize that a big team could not only rebound but run a good fast break as well."[16]

The season began on a significantly sobering note: The Japanese military attack on Pearl Harbor occurred during the first month of the 1941-42 season. There were blackout curtains on the windows in Stanford dormitories. The entire West Coast was on alert for a possible Japanese attack. Gasoline was subject to rationing.

The first few games of the 1941-42 Stanford Basketball season began with three consecutive wins at home, followed by a 10-point loss to Santa Clara. But then the team began to find cohesion on offense, winning 13 consecutive games, including the first 4 of its 12 PCC Southern Division conference games.

After losing two of its next three games at home, one to USC and the other to the Athens Club, the 1941-42 Stanford Basketball team reeled off six consecutive conference wins to close the conference season with an 11-1 record and possession of the PCC Southern Division title.

In the best-of-three playoff with PCC Northern Division champion Oregon State held at the Stanford Pavilion—with the winner to receive a berth in the still nascent NCAA Tournament—the Indians won the first game 41-28. The Beavers took the second game, 42-33. In the decisive third game, home-court toughness won the day as Stanford pulled out a five-point win, 40-35, with Howie Dallmar and Ed Voss scoring back-to-back baskets in the second half to break a 33-33 tie and provide Stanford with a lead that it would not relinquish.

For the first time, Stanford would play in the tournament that would determine the college basketball champion. The NCAA postseason basketball championship tournament, which had begun only in 1938-39, was in 1941-42 just an eight-team competition (remaining at that modest number until the 1950s when expansion increased the number of teams in the tournament).

The NCAA Basketball Tournament in 1942 was divided into two regions. In the East Region, the four teams were Dartmouth, Kentucky, Illinois, and Penn State. The East Region games were played at Tulane Gym in New Orleans. In the West Region, the four teams were Colorado, Rice, Kansas, and Stanford. The West Region games were played at Municipal Auditorium in Kansas City.

In the East Region, the first-round NCAA Tournament games saw

Dartmouth defeat Penn State, 44-39, and Adolf Rupp's Kentucky Wildcat team prevail over Illinois, 46-44. In the regional final, the Ivy League's Big Green dominated Rupp's Kentucky squad, winning 47-28.

In the West Region, Stanford got past Rice, 53-47, with Jim Pollard scoring 26 points and Ed Voss tallying 17 points for the winners. In the other regional semifinal, Colorado upended Kansas, 46-44, thus keeping Stanford from having to play Kansas in front of a legion of Jayhawk fans in Kansas City. Without having to face a hostile crowd, Stanford got past Colorado in the regional final, 46-35, with Pollard scoring 17 points to lead the way.

Difficulties descended upon the Stanford Basketball team prior to the March 28, 1942, NCAA championship game in Kansas City's Municipal Auditorium. Jim Pollard had a bad case of the flu and would not play. Don Burness had an injured ankle, was unable to start, and would play only nine minutes in the game. Pollard and Burness were the team's top two scorers. Who would pick up the scoring load for Stanford?

The answer was that the scoring load was shouldered by multiple players. Coach Everett Dean started junior and "sixth man" Jack Dana in place of Pollard, and junior guard Fred Linari started in place of Burness. It was a roll of the dice, but Everett Dean had no choice.

Stanford led by just two points at halftime, 24-22. But the second half was a completely different story. The team's nickname heard frequently in Kansas City, the "Tall Redwoods of California," was cemented in memory in a Stanford-dominant second half, with the Stanford big men able to score again and again. When it was over, Everett Dean's team had nearly doubled the Dartmouth scoring output in the second half. The final score of the 1942 NCAA title game: Stanford 53 – Dartmouth 38. Despite its various obstacles, Stanford had prevailed and was NCAA champion!

Howie Dallmar scored 15 points, Jack Dana 14 points, and Ed Voss 13 points. In the backcourt, Fred Linari contributed 6 points and Bill Cowden added 5 points. Cowden, speaking decades later to Dwight Chapin of the *San Francisco Examiner*, described how his Stanford team was able to overcome both its own injury-plagued situation as well as the Big Green opposition that March 1942 evening in Kansas City:

> *Yes there was some apprehension, but Coach Dean was a very observant man and he was able to pinpoint some of Dartmouth's weaknesses. It really helped, too, that we had all learned from watching Hank Luisetti. We were throwing up*

shots left-handed and right-handed, while Dartmouth was still working with set shots.[17]

Howie Dallmar, the leading scorer for Stanford in the championship game, was named the Most Outstanding Player of the 1942 NCAA Tournament. His teammate Jim Pollard was the tournament's co-leading scorer, along with Rice's Chet Palmer. Pollard had scored his tournament-high-tying 43 points despite having not even played in the title game.

Comparisons of Stanford's 1942 NCAA championship team with decades-later championship Stanford Basketball teams are futile; the style of basketball was much different in the 1940s than it was in the late 1990s and early 2000s. But one thing was the same then as it is now. As researched and reported by *San Francisco Chronicle* reporter Tom Fitzgerald decades later, a Kansas City writer at the 1942 NCAA Tournament had this to say about the Stanford Basketball players:

Strangely enough, the boys actually study. When they left their home campus, examinations were starting and books became an important part of their luggage. Most of the team members will take their tests upon arriving home next week.[18]

As far as on-court comparison, it is natural to want to compare the 28-4, NCAA-champion 1941-42 Stanford team with the 1936-37 Luisetti-led Stanford squad that produced a 25-2 record and was named the national champion by the Helms Foundation. To compare these two outstanding FDR-era Stanford Basketball squads, eyewitness Don Liebendorfer in *The Color of Life Is Red* had this to say: "Aside from Hank, the teams were dead even in balance, offense, defense, spirit, condition, size, and just about any department you could mention."[19]

Liebendorfer further likened the comparison of the 1936-37 and 1941-42 Stanford Basketball teams to the Stanford Vow Boys football team in 1935 and the undefeated Wow Boys football team in 1940. Just as each of those two football teams had been both conference champions and end-of-season Rose Bowl champions, each of the 1936-37 and 1941-42 Stanford Basketball teams won a conference title and earned a *national champion* designation by the end of the season.

A two-time national player of the year, Hank Luisetti was, as of the late 1930s, the best player ever to have played basketball.

III. Postwar and Early Dallmar Coaching Years

Future NBA Players and Olympians

World War II heavily impacted Stanford Basketball during the 1942-45 period. In 1942-43, there was basketball, but due to travel restrictions the schedule was significantly different from the norm. Only eight—as opposed to the usual twelve—PCC Southern Division games were played collectively against Cal, USC, and UCLA. Most of the 21 games, whether at home or on the road, were played in the Bay Area.

Of the 21 games in 1942-43, six were played against U.S. military service-related teams. In fact, Stanford lost to a U.S. Navy Pre-Flight squad led by Hank Luisetti and later won a game against a Coast Guard team on which Jim Pollard played. The 1942-43 team finished with a 10-11 record, with both Howie Dallmar and Ed Voss being named to the All-PCC-Southern-Division team at season's end. Due to the United States' war effort, there was no Stanford Basketball in 1943-44 or 1944-45.

With World War II having subsided by the fall of 1945, intercollegiate basketball returned to the Farm. But that first season of resumed play (1945-46) found a Stanford roster filled with inexperienced players, including freshmen. Exceptions to the rule prohibiting freshmen from playing varsity basketball were occasionally made during and immediately following U.S. wartime involvement, and this was the case in the mid-and-late 1940s following the end of World War II. The results were surprising neither to Stanford fans nor to head coach Everett Dean. The team went 6-18 in 1945-46, losing all 12 PCC Southern Division games.

Some help in the talent department came in 1946-47. In addition to having a cornerstone talent in junior John "Babe" Higgins, the team had a couple of underclassmen, Dave Davidson and George Yardley, who were good players and in later years would improve to become All-Conference level performers on the court. Higgins, a guard, was the team's leading scorer in

1946-47. The team finished 15-16 overall, including 5-7 in the PCC Southern Division, and Higgins was named to the All-PCC-Southern-Division team.

A milestone of sorts occurred during that 1946-47 season. In Stanford's second game, the Indians lost to Santa Clara 107-76—the first time a Stanford Basketball team had played in a game in which a team scored at least 100 points. It would be five years before the second such Stanford game was played.

The next two seasons, Everett Dean's Stanford Basketball teams produced won-loss records that exceeded the .500 mark. In 1947-48, with Babe Higgins again leading the team in scoring and earning All-PCC-Southern-Division honors, Stanford won 15 of the 26 games on the schedule. The team, however, won only 3 of 12 PCC Southern Division games. Senior forward Morley Thompson and junior center Bill Stephenson were also top scorers on the team.

The 1948-49 Stanford Basketball team improved on the prior year's performance with a 19-9 won-loss record, including a 5-7 mark in the PCC Southern Division. This was the best of Everett Dean's post–World War II teams—only two of the nine losses were by more than 10 points, and three of the seven conference losses were by two points or fewer. Guard Dave Davidson earned All-PCC-Southern-Division honors and led Stanford in scoring in 1948-49.

In addition to the all-around excellence of seniors Dave Davidson and Bill Stephenson, a key senior was guard and defensive standout Bob Lewis, who had transferred three years earlier from Utah, where he had been one of the four freshmen starters—along with the great Arnie Ferrin—on Utah's 1944 NCAA championship team. Another feature of the 1948-49 campaign was the emergence of forward George Yardley.

A thin, gangly player whose nickname was "Bird," Yardley did not play much his freshman season in 1946-47—in fact, Yardley was sufficiently awkward that Coach Dean would play Yardley only at the end of games. But the Stanford head coach was bullish on Yardley's potential and exercised the requisite patience as his young frontcourt player matured into his body; beginning in 1948-49, Yardley became a factor in Stanford games. As a junior in 1948-49, Yardley finished eighth among all PCC Southern Division players in scoring (with senior teammates Davidson and Stephenson finishing second and seventh).

Despite the losses to graduation of Davidson and Stephenson and the uncertain prospects for the Stanford Basketball team given such losses, Yardley was poised for a big senior season in 1949-50. And he didn't disappoint. In the history of the four-team (Stanford, Cal, USC, and UCLA) and 12-game PCC Southern Division seasonal schedule alignment, the season scoring record for conference-only games was 232 points, set by Stanford's Hank Luisetti back in 1937-38. Going into the 1949-50 season's final game against Cal, Yardley needed 12 points to break Luisetti's record. Playing in a raucous Stanford Pavilion, where the patrons were well aware of Yardley's pursuit of Luisetti's record, Yardley exploded for 26 points to set a new conference-play-only scoring record of 237 points.

Unfortunately, Yardley's record lasted only a half-hour. In Los Angeles, USC guard Bill Sharman was piling up points in his team's finale against UCLA, and the Trojan guard finished the season one point ahead of Yardley with 238 points in twelve conference games. Still, George Yardley's stellar senior season earned him a spot on the All-PCC-Southern-Division team, despite Stanford's overall record of 11-14 and its 5-7 mark in PCC Southern Division play.

The next season, 1950-51, would mark the final season of Everett Dean's tenure as Stanford Basketball's head coach. The loss of George Yardley—as well as seven of the other 11 letter-winners—would require contributions from new talent if Stanford was to have a decent year in 1950-51. Returning starters Jim Ramstead (13.8 ppg) and junior guard Jim Walsh (12.8 ppg), both juniors, shouldered some of the scoring load in 1950-51. But the big boost in scoring—and a big reason why Stanford improved its PCC Southern Division won-loss record by a couple of games as compared to the prior season—was the play of a newcomer to the program, Sebron "Ed" Tucker.

Tucker, a junior forward and a transfer student from Compton Junior College, immediately won a starting spot and led the 1950-51 Stanford Basketball team in scoring with 16.5 points per game. Stanford's first African-American scholarship athlete who later became a prominent physician, Tucker finished second among all PCC Southern Division players in scoring in 1950-51.

Ed Tucker's greatest moments—in a two-year career that featured more than a few—came on Friday and Saturday February 23 and 24, 1951, at the Stanford Pavilion. In the Friday night game, Tucker calmly hit two free throws with two seconds remaining to give Stanford a win over USC. In the Saturday night game against UCLA, the junior forward set a Stanford Pavilion single-game scoring record of 31 points in a 68-65 loss to UCLA, breaking Hank Luisetti's Stanford Pavilion scoring record of 30 points set in 1937-38.

However, undone by two losing streaks of five and six games at different junctures during the season, the 1950-51 Stanford squad finished 12-14 overall and 5-7 in the PCC Southern Division. The two talented Stanford Basketball frontcourt guys named Jim—Walsh, a guard, and Ramstead, the center—earned spots on the All-PCC-Southern-Division team.

Everett Dean's departure as basketball coach—he remained Stanford's head baseball coach—was prompted by a heart condition and the concomitant advice of his physician to lighten his coaching responsibilities. By all measures, Dean's tenure had been a successful one, having compiled a 166-119 won-loss record and having coached the 1941-42 team to the NCAA Basketball championship. Little wonder that Everett Dean, subsequent to his retirement, was elected to both the Naismith Basketball Hall of Fame (1966) and the College Basketball Hall of Fame (2006). He remains the only coach with an undefeated record (3-0) in the history of NCAA Tournament play.

Dean's successor was Bob Burnett, a reserve player on the Hank Luisetti–led Stanford Basketball teams of the late 1930s. Burnett was a fiery head coach in personality; as to his team's on-court style, he favored a fast pace and lots of scoring, even at the expense of defense if necessary. And he could be very creative as a strategist. Coach Burnett's first year, 1951-52, figured to be a good one, with Ed Tucker, Jim Ramstead, and Jim Walsh all returning starters. And added to that solid core of starters was a prolific-scoring 5′ 11″ freshman guard from Oakland named Ron Tomsic.

Despite winning 10 of its first 11 games, the 1951-52 Stanford Basketball team could manage only a 19-9 overall won-loss record, including a 6-6 mark in the PCC Southern Division. Ed Tucker, however, was a bright spot; not only did he lead the team in scoring with a 15.3 points-per-game average, he also led the entire PCC Southern Division in scoring. Despite this, he was not named to the All-PCC-Southern-Division team, although Jim Ramstead and Jim Walsh were named to the team with lesser scoring averages of 14.8 and 11.6, respectively. Ron Tomsic, though just a freshman, also averaged in double figures with 11.5 points per game.

The most colorful event during Bob Burnett's maiden season as head coach was a home game against USC on February 22, 1952. With Stanford having broken out to a 26-12 early lead, Burnett ordered his team to stall, with one of his players—Jim Walsh—holding the ball near midcourt and the other four Stanford players simply standing motionless elsewhere in the front court.

Forrest Twogood, the USC coach, was furious at Burnett and the "stall" tactic, apparently deeming it not sporting or sportsmanlike. For several minutes, he instructed his team to do nothing, and during this time—perhaps due to the stress of the situation—he walked out of the Stanford Pavilion, while play was going on, to smoke a cigarette. Eventually Twogood came back inside and ordered his defenders to aggressively contest the stalling Stanford offense. The predictable result was that USC was whistled for a total of 39 fouls during the game. A worse result for the Trojans was that the strategy was not good enough to overcome Stanford, which won the game by the score of 51-41.

For good measure, in the next night's game against USC, Bob Burnett called for the stall again. The combination of the stall, and Burnett's "platoon" strategy—removing starters Tucker, Walsh, Ramstead, Tomsic, and Oleg Suzdaleff and replacing them with an effective second unit of George Zaninovich, Don DeLong, Dave Epperson, Bruce Iversen, and Paul Johnson—was effective. Again, the result was a Stanford win over the Trojans, 75-64. These two unorthodox, back-to-back wins over USC at the Stanford Pavilion were the highlight of the 1951-52 campaign.

Graduation losses following that 1951-52 season were heavy. Ed Tucker's career scoring average of 15.8 points per game was second only to Hank Luisetti's in Stanford Basketball history. The departing Jim Walsh had become so good a player that, following graduation, he would make a U.S. Olympic Basketball team. The graduated Jim Ramstead had been a career double-digit per-game scorer. Predictably, the next two seasons were struggles for Stanford, particularly in conference games. In 1952-53, Stanford Basketball went 2-10 in PCC Southern Division play, and in 1953-54 Stanford's PCC Southern Division record was 3-9.

A bright spot on the 1952-53 team was the play of sophomore Ron Tomsic, who scored a Stanford-record 515 points to shatter Luisetti's single-season record of 465 points. Despite Stanford having just a 6-17 overall won-loss record in 1952-53, Tomsic earned All-PCC-Southern-Division honors. In 1953-54, with Tomsic poised for another big-scoring year, Stanford ripped off seven straight wins to begin the season. But in that seventh game, Tomsic suffered a season-ending knee injury. From that point forward, Stanford won only 6 of the 16 remaining games.

Filling the enormous scoring void caused by Ron Tomsic's absence seemed impossible, but 5′ 8″ sophomore guard George Selleck assumed the vacated spot and had a remarkable season in 1953-54, averaging nearly 14 points per game. Shouldering an even larger portion of the scoring responsibility was junior center Russ Lawler, who averaged 16.3 points to lead Stanford in scoring in 1953-54. Lawler's 408 total points in 1953-54 made him just the fifth Stanford Basketball player to score at least 400 points in a season, the others having been Hank Luisetti, George Yardley, Ed Tucker, and Tomsic.

That 1953-54 season was the last for coach Bob Burnett, who resigned to enter private business. Unlike prior Stanford Basketball head coaching searches, where some level of vetting of candidates was necessary, the search in the spring of 1954 required no such labor. The initial list of candidates yielded an obvious choice. He was 32 years old. He had just completed his sixth year as head coach at Penn. And, oh yes, he was a former Stanford Basketball player—a very good one, in fact. He was the Most Outstanding Player of the 1942 NCAA Basketball Tournament won by Stanford.

The justifiable, popular, and obvious choice for the next Stanford Basketball head coach was Howie Dallmar.

Dallmar enthusiastically accepted Stanford's offer and, as the new head coach, returned home to a good situation in his inaugural 1954-55 campaign. The returning talent—particularly at the guard position—was significant. Guard Ron Tomsic's knee had healed; he and fellow senior Russ Lawler would be co-captains as well as the primary scoring threats. Guard George Selleck, fresh off his productive sophomore campaign, returned and would form a dynamic, if somewhat undersized, backcourt with Tomsic.

Dallmar took advantage of the returning talent and led Stanford Basketball to a fine 16-8 record, including a 7-5 mark in the PCC Southern Division. It was the first winning record for Stanford in conference play since the 1942 NCAA championship season. For the second time in his four years as a Stanford Basketball player, Ron Tomsic averaged over 19 points per game in 1954-55, closing out his Stanford career by being named to the All-PCC-Southern-Division team for a third time. Tomsic also set the all-time Stanford career scoring record with 1,416 points, bypassing Hank Luisetti's 1,291 points (Luisetti, unlike Tomsic, played only three varsity seasons).

A comparison of Tomsic to Luisetti is at least somewhat apt, if for no other reason than the similarity of each man's scoring and shooting abilities. Don Liebendorfer, in *The Color of Life Is Red*, offered this opinion as to the shooting prowess of the two Stanford greats:

> *[Tomsic] was second to Hank Luisetti as a marksman, and I know some folks who would reverse that order. I must admit that if it were possible to bring this pair together in a purely*

shooting accuracy contest when each was in his prime the result would be very close, both from a set position and in motion.[20]

Liebendorfer hastened to confirm a well-known difference between Luisetti's and Tomsic's playing styles: "Ron shot more often than Luisetti did."[21]

Both co-captains, Tomsic and Lawler, graduated following the 1954-55 season, leaving just three starters for coach Howie Dallmar going into the 1955-56 Stanford Basketball season. (Tomsic, along with former teammate Jim Walsh, would earn a spot on the 1956 U.S. Olympic Basketball team after graduating from Stanford.) It seemed highly unlikely that Howie Dallmar's 1955-56 team could repeat the success level of the previous year's 16-8 won-loss standard.

For the 1955-56 season, a change in conference alignment occurred. No longer were there two divisions (North and South) of the Pacific Coast Conference; the two were merged into one Pacific Coast Conference comprising of Stanford and Cal, USC and UCLA, Oregon and Oregon State, Washington and Washington State, and Idaho. Led by senior captain George Selleck, who averaged 16 points per game and won All-Conference honors, the 1955-56 Stanford Basketball team went 18-6 overall and 10-6 in conference play, finishing tied for third (with Cal) behind UCLA (16-0) and Washington (11-5). Also averaging double figures for the season were juniors and starting forwards Barry Brown and Bill Bond, who each averaged an impressive 15 points per game.

The graduation of the great floor leader Selleck following the 1955-56 campaign was a loss the 1956-57 Stanford Basketball team could not overcome. Howie Dallmar suffered his first losing season in 1956-57 as Stanford went 11-15 overall and 7-9 in Pacific Coast Conference play. The leading scorers were Bill Bond, at 16.4 points per game, and sophomore starting guard Paul Neumann, who averaged 12.4 points per game in his first varsity season. The leading rebounder was also a sophomore, starting center Dick Haga, who averaged 6.5 rebounds per game.

Stanford notched almost an identical record the following season. The 1957-58 Stanford Basketball team finished 12-13 overall and 7-9 in the Pacific Coast Conference. Neumann shared team scoring leader honors with sophomore starting forward John Arrillaga—each of them averaged 12.3 points per game in 1957-58.

In 1958-59, with four upperclassmen starters consisting of junior John Arrillaga and seniors Paul Neumann, Dick Haga, and Doug Warren, Stanford bounced back with a solid 15-9 overall record including a 10-6 mark in the Pacific Coast Conference. Aided by the play of reserves—including football star Chris Burford, big man Neal Brockmeyer, pesky guard John Stahler, and free-throw shooter extraordinaire Jerry Thuesen—the 1958-59 Stanford squad did not lose more than two games in a row at any point during the season. They were only the second Stanford Basketball team since the 1942 NCAA championship team that could make that statement.

Paul Neumann, the 1958-59 team's leading scorer at 16.2 points per game, earned not only All-PCC honors but also second-team All-America honors in his final college season. Neumann would be a fourth-round NBA Draft selection that spring (by the Syracuse Nationals) and would play several seasons in the NBA with the Nationals and later with the San Francisco Warriors. An interesting note about Paul Neumann's NBA career is this: In 1965 Neumann was part of an NBA trade that involved the legendary Wilt Chamberlain, in which Chamberlain was dealt from the Warriors for three players including Neumann.

The 1959-1960 Stanford Basketball team fell back to a sub-.500 won-loss record, winning just 11 of 25 games. Another conference change had occurred: Stanford, Cal, USC, UCLA, and Washington joined to form the five-team Athletic Association of Western Universities (AAWU). Stanford's maiden AAWU conference record was 4-7. John Arrillaga, the team's senior captain and leading scorer in 1959-60, was named All-Conference and third-team All-American.

Following graduation, Arrillaga enjoyed a landmark career in real estate development in the burgeoning Silicon Valley region within which the Stanford campus is centered. That success, in turn, enabled the 1960 Stanford graduate to become a prominent benefactor to Stanford University for over half a century, and he remains actively so as of the publication of this book. John Arrillaga's desire to—within the strict bounds of the University's charitable donation and participation rules—participate as a lead donor and advisor with respect to dozens of major Stanford University initiatives, such as scholarship endowments and on-campus infrastructure projects (both athletics and non-athletics focused), has been historically meaningful not only for its significant dollar amount but also for its complete lack of self-seeking publicity or fanfare.

ABOVE, CLOCKWISE FROM TOP LEFT: *Ron Tomsic, three-time all-conference and U.S. Olympic team selection; George Selleck, captain and top scorer of 18-6 team in 1956; Paul Neumann, 1959 All-American; and John Arrillaga, 1960 All-American.* RIGHT: *George Yardley, first great big man in Stanford history and six-time NBA All-Star selection.*

IV. Dallmar's '60s and '70s Seasons

A Dose of a Championship, a New Pavilion, and a Miracle Weekend

For the most part, the 1960s were a high point in the Howie Dallmar coaching era at Stanford. From 1961-62 through 1966-67, the Stanford Basketball team averaged 16 wins per season and produced a collective 48-33 conference won-loss record, finishing no worse than fourth place in any of those seasons. This is remarkable because the 1960s coincided with the rise of UCLA as the nation's #1 college basketball power. In each of 1963-64, 1964-65, and 1966-67 seasons, UCLA went undefeated and won the NCAA championship—a stretch that constituted the beginning of the peak of the John Wooden coaching era at UCLA.

Despite a difficult 1960-61 campaign in which Stanford's won-loss record ended up being 7-17, there was a quiet optimism prior to the start of the 1961-62 Stanford Basketball season. A young big man had starred on the 1960-61 freshman team and was now eligible for varsity play. His name was Tom Dose. He was 6′ 8″ and he had erased many of Hank Luisetti's single-game and other freshman scoring records. According to Don Liebendorfer in *The Color of Life Is Red*, "Tom had a fine jump shot, could hook with either hand and was very strong on the boards."[22]

Even in its glory years, Stanford Basketball had never had anything close to a great big man, with the possible exception of George Yardley in his senior season in 1949-50. Dose had been informed of that historical "deficiency," and he and head coach Dallmar were determined that Dose would change that. With Dose ready to be a significant—and potentially dominant—contributor in his first varsity season, Stanford Basketball's starting lineup in 1961-62 featured players with solid and complementary skill sets. The forwards were senior co-captain John Windsor and sophomore newcomer and defensive specialist Hollis Moore. Dose was the center. The guards were junior Don Clemetson and two-sport (baseball and basketball) player Darrell Sutherland. The other co-captain, senior Phil Kelly, was a reliable scorer from the bench.

This roster of complementary players in 1961-62 produced an overall won-loss record of 16-6, including 8-4 in the AAWW, which was good enough for second place in the conference standings. John Windsor, who averaged 11 points and 10 rebounds per game, was named to the All-AAWU team. Dose led the team in scoring with 17 points per game, with a high of 29 points against USC, but somehow the sophomore center was not selected to the All-Conference team. A highlight of the 1961-62 campaign was an 82-67 home win over John Wooden's UCLA Bruins on March 9, 1962, which avenged two road losses at UCLA earlier that year. Guard Darrell Sutherland had a career-high 30 points in the win over the Bruins at the Stanford Pavilion.

With only John Windsor departing following the successful 1961-62 season, Stanford Basketball fans eagerly anticipated the coming of the 1962-63 campaign. Senior guards Don Clemetson and Darrell Sutherland were the co-captains. Tom Dose, now a junior, was primed for even bigger scoring and rebounding achievements. And one more thing: Stanford's defense in 1961-62, with Hollis Moore the best defender, had led the AAWU and had finished seventh in the nation in defensive statistics. With nearly everyone returning, the defense figured to be as good or even better in 1962-63.

As things turned out in 1962-63, not only did Stanford essentially equal the impressive achievements of the 1961-62 squad, it also came within one game of reaching the NCAA Tournament. Through the first ten games of the AAWU conference schedule in 1962-63, Stanford had a 7-3 record and was alone in first place. The three losses had been by a combined total of six points. With one weekend remaining in the regular season, Stanford had a two-game lead in the conference race with just two games left to play—road games at UCLA and USC. Stanford just needed to win one of the two games to clinch the AAWU title and the NCAA Tournament berth.

On March 8, 1963, at UCLA, Stanford got off to a rough start, not making its first field goal until nearly four minutes had elapsed in the game, and trailing 38-27 at halftime. Although Dose was on his way to a 31-point scoring performance and fellow Stanford big man Clayton Raaka was having a 16-point scoring night, it wasn't enough to win against the John Wooden–coached Bruins. Final score: UCLA 64 – Stanford 54. The loss cut Stanford's lead over UCLA in the standings to just one game. One game remained on the regular season schedule at USC. Any combination of a Stanford win or a UCLA loss (at home to Cal) would give Stanford sole possession of the AAWU championship.

Things started better against USC than they had against UCLA the previous night. Stanford led by ten points at halftime, 37-27. Although Dose fouled out with just over six minutes remaining, Stanford managed to maintain its lead and led by four points, 59-55, with 51 seconds to go in the game. But baskets by USC's Bill Morris and Gary Holman brought the Trojans even and sent the game into overtime. In the extra period, USC dominated Stanford, outscoring the visitors 8-2 and winning the game by the score of 67-61.

Meanwhile, on the west side of Los Angeles, UCLA thrashed Cal 72-53. Stanford and UCLA had finished the AAWU regular season as co-champions, with identical 7-5 conference records. A one-game playoff, three days later on Tuesday, March 12, 1963, in Los Angeles, would decide who the NCAA Tournament representative would be from the AAWU.

As it had four nights earlier, UCLA jumped Stanford early. The Bruins led at halftime and held a 40-26 advantage midway through the second half. Stanford then rallied, putting together a 14-4 run to slice the Bruins' lead to 44-40 with six minutes to go in the game. But Bruin coach John Wooden then employed a stall, which forced Stanford to foul. UCLA made its free throws upon being fouled, scoring the next five points to expand its lead to 49-40 with three minutes remaining in the game. Stanford could not rally further and fell, 51-45.

So UCLA, not Stanford, received the 1962-63 NCAA Tournament berth—the fifth for John Wooden in his 15-year UCLA coaching career but just his second in the previous seven seasons. His teams thereafter, beginning in the ensuing 1963-64 season, would advance to the NCAA Tournament in eleven of the next twelve seasons and would win an incredible 10 NCAA championships during that span. This Wooden greatness was not yet apparent in March of 1962-63. But that was little consolation to a Stanford team that had just lost its 17th consecutive game to UCLA in Los Angeles. Dose, who had averaged 30 points per game in the prior three games against UCLA in 1962-63, was held to 19 points in the playoff game loss.

The disappointment of missing the NCAA Tournament certainly did not diminish the luster of Tom Dose's junior season accomplishments. Dose scored 520 points in the 25 games, breaking Ron Tomsic's single-season record of 515 points set eight seasons earlier. Dose's scoring highs of 35 and 31 points were achieved, fittingly, against UCLA, the most difficult opponent for Stanford. Dose also averaged 10.8 rebounds per game. Dose and Don Clemetson, who averaged 12.4 points per game, were named to the All-AAWU team. Dose also was named a second-team All-American by the Helms Foundation. His 20.8 points-per-game average represented the first time a Stanford Basketball player had averaged at least 20 points per game in a season.

Despite the losses of co-captains and starting guards Don Clemetson and Darryl Sutherland, the 1963-64 Stanford Basketball team still had Tom Dose, and that alone made Stanford a contender for the conference title. He and fellow senior starter Hollis Moore were named co-captains for the 1963-64 season. Despite a more ambitious non-conference schedule that included a matchup with Kansas, Stanford nonetheless won 15 games overall and lost 10 in 1963-64, finishing in second place in the AAWU with a 9-6 record. This being the first of John Wooden's many undefeated seasons at UCLA, three of Stanford's conference 10 losses were to the eventual national champion Bruins.

Tom Dose again was named a Helms Foundation All-American at season's end, to go along with another All-AAWU citation. Dose again averaged 20 points per game, and he finished his glorious Stanford career as the program's all-time leading scorer with 1,441 points, 25 ahead of Tomsic's 1,416 points. On March 2, 1964, in his penultimate home appearance at the Pavilion, Dose poured in a career-high 42 points in a win over Washington State—a single-game scoring total that at the time ranked second in Stanford Basketball history, behind only Luisetti's 50-point game against Duquense in 1937-38.

A remarkable feat of the 1960s in Stanford Basketball was the fact that in the year after Tom Dose's departure from the program—that being the 1964-65 season—Stanford actually produced better overall and conference records. Two returning starters, junior forward Bob Bedell and senior guard Kent Hinckley, were the key pieces. Bedell averaged over 16 points per game while Hinckley contributed nearly 14 points per contest. Bedell was honored as an All-AAWU selection at the conclusion of the 1964-65 campaign. Another reason for Stanford's 15-8 overall and 9-5 AAWU record in 1964-65 was the play of junior starting center Ray Kosanke, a 6′ 9″ and 232-lb. backup to Dose the prior season. Kosanke averaged a solid 12 points and 8 rebounds per game in 1964-65.

For two more seasons, in 1965-66 and 1966-67, Stanford Basketball would continue its string of solid won-loss-record performances, thanks in part to one key newcomer in each season. In 1965-66, Bob Bedell returned for his senior campaign and was his usual highly productive self, averaging 16.8 points and 9.1 rebounds per game. Kosanke, also a senior, started once again at center and was even better than the prior year, producing 14 points-per-game and 9-rebounds-per-game averages. But perhaps the biggest reason for Stanford's 13-12 overall and 8-6 AAWU records was the play of a sophomore guard who had broken several of Tom Dose's freshman-team scoring records.

His name was Arthur Harris. At 6′ 4″, with perhaps the best vertical leap of any Stanford Basketball player who had preceded him, Art Harris authored one of the greatest sophomore seasons in Stanford history, averaging 16 points and 5 rebounds per game. Starting alongside fellow sophomore guard Gary Petersmeyer, with whom Harris would serve as co-captain two years later, Harris the newcomer was so good that he was named to the 1965-66 All-AAWU team. Sophomore Harris and senior Bob Bedell each scored more than 400 points in that 1965-66 season—just the second time in Stanford Basketball history that two players on the same team had done that, Ed Tucker and Ron Tomsic having done so in 1951-52.

Coach Dallmar's streak of consecutive winning seasons would reach six the next year, 1966-67. Bedell had graduated, but sophomore newcomer Don Griffin—up from the freshman team—joined the starting lineup at guard, Dallmar having moved Art Harris from guard to forward. Like Harris had done the year before, Don Griffin put together a tremendous sophomore campaign in 1966-67, averaging a team-high 15.6 points per game. With Harris contributing 14.9 points and a team-high 7.5 rebounds per game, and with Petersmeyer increasing his scoring to nearly 10 points per contest, this decidedly smallish Stanford Basketball team was able to achieve well more than was expected. The squad compiled a 15-11 won-loss record, including a 7-7 AAWU mark in a year in which UCLA and sophomore sensation Lew Alcindor dominated not only the AAWU but also the entire college basketball world with a perfect 30-0 record and an NCAA championship.

For the first time in six seasons, no Stanford player received All-Conference honors, although, based on statistics, a good case could be made for either Art Harris or Don Griffin to have been named to the All-Conference team. Griffin's big-scoring games included 33 points versus Washington and 30 points against USC. Nine times the sophomore scored 21 or more points in 1966-67. And, as observers of the 1966-67 Stanford Basketball team tell it, Griffin's defense was often as impressive as his offense.

As the calendar turned to 1967-68, Stanford Basketball faced even greater "size" challenges than it had faced the previous year. No Stanford starter stood taller than 6′ 6″, and only one weighed more than 210 lbs., that being 6′ 6″ sophomore center Steve Kuchenbecker. The conference did not yet have the full complement of talented big men—other than UCLA's Alcindor—that it would have in the coming seasons. Stanford's height problems in 1967-68 caused it to suffer its first losing season since 1960-61, with an overall won-loss record of 11-15, which included a 5-9 mark in the AAWU.

Not compromised in 1967-68, however, was the display of senior Art Harris's talent. Harris averaged 20.8 points per game, and he scored 540 points for the season, setting a new Stanford single-season record.

The 1968-69 Stanford Basketball season was best known for the mid-season opening of Stanford's new multisport athletics arena. Known as Roscoe Maples Pavilion and built at a cost of $3,300,000, the 7,500-seat facility was designed primarily for basketball but was capable of hosting volleyball, tennis, gymnastics, and wrestling events as well.

The new Maples Pavilion had a flat roof and concrete walls—the better to make the venue as noisy as possible. But the floor was the most innovative and talked-about feature of the new arena. The floor was unusually springy, due to its composition of cross-thatched layers of wood.

In the new arena, students were given the lower-level section of seats located directly across from the scorer's table and team benches. A popular early tradition at Maples was for the Stanford starters, upon being introduced by the public address announcer, to run over to the student section to slap hands with their fellow students. These various features of the new Maples Pavilion would prove, in time, to be huge venue advantages for Stanford. Unfortunately, in the first few years of its existence, the home team often was unable to take advantage of them.

On January 3, 1969, Maples Pavilion hosted its first Stanford Basketball game—Stanford vs. BYU. The Cougars prevailed, 95-89, but the next night Stanford evened the ledger, winning 94-78. In many ways, the opening of Maples was the highlight of the season. Stanford finished with an 8-17 record overall and a 4-10 mark in conference play in 1968-69, the final year of the Alcindor-era dominance at UCLA. Don Griffin went out with a flourish in his senior season in 1968-69, averaging 20.8 points per game. Fellow senior Mal McElwain—a skinny 6′ 5″ forward with a reliable jump shot—helped out by averaging 12.7 points per contest.

As compared to other Pac-8 teams—the conference name having been changed from AAWU to Pac-8—Stanford remained a relatively undersized team for the next two seasons, 1969-70 and 1970-71. Whereas Stanford was starting 6′ 7″ Bill Palmer at center, UCLA had three starters 6′ 8″ or taller, including the great frontcourt triumvirate of Sidney Wicks, Curtis Rowe, and Steve Patterson. Oregon had 6′ 9″ Stan Love—a future five-year pro and father of a future great in Kevin Love—as its big man. USC had 6′ 9″ Ron Riley, an All-American candidate and a key reason USC was able to upset mighty UCLA twice during those two seasons. Washington, too, had a talented big man, a future NBA player in 6′ 10″ Steve Hawes.

Against this seeming legion of talented big men residing on various Pac-8 opponent rosters, Howie Dallmar's talented shooters and sound defensive schemes did not have much of a chance. Stanford Basketball won only five games in 1969-70 and only six games in 1970-71. In both seasons, Stanford's Pac-8 record was 2-12. Amid these persistent difficulties in the early 1970s, however, were moments of Stanford Basketball brilliance on the court. Many of these moments were produced by a 6′ 5″ sharpshooting guard from California's Central Valley named Claude Terry.

Right from the start, as a debuting sophomore up from the freshman team, Terry established himself as the team's go-to scorer in 1969-70. Despite being the focus of virtually every Stanford opponent's defensive efforts, Terry was Stanford's leading scorer in each of his three seasons on the Farm, averaging 19.6, 20.9, and 21.2 points. His career shooting percentage was 47%—a remarkable feat for a player whose field-goal attempts typically were deep jump shots and who was defended with more vigor than any other Stanford player.

Maybe the most impressive of Claude Terry's qualities was his indefatigable spirit. Despite the many losses, despite the lack of consistent scorers around him to help out—with the exception of fellow guard Dennis O'Neill, a career double-digit scorer—Terry never ceased competing aggressively on the court.

That competitive spirit nearly resulted in a mammoth upset of UCLA at Maples Pavilion. On Friday night, January 15, 1971, the #1-ranked Bruins faced Stanford in Palo Alto in what was Stanford's Pac-8 home opener. With the Maples crowd roaring with every Stanford made basket and defensive stop, the undersized Indians nearly pulled off the upset and lost by just five points, 58-53, to a UCLA team that would later that season win its fifth consecutive NCAA championship.

In 1971-72, Howie Dallmar's team made progress on multiple fronts.

On the court, Stanford Basketball nearly doubled its overall win total from the prior year, winning a total of ten games. In Pac-8 play, Stanford produced a 5-9 record, which with a little luck could have turned out even better. Three of Stanford's conference losses were by four points or less. Terry, in his senior season, was named to the All-Pac-8 team, becoming Stanford's first All-Conference selection in five seasons.

Off the court, Howie Dallmar's effort to develop productive big men was beginning to pay dividends. Seven-foot Rich Kelley was preparing for future varsity action as a member of the 1971-72 freshman team. On the recruiting front, Dallmar was making decisive inroads with 6′ 8″-and-taller prep stars such as Ed Schweitzer and Tim Patterson, the latter of whom was the brother of former UCLA great Steve Patterson. Each of the 6′ 8″ Schweitzer and 6′ 10″ Patterson would decide to attend Stanford, and both would become Stanford frontcourt starters alongside Kelley in future seasons.

The payoff initially came in 1972-73. Kelley, who played his high-school ball just five miles from campus at Woodside High School, immediately became the starting center upon joining the varsity team. And what a difference-maker Kelley was. For the first time in six seasons, Stanford in 1972-73 had a winning record (5-4) through the non-conference portion of the schedule. For the entire year, the Cardinal—effectively the school's new nickname as of 1972-73 school year—finished above .500 for the first time in six seasons, with an overall won-loss record of 14-11. In conference play, the improvement was even more starkly seen. Stanford ended up 7-7 in the Pac-8, with each of the last four conference losses being by seven points or less.

On March 3, 1973, in a game at UCLA's Pauley Pavilion against the #1-ranked Bruins, who were then riding a 69-game winning streak, Stanford rose up. In a game that featured the second-ever matchup between Stanford sophomore Rich Kelley and UCLA junior All-American center Bill Walton, the Cardinal actually led by seven points at halftime, putting newsrooms on "upset alert" all over the country.

In that first half, Kelley had been able to score inside on Walton. UCLA coach John Wooden addressed that issue with a schematic change at halftime, implementing a 3-1-1 halfcourt trap in the second half that impaired Stanford's efforts to get Kelley the ball on the block near the basket. The UCLA strategy worked—the Bruins overcame the deficit and managed a six-point win, averting the upset.

Inside the Stanford locker room, having come close to taking down the mighty Bruin team, Rich Kelley spoke of his desire to take down UCLA and his resolve to make it happen at least once before his college career ended. This game taught Kelley, his teammates, and Coach Dallmar that it could be done.

Rich Kelley finished his sophomore season as Stanford Basketball's leading scorer at 17.3 points per game. Even more impressive was Kelley's season average of 13.2 rebounds per contest, a Stanford Basketball record. Kelley also shot nearly 52% from the field, and he converted better than 70% of his free-throw attempts. When the five-man All-Pac-8 team for 1972-73 was announced, Stanford sophomore Rich Kelley was on it, along with Walton, UCLA's Keith Wilkes, Oregon's Ron Lee, and Washington's Louie Nelson. One can count on one hand the number of Stanford sophomores who, as of 1975, had been All-Conference selections in their sophomore seasons.

In 1973-74, Rich Kelley repeated as an All-Conference selection, averaging over 18 points per game. He even improved his free-throw shooting percentage to 80.6%—an unheard-of accuracy level for a seven-footer. As far as rebounding, not only did Kelley again lead the team in that statistical category, he also put forth the greatest single-game rebounding effort a Stanford Basketball player had ever produced. On December 22, 1973, at Kentucky, Rich Kelley set a Stanford single-game record with an incredible 27 rebounds in a loss to the Wildcats.

Despite Kelley's individual success and accolades, the Cardinal stumbled a bit in 1973-74 as far as the won-loss record was concerned, winning 11 games and losing 14. In conference play, the Cardinal record was 5-9. Dallmar's starting lineup was his tallest ever, with 7′ 0″ Kelley at center, 6′ 11″ Tim Patterson and 6′ 8″ Ed Schweitzer at the forward slots, and 6′ 6″ David Frost and 6′ 3″ Melvin Arterberry at the guard positions.

Besides Rich Kelley, two other Stanford starters averaged double figures in 1973-74. Ed Schweitzer, a sophomore, averaged 12 points (along with 8 rebounds) per game. David Frost, a senior from Long Beach who also played baseball on the Farm and who five years later would be a starting pitcher for the 1979 American League West champion California Angels, averaged nearly 14 points per game.

If anything, Stanford may have been oversized in 1973-74. That year, it had trouble with teams featuring high scoring, smallish perimeter players such as USC (Dan Anderson), Oregon (Ron Lee), and Oregon State (Ricky Hawthorne). Against those three Pac-8 foes, Stanford won just one of six games in 1973-74.

For Rich Kelley, there was still that "UCLA thing" nagging him—a Stanford Basketball team had not beaten the Bruins in a very long time. The Bruin dynasty had begun to show cracks in 1973-74. UCLA saw its 88-game winning streak end in a January 19, 1974, loss to Notre Dame, and four weeks later UCLA suffered its first Pac-8 losses in four years, losing both games in a weekend road trip to Oregon and Oregon State. But Stanford once again fell short—just short—of slaying the UCLA dragon in 1973-74. On March 2, 1974, at Maples Pavilion, Kelley and Stanford gave the Bruins all they could handle before succumbing by a mere two points, 62-60.

That two-point loss game to UCLA was Stanford's final home game of 1973-74. Having just concluded his junior season, Rich Kelley knew that he had just two more chances—and just one more at Maples Pavilion—to realize his, his teammates', his coach's, and Stanford fans' collective goal of defeating John Wooden and UCLA.

Within 46 weeks, that goal would be achieved.

What occurred 46 weeks later, early in the 1974-75 conference schedule, was the first of the truly amazing games in Maples history: the first time the noise in the arena was truly deafening, the first time the fans rushed the court after the game, the first time a Stanford win in Maples made instant national news. This first of what has become a long line of incredible Maples Pavilion performances by a Stanford Basketball team happened in mid-January 1975. It is known, simply and fondly, as the Miracle at Maples.

The background: UCLA had won nine NCAA titles in the previous eleven seasons, and the Bruins were on their way to national championship #10 in 1975. Coach John Wooden had led UCLA to 57 conference wins in its most recent 59 games. With this formidable résumé, UCLA traveled to Palo Alto for a Friday night, January 17, 1975, Pac-8 contest against Stanford. The Bruins—featuring future NBA star Marques Johnson, future pros Dave Meyers and Richard Washington, and a seven-foot center in Ralph Drollinger—brought a perfect 12-0 record and a #2 national ranking into the game at Stanford. Stanford countered with a veteran-laden starting lineup featuring four seniors—Kelley, forward Scott Trobbe, and guards Melvin Arterberry and Mark Gilberg—along with junior forward Ed Schweitzer.

With a standing-room-only crowd of 7,913 behind it, Stanford got off to a strong start, building a double-digit lead early in the first half. With roof-rocking crowd noise accompanying every Cardinal basket, Stanford maintained its momentum and the first half ended with Stanford ahead of the Bruins, 37-24, despite the Cardinal having committed 10 turnovers. At the start of the second half, with the Maples roars seemingly reaching El Camino Real a half-mile away, the Stanford lead grew to 15 points. UCLA center Drollinger drew his fourth foul early in the half, aiding the Cardinal hopes for the upset.

Then UCLA came storming back, with its vaunted full-court press suddenly becoming effective. Bruin forward Richard Washington made a basket, then scored again. Suddenly UCLA had reeled off 11 straight points. With ten minutes remaining in the game, Stanford's lead had been sliced to four points, 45-41. Like so many times before, at home and on the road, the talented and poised Bruins of John Wooden seemingly were ready to take hold of a college basketball game. But with the screaming Maples fans behind them, the Stanford players held their ground during the final frenzied minutes. Stanford was able to convert field goals and free throws at the same rate as UCLA down the stretch, with Kelley and Schweitzer getting the big baskets and key rebounds. The Bruins could get no closer than within four points of the Stanford lead.

As the final few seconds ticked away, it suddenly sunk in to Stanford players, coaches, and fans—Stanford was not going to be denied on this night. The final score: Stanford 64 – UCLA 60. For the first time in 17 games since the mid-1960s, Stanford had beaten a UCLA team. As the final buzzer sounded, the ecstatic Maples student section—as one body—streamed off of the lower-level bleachers and engulfed the Stanford players. The court became a sea of humanity, bouncing on the springy Maples floor as the Stanford Band lustily and repeatedly played choruses of "All Right Now."

Rich Kelley was the difference-maker, finishing with 22 points, 13 rebounds and a perfect eight-for-eight from the free-throw line. Ed Schweitzer added 22 points, making 9 of 12 field goals and also contributing 8 rebounds. The Stanford big men, in their final collective chance to knock off UCLA at Maples Pavilion, had met the challenge.

News of the Stanford upset of #2-ranked UCLA immediately rocked newsrooms across the country late that Friday night and early the following Saturday morning. Any team beating UCLA in those days made for huge headlines. It was only the ninth Bruin loss in nine seasons. And it wouldn't be the only magic produced by Stanford Basketball that January 1975 weekend at Maples Pavilion.

In the 1970s, Pac-8 teams played conference games on Friday and Saturday nights. Then, as now, the conference schools traveled in pairs—UCLA and USC in one pair, Oregon and Oregon State in another, with Washington and Washington State as the third geographic pair that Stanford teams faced on conference-play weekends. Given the Friday-and-Saturday playing arrangement, Stanford had only 24 hours to savor the UCLA upset.

Another titan was coming to Maples: the nation's #5-ranked team, the USC Trojans. Would Stanford Basketball suffer a letdown after such an epic victory the previous evening? As freshman reserve guard Jay Carter later told the *Stanford Daily* about the Saturday morning and afternoon that followed the UCLA win and preceded the USC challenge, "all day long I had to calm myself down."[23]

Fortunately a Stanford senior—starting guard Mark Gilberg, who had scored nine points in the UCLA win and whom the *Stanford Daily* referred to as the "best guard on the floor" in the UCLA game—had used the right words in the locker room moments following his team's big upset of UCLA. To prepare his younger teammates mentally for a second consecutive evening of formidable competition, the veteran Gilberg had issued a warning: "If we don't win tomorrow [against USC]," Gilberg told his teammates sternly, "this [UCLA victory] doesn't mean a thing."[24]

Saturday night, January 18, 1975. Stanford versus USC. Once again a raucous, sellout crowd filled Maples Pavilion hoping for another upset win and another wild postgame celebration. The USC-Stanford game was tightly contested, right from the start. Avoiding the feared letdown, Stanford was able to forge an early lead, but only by single digits. Both Rich Kelley and USC guard Gus Williams were scoring points in bunches. Stanford led by a small margin at halftime, but a second straight Stanford upset victory over a highly ranked opponent was far from certain.

With 1:20 remaining in the game, Stanford held only a one-point lead, 63-62. With the shot clock not yet in existence, USC's strategy was to foul Stanford and hope for missed Cardinal free throws in the final minute. The Trojans chose Stanford center Rich Kelley as the target to foul and send to the free-throw line.

Bad decision by USC coach Bob Boyd.

Kelley, though fatigued from being pushed and leaned on for a second consecutive night, would prove that he had enough left in the tank and enough ice left in his veins—to shamelessly quote a couple of clichés—at the end of the USC game. Kelley coolly hit four consecutive free throws in the final minute—including both ends of a pressure one-and-one free-throw opportunity with 18 seconds remaining in the game and Stanford clinging to a one-point lead—to keep his team ahead on the scoreboard.

USC could not answer Rich Kelley's clutch free-throw shooting. Final score: Stanford 67 – USC 66. Again a wild, fans-rushing-the-court, band-rocking celebration accompanied the final buzzer. Kelley finished with 30 points and 15 rebounds, Ed Schweitzer added 19 points with another excellent (9-of-14) shooting performance, and Jay Carter was a perfect 5-for-5 from the floor for a very important 10-point contribution. Said Dallmar of Carter: "Freshmen are supposed to fold in situations like this, Jay didn't."

As Rich Kelley, who had tallied 52 points, 28 rebounds, and a perfect 18-of-18 from the free-throw line for Stanford in the two epic Cardinal victories, succinctly put it: "It was quite a weekend." Indeed, it had been the most amazing weekend in Stanford Basketball history: two wins in two nights over two national top-five-ranked teams. It had never happened before at Maples Pavilion. It has not happened since. Little wonder the January 1975 weekend was dubbed then—as it is remembered now—as the Miracle at Maples.

For head coach Howie Dallmar, the Stanford playing legend of the early 1940s and the beloved Stanford head coach since 1955, the win would provide a particularly sweet memory. Dallmar's final season as Stanford Basketball's head coach would be 1974–75. Dallmar could not have scripted a better signature game in that final season: a win over Hall of Famer John Wooden and eventual 1975 national champion UCLA at Maples Pavilion. Howie Dallmar had decades earlier achieved the rare feat of winning an NCAA championship as a player, and now as a departing coach, he had defeated an NCAA championship team in an era when hardly any opposing coach ever did. And he had done them both for Stanford Basketball.

Opposite, clockwise from top left:
Don Griffin finished among the top three scorers in the Pac-8 in 1969; Rich Kelley, three-time All-Pac-8 honoree and engineer of 1975's Miracle at Maples weekend; Coach Howie Dallmar and Tom Dose, star Stanford center of the early 1960s.

STANFORD
CLA
35

STANFOR
55

V. The DiBiaso and Dr. Tom Years

Transitions, Upsets, and Cornerstones of Renaissance

Howie Dallmar's 21 years (1955–1975) constituted the longest tenure of any Stanford Basketball head coach. Beloved and embedded, Dallmar remained on campus after leaving the head coaching post, becoming director of Stanford's popular intramural sports program. Who would be his successor?

Athletic Director Joe Ruetz decided in the spring of 1975 that the coaching reins would be handed over to 34-year old Dick DiBiaso. DiBiaso had been an assistant at Notre Dame under coach Digger Phelps since 1971. The Fighting Irish had become a very high-profile program in the early 1970s, with more victories over John Wooden's UCLA teams—including the historic win in January 1974 that halted the Bruins' 88-game winning streak—than any other team in the nation during that span of years. Notre Dame's success was a certainly a factor in Stanford's decision to hire the enthusiastic and expressive DiBiaso.

Dick DiBiaso's first year, 1975-76, would be burdened by the absence of the graduated center Rich Kelley. Nonetheless, new players to the program—such as freshmen Kimberly Belton and Paul Giovacchini as well as junior-college transfer George Schader—made immediate and positive impacts. Meanwhile, roster holdovers such as Mike Bratz, Tim Patterson, Jay Carter, and Melvin Arterberry ensured that, even in the brutal Pac-8 Conference, the Cardinal would be competitive in games. Unfortunately, being competitive didn't always equate with winning.

From 1975-76 through 1977-78, DiBiaso's teams put up won-loss records of, respectively, 11-16, 11-16 and 13-14. To be sure, this performance was not an improvement from the Rich Kelley–era Stanford Basketball teams. But Maples Pavilion—still less than ten years old yet already a well-recognized college arena name, due to Stanford's big home wins in the mid-1970s—continued to grow in reputation as a place where interesting and sometimes amazing things happened, despite Stanford's struggles in the won-loss department.

In those lean years of the late 1970s, sometimes the amazing things at Maples Pavilion occurred not while the game was going on but, instead, at *halftime*. Take, for instance, the final game at Maples during the 1976-77 season. There were 14 home games that season, and at each game $100 was offered to a randomly selected fan who could make a half-court shot in the one attempt allowed. If the shooter failed to make the shot, the prize amount increased by $100 at the next home game. There was just one contestant permitted per game.

Predictably, at the March 3, 1977, home game—the 14th and final home game that year—the prize amount had increased to $1,400 as no fan in the prior 13 games had made the half-court shot. Stanford was leading California, 37-31, as the team went off the court for halftime. The randomly selected contestant for the halftime half-court shot was a freshman tennis player named Peter Rennert—the Peter Rennert who would become a two-time tennis All-American before graduating in 1980. Rennert took the ball at midcourt, smiled and—with an unorthodox underhanded fling of the ball—swished the shot attempt! And then he celebrated his accomplishment minutes later by buying food and drink for fellow game attendees at one of the Maples Pavilion concession stands!

The next games at Maples—which happened to be the first two games of the ensuing 1977-78 campaign—were interesting for what was happening *during* the games. In perhaps the most impressive debut a Stanford Basketball freshman has *ever* had on the Farm, guard Mark Pitchford scored 41 points in the two games combined to help lead the Cardinal to thrilling one-point wins over Cal Poly Pomona and San Jose State. Pitchford dazzled in the opener, coming off the bench to score 28 points as Stanford edged Cal Poly Pomona 92-91 in overtime, winning the game on two Jeff McHugh free throws in the final seconds. The next night, Pitchford hit a corner-of-the-key jump shot with six seconds remaining to cap a five-point Stanford comeback in the final 30 seconds as the Cardinal nipped the Spartans, 81-80.

In what would symbolize, perhaps, the ill-luck that all-too-often afflicted a Dick DiBiaso–coached Stanford Basketball team, Pitchford subsequently would suffer a back injury that limited his playing career to just that freshman season in 1977-78, in which he was able to score just 151 more points after that thrilling two-game freshman debut.

The first truly amazing DiBiaso–era game at Maples took place on December 27, 1978. The opponent was once again UCLA, always a top draw and always a big target for Stanford. It was a Bruin team that was once again a top-five-ranked team nationally and one that would reach the NCAA Tournament Elite Eight in March of that 1978-79 season. Boasting a roster of future NBA players such as David Greenwood, Kiki Vandeweghe, and Brad Holland, UCLA seemed on paper too much for a relatively untested Stanford Basketball squad.

Stanford's starting guards in 1978-79 were Lieutenant "Wolfe" Perry, a 6′ 8″ shooting guard, and point guard Paul Giovacchini. Both were seniors. Returning All-Conference junior Kimberly Belton started at forward alongside freshman forward Brian Welch, and junior Tom Schmalzreid was the starter at center. Key reserves included junior guard Daryle Morgan, sophomore forward Jeff Ryan, freshman forward Orlando Ward, and freshman guard Doug Marty.

With the additions of Arizona and Arizona State to the conference in 1978-79, the Pac-8 was renamed the Pac-10. The number of conference games each league member would play increased from 14 to 18 games, and because of this expanded schedule, it became necessary for teams to play Pac-10 games in December. One of Stanford's December Pac-10 games in 1978-79 was against UCLA—a December 27, 1978, matchup at Maples Pavilion.

UCLA entered the game with a 6-1 record and a #3 national ranking. As had been the case with every Stanford game against UCLA since Stanford's 1975 upset win over the Bruin, a sellout crowd was on hand at Maples Pavilion. The Bruins played solid basketball in the first half but, amazingly, so did the upset-minded Cardinal, and the game was tied 34-34 at halftime. With 4:11 remaining in the game, Kiki Vandeweghe scored to give UCLA a 72-68 lead. Stanford answered with a basket at the 3:49 mark, cutting the Cardinal deficit to two, 72-70.

Then the Bruins went into "protect" mode. It being still eight years away from the advent of a shot clock in college basketball, UCLA coach Gary Cunningham was free to have his team employ a stall, and he directed his team to do just that. As opposed to earlier versions of the stall, in the 1970s a stall meant stationing four players near the four corners of the front court, with a fifth player positioned near the free-throw line to create maximum spacing. If unchallenged, the stalling team could literally go several minutes keeping possession of the ball by simply having a player dribble the ball or having players pass the ball among themselves.

Stanford allowed UCLA to maintain stall for a couple of minutes. Then, with 1:37 remaining in the game, the Cardinal opted to foul UCLA's David Greenwood. The Bruin senior All-American missed the front end of a one-and-one free-throw opportunity, and Stanford grabbed the rebound. On the attack in the frontcourt, Stanford's Orlando Ward was fouled. The freshman made the first of two free throws to cut UCLA's lead to 72-71. One minute and 11 seconds remained in the game. Ward had a second free throw to try to tie the score.

Ward's second free throw missed, but the ball bounced off Greenwood and out of bounds. The Cardinal inbounded the ball and immediately went into a stall of its own, setting up one final possession and a chance for a basket or free throws to win the game. What happened next might be best described as a dream scenario for Stanford—literally. One of Stanford's key players, sophomore Jeff Ryan, told reporters that the night before the UCLA game that he had had a *dream* that Stanford would upset the Bruins and win by one point.

Fittingly, on Stanford's final possession, with Stanford trailing by one point, the ball found its way into the hands of Jeff Ryan. Less than five seconds remained in the game. Ryan sighted the hoop and tossed up a short jump shot—good! And he was fouled! Stanford now led by one point, 73-72, with Ryan going to the free-throw line for one free-throw attempt. Just two seconds remained in the game. UCLA was out of timeouts.

Ryan, being a savvy Cardinal hoopster, intentionally missed the free throw, knowing that the timeout-less Bruins could do no more than rebound the miss and—at best—heave the ball 80 feet toward the goal with virtually no chance of scoring. Everyone expected, therefore, a one-point Stanford victory, just as Jeff Ryan had dreamed the night before. Well, the ending *almost* happened that way.

Instead of Jeff Ryan's dreamed-of one point Stanford win, the final margin of victory ended up being three points. Orlando Ward rebounded Ryan's intentionally missed free throw and in one motion dunked the ball through the basket as time expired. Final score: Stanford 75 – UCLA 72. Screaming and deliriously happy Cardinal fans—for the first time since the 1975 upset over the #2-ranked Bruins—streamed onto the Maples court in celebration of the epic upset of #3-ranked UCLA.

Jeff Ryan and Orlando Ward's late-game heroics did not diminish the luster of Wolfe Perry's performance that evening. If the game was Jeff Ryan's dream ending, it was also Wolfe Perry's dream *game*, period. Perry scored 34 points on 15-of-20 field-goal shooting plus four made free throws. Had the three-point line been in effect, Perry would have scored at least 40 points. Stanford, as a team, made 18 of its 27 shots in the second half, with Perry hitting 7 of his 9 second-half field-goal attempts.

The win was UCLA's first conference loss in three seasons, and it was Dick DiBiaso's first win over the Bruins in seven tries. Stanford showed, as it had three years earlier when the Stanford head coach was Howie Dallmar and the headline player was Rich Kelley, that it again could rise up and knock off a top-five-ranked team, regardless of the star power on the opponent's roster.

"That's the most points I ever scored in my life," said Wolfe Perry, "and that includes summer ball and playing around with my little brother." As of Stanford Basketball's 100-year anniversary, Perry is one of only twenty Stanford Basketball players to have scored 34 or more points in a game. Following his graduation from Stanford, Perry did not have a career in professional basketball but nevertheless was able to maintain a connection with basketball in his working life—he became an actor and one of his prominent roles was as the Teddy Rutherford character in the popular high-school basketball sitcom *The White Shadow*, which aired for several seasons on the CBS network.

The other UCLA game hero, Jeff Ryan, did not limit his late-game magic to just the Bruins. Just two nights following the UCLA game, on December 29, 1978, Ryan "replicated" his dream ending against UCLA with *another* last-second-shot masterpiece. This time it was an end-of-game basket in San Diego to enable Stanford to knock off San Diego State, 85-84, in the latter's holiday tournament. Although many are curious, there has been no inquiry as to whether Ryan foresaw the San Diego State game's outcome in a dream, as he had done prior to the UCLA win. Those back-to-back December wins were the highlight of the 1978-79 season.

Coach Dick DiBiaso's final three seasons on the Farm, from 1979-80 through 1981-82, featured still more memorable games at Maples. The first of these was the game still remembered as the "Stall Game." It was, and remains, one of the most unique college basketball games of the pre-shot clock era. It happened on Monday, January 28, 1980, at Maples Pavilion.

Stanford, with an overall record of 3-13 including a last place 1-7 record in Pac-10 conference play, hosted the nation's #2-ranked team, 18-1 Oregon State. It was a mismatch, on paper, and the expected-to-be-sparse Maples Pavilion crowd didn't figure to be much help to the underdog Cardinal. DiBiaso concluded that a conventional game approach would not work against coach Ralph Miller's powerful Beaver squad, so he opted to employ the stall strategy. Said DiBiaso of his strategic choice: "It was our goal to have the game come down to the final two minutes. Our strategy was to stay in the delay even if we were down by as many as six to eight points."

Stanford held the ball on each possession in the first half, sometimes for minutes at a time. Unless a wide-open driving lane to the basket presented itself, or a teammate away from the ball flashed to the basket for a high-percentage backdoor pass-and-layup opportunity, the Cardinal player with the ball had been instructed to simply stand in place and hold the ball. On defense, Oregon State did not apply pressure against the Stanford stall strategy, except in select circumstances when a turnover possibility presented itself. And in those few instances when Oregon State did apply pressure to a Cardinal ball handler, the Cardinal player with the ball simply passed the ball backward to an open teammate standing alone near the half-court line. The Beavers simply weren't going to guard Stanford players situated 25 feet or more from the basket.

For its part on offense, Oregon State was not playing a delay game, but the keep-away strategy employed by Stanford meant very few opportunities for the Beavers to score in the first half. Predictably, the two teams took less than fifteen shots, combined, in the first half. Instead of a first half played in the typical 50-60 minutes of real time, it was played in less than 30. The predictably low-score halftime tally was 12-12.

The Stanford stall strategy remained unchanged in the equally speedily played, and no less fascinating, second half. Each team scored four points in the first ten minutes of the second half. With eight minutes remaining in the game, Beaver forward Dwayne Allen scored a basket to make the score 18-16 in favor of Oregon State. After Stanford did not score on its next stall-ball possession, Oregon State suddenly decided to go into a stall game of its own—to "protect" its now two-point advantage. For the next seven minutes, Stanford simply stood around on defense, content with allowing OSU to stall and the clock to wind down.

The score was still 18-16 when, with less than one minute to go in the game, the Cardinal finally decided to foul OSU's Dwayne Allen. Allen missed the front end of the one-and-one free-throw opportunity, and Stanford rebounded the miss. The Cardinal now had a chance to tie the game. With less than fifteen seconds left to play in the game, sophomore point guard Doug Marty had the ball in the frontcourt, attacked the free-throw lane area with the dribble, and then threw a pass to freshman forward

Brian Welch, who was moving toward the basket as he received the ball. But Welch bobbled the pass and was called for traveling with nine seconds remaining in the game.

Following the inbound pass, Oregon State tried to play "keep away" for the final nine seconds, but Stanford managed to foul OSU's Jeff Stout with two seconds remaining. Stout missed the front end of the one-and-one, but in the remaining two seconds the Cardinal was not able to get off a potential game-tying shot attempt. The game ended with the final score being Oregon State 18 – Stanford 16. It was, and remains, the lowest scoring basketball game in Maples Pavilion history. No Stanford team had scored fewer points in a game since the end of World War II. The Cardinal finished 7-for-12 in field-goal shooting for the *entire game*. Doug Marty scored eight points, Brian Welch added six points, and Orlando Ward had two free throws for two points. That was the extent of the Stanford scoring.

The Cardinal struggled the remainder of that 1979-80 campaign, but did finish the home schedule with a flourish. On Saturday night, March 1, 1980—Senior Night for the Stanford Basketball senior quartet of Kimberly Belton, Tom Schmalzried, Doug Barnes, and Daryle Morgan—Belton had a Maples finale for the ages. Twice a second-team All-Conference performer and once a first-teamer, Belton scored a career-high 41 points in a thrilling 93-91, Stanford overtime win over USC.

The final high-water mark of the DiBiaso era would come the next season, 1980-81. Never in any prior year in Stanford Basketball history had a freshman class had such a dominant role on a Stanford team. The four freshman recruited by DiBiaso who entered Stanford as freshmen in 1980-81 were the following: Keith Jones from Phoenix, AZ; Roger Lemons from Anaheim, CA; John Revelli from Scarsdale, NY; and Hans Wichary from San Diego, CA.

Due to, among other things, graduation losses from the previous season, Jones, Revelli, Wichary—and to a lesser extent Lemons—received playing time right away. The group performed solidly, if not spectacularly, during the first two months of the season. Stanford's won-loss record at the end of the non-conference portion of the 1980-81 schedule was 4-5.

Not much changed as the calendar turned to January, except that Jones turned some heads with a breakout 23-point scoring night against Washington State at Maples Pavilion on January 17, 1981. Jones, Revelli, and Wichary were starting and playing solidly, but they weren't putting up extraordinary numbers or wowing Stanford fans. At least not yet.

But then came February of 1981, a month in which these freshmen would come of age and become protagonists in two more amazing Maples Pavilion basketball nights. The two February 1981 games presented opportunities for a seemingly undermanned Stanford to knock off not one but two top ten-ranked teams, as had been the case in the two "Stanford-as-David" versus "UCLA-as-Goliath" games in 1975 and 1978. Only this time, in 1981, the David metaphor *really* fit. The key players for Stanford Basketball in 1981, unlike as in 1975 and 1978, were freshmen.

The first of these David-versus-Goliath games occurred on Saturday, February 7, 1981. A sellout crowd of 7,500 packed Maples Pavilion. Once again the opponent was Ralph Miller–coached Oregon State. Once again, as was the case the prior season in the Stall Game, the Beavers came to Maples as the nation's #2-ranked team. The Beavers were anchored, as in the prior season, by senior center Steve Johnson, who would finish his career as the most accurate field-goal shooter in NCAA history, and two senior All-Pac-10 guards in Ray Blume and Mark Radford.

Stanford countered with a starting lineup of three freshmen—Keith Jones, John Revelli, and Hans Wichary—and two juniors, Brian Welch and Doug Marty. Questions abounded within Stanford Basketball fandom. Would Stanford stall again? If not, could the Cardinal keep the game margin within 20 points and make the anticipated loss seem less embarrassing?

What happened instead was 40 minutes of drama. Although Stanford trailed 12-3 to start the game, it fought back to tie the game 15-15 with nine minutes remaining in the first half. The Beavers forged ahead by four points at halftime, but again Stanford came back to trail by just two points, 43-41, a few minutes into the second half. The Maples crowd was in a frenzied state once again, hoping for another epic upset victory and raucous postgame celebration.

The upset didn't happen, although the Cardinal came close.

In the final minutes of the game, the upperclassmen-dominated Beavers were the more poised team. OSU led by six points with five minutes remaining, and although Stanford was able to get within four points, 55-51, with 1:16 left, it could get no closer. The nation's #2 team, for a second straight season, had managed to escape Maples Pavilion with a narrow margin of victory, 62-57. But this had not been a stall-ball game. How was this inexperienced, freshman-dominated Stanford Basketball team able to almost take out the undefeated and #2-ranked Beavers? Two weeks later, the nation would find out.

The date was Saturday, February 21, 1981. The opponent was #10-ranked UCLA. Coached now by Larry Brown, the Bruins had eleven en months earlier played in the 1980 Final Four, reaching the national championship game against Louisville and leading in the final minutes of the game before falling by single digits. The majority of UCLA's starting lineup in 1980-81 featured returnees from that 1980 national championship game. Again Maples Pavilion was packed to the rafters. Many fans had seen Stanford's near upset of #2-ranked Oregon State two weeks earlier. Could the freshmen-laden Cardinal repeat, or perhaps even exceed, that effort against UCLA?

UCLA had the veteran and future NBA forward Mike Sanders to do battle against John Revelli in the "low post" area (near the basket). On the perimeter, the Bruins had two starting guards who the prior season had been starters and freshmen All-Americans, Rod Foster and Michael Holton. Both superb defenders, Foster and Holton could take turns defending Stanford's fledgling freshman guard Keith Jones. In other words, the matchups did not look promising for Stanford. But from the opening tip, the Cardinal youngsters played with confidence and hunger, and none more so than Keith Jones.

The frosh phenom Jones went wild from the start, scoring in all kinds of ways—blow-by drives to the rim, stop-on-a-dime pull-up jumpers from the 10-15-foot range, and an occasional long-range jump shot. And Jones had help. In the paint, freshman Revelli was able to get putback baskets and score with power moves. And fellow freshman Wichary was able, on this night, to score not only inside with his 6′ 9″ frame but also step outside and drill multiple midrange jump shots.

Stanford led in the first half, but the game was tied 38-38 at halftime. The Bruins scored the first four points of the second half, but immediately thereafter the Cardinal—with Jones leading the way—went on a 10-0 run to go up by six points. The Stanford lead was five points, 73-68, going into the final minute of the game. The Bruins then scored the next four points, the latter two with 16 seconds remaining, to slice the Cardinal advantage to just one point, 73-72.

John Revelli was fouled by UCLA's Darren Daye on the ensuing inbounds play but missed the front end of the one-and-one free-throw opportunity. The Bruins came downcourt bent on getting a game-winning basket or free throws. But, with ten seconds remaining in the game, Bruin Michael Holton's shot attempt was blocked by Hans Wichary. Stanford seized possession of the ball following the block, and five seconds later Stanford guard Doug Marty was fouled upon catching a length-of-the-court pass.

Marty made one of two free throws. The score was now 74-72

Cardinal, with five second remaining. UCLA rushed upcourt. Rod Foster, who would finish with a game-high 24 points, got open for a 10-foot shot attempt that would have sent the game to overtime, but the shot fell short. Game over. Final score: Stanford 74 – UCLA 72.

The loud and celebratory crowd reaction as the final buzzer sounded was not new: A student-led postgame court rush, with Stanford Band accompaniment, engulfed the Maples Pavilion floor, just as had occurred in January 1975 and December 1978, when Stanford teams likewise had upended highly ranked and heavily favored UCLA teams. But the way Stanford had architected the upset *was* new. Stanford had taken out top -ten-ranked UCLA almost exclusively with freshmen.

Keith Jones finished with 23 points, shooting a stunning 9-of-10 from the floor against, in Rod Foster and Michael Holton, perhaps the quickest, most athletic and defensively gifted a guard tandem as a Stanford Basketball team had ever faced. John Revelli added 16 points and Hans Wichary contributed 14 points. Those three freshmen starters for Stanford not only led the team in scoring, they also scored 53 of Stanford's 74 points!

From Los Angeles to New York, evening sports reports that Saturday night and newspaper headlines the next morning led with the following opening paragraph, or variations thereof: "Top 10-Ranked UCLA falls to a Cardinal team with twice as many losses as wins. Who *are* these Stanford kids?" Unfortunately, there would be no further epic wins for Stanford the remainder of that 1980-81 season—although the Cardinal did conclude the campaign with a satisfying home win on March 7, 1981, over a solid Cal team by a score of 81-72, with multiple freshmen again dominating play for Stanford.

In contrast to 1980-81, there would not be any memorable wins in 1981-82, during which Stanford Basketball experienced the pain and frustration of a 7-20 season. With a month left in the season, Dick DiBiaso announced that, effective at the end of the regular season, he would resign as Stanford Basketball head coach.

DiBiaso, in certain ways, clearly left a positive mark on Stanford Basketball. During his seven-year tenure on the Farm, the coach the players called "DEE-bo" led Stanford Basketball to two wins over top-ten-ranked UCLA teams, had nearly knocked off two different #2-ranked Oregon State teams, had produced a couple of NBA players in Mike Bratz and Kim Belton, and in 1980 had recruited the most productive freshman class yet seen at Stanford.

Athletic Director Andy Geiger conducted a brief search following

DiBiaso's departure. Dr. Tom Davis, holder of a doctorate in athletics history and head coach of a Boston College team that in 1981-82 came within one game of reaching the Final Four, was named the new Stanford Basketball head coach in late March of 1982.

Dr. Tom would have a four-year run on the Farm. But several obstacles confronted the new coach even before he coached his first game. The roster was depleted. Senior starters Brian Welch and Doug Marty were gone to graduation, and key reserve Roger Lemons had sustained a career-ending knee injury. Recruiting had suffered. No player taller than 6′ 5″ having been signed to a national letter of intent during the prior year's recruiting period, only one player on the roster was 6′ 10″ or taller—reserve center David Nussbaum. In other words, the roster for 1982-83 was a bit short-handed even before practice began in the fall of 1982.

The maiden Davis season was notable for a handful of reasons. One was the liberal substitution of players during games; routinely ten or more Stanford players would play in a game, with three-or-more subs at a time often checking into the game simultaneously. Another was a steady diet of full-court pressure applied against the opponent, which was one of the reasons frequent Cardinal subs were necessary. The energy-intensive style of play demanded hustle and a large in-game rotation. Even end-of-the-bench guys such as senior Darin Maurer, a high-school classmate and teammate of future U.S. President Barack Obama at Punahou High School in Hawaii, would find themselves in games more often than they thought they would when the season began.

Tom Davis rewarded production, not reputation, in doling out playing time. Thus three freshmen—guard Keith Ramee, forward Earl Koberlein and nonrecruited walk-on forward Andy Fischer—were in the starting lineup together during the first three weeks of the season, which saw Stanford surprise many by bursting out to a perfect 6-0 record. Fischer was the poster-boy for the ultrakinetic and full-court style of play that Tom Davis was forced to emphasize in 1982-83 with only two reliable half-court scorers, juniors Keith Jones and John Revelli, in his lineup.

The Davis retooling worked, at least on the offensive end of the court. The hectic pace of play produced nearly 76 points per game, 41st best among the 274 Division 1 teams. The 1982-83 team shot an exceptional 54.8% for the season, though it did allow opponents to shoot 51.3%. In January 1983, in a road game at Oregon, Stanford set a single-game record for shooting percentage, 76.9%, in a win over the Ducks.

Besides Jones and Revelli averaging nearly 20 points per game each, two sophomores—sharpshooting forward Johnny Rogers and versatile wing Steve Brown—each averaged ten points per game for the Cardinal in 1982-83. The productivity on offense led to one thing: an immediate end to the streak of losing seasons. In Tom Davis's first season on the Farm, a Stanford Basketball team finished the season with a nonlosing record (14-14) for the first time in ten seasons.

Had John Revelli not suffered a season-ending knee injury in February, the 1982-83 Stanford Basketball team may have recorded *even more* wins. Keith Jones was brilliant all season, shooting nearly 56% from the floor—an incredibly high percentage for a 6′ 2″ guard—and had a 36-point career-high scoring night at Arizona late in the season. So what was the takeaway from the initial Dr. Tom coaching year in 1982-83? Davis looked like he could win at Stanford, and Revelli and Jones—his two stars—clearly were primed for big senior seasons in 1983-84.

The elevated predictions for 1983-84 were initially fulfilled. The Cardinal raced out to an 11-1 non-conference record. The lone loss? Saturday evening, December 3, 1983, at Maples Pavilion against #1-ranked North Carolina in the championship game of the four-team, two-night Hewlett-Packard Stanford Invitational. Before a Maples Pavilion all-time record crowd of 8,000—500 over capacity—the Michael Jordan and Sam Perkins–led Tar Heels won the game by 13 points, 88-75, although the Cardinal were down by only six points late in the second half. But Michael Jordan was not, as things turned out, the weekend headliner at Maples—not by a longshot.

The first night of games of that December 1983 Stanford Invitational featured Fordham against North Carolina and San Jose State against Stanford. Fordham lost the opener to Carolina, 73-56, but during that game the heavily pro-Stanford fans at Maples Pavilion fell in love with a Fordham junior guard named Jerry Hobbie. Hobbie's appeal wasn't his so much on-court productivity—he tallied only a modest eight points against the Tar Heels—but rather his on-court hustle and workman-like flair.

Hobbie became a Maples darling almost instantly, stealing the ball from North Carolina superstar Michael Jordan on the first play of the game and going the length of the court for a layup. The infatuation grew with each unorthodox left-handed jump shot that Hobbie attempted. By the next night's consolation game against San Jose State, Hobbie was the center of attention at Maples Pavilion. Fans squealed with delight whenever Hobbie had possession of the ball, and whenever he scored a thunderous ovation cascaded throughout Maples. When the San Jose State game was over,

Hobbie had scored a career-high 21 points, his team had won by 15 points, and the Maples Pavilion student section was chanting "*M-V-P, M-V-P*" and "*Transfer, Transfer*"! And that wasn't the end of the Hobbie love.

At halftime of the Stanford-North Carolina game that followed his team's game with San Jose State, Jerry Hobbie emerged from the Fordham locker room and, clad in street clothes, was standing with his teammates near the Stanford student section. He was immediately surrounded by autograph-seekers. While this was going on, Stanford President Donald Kennedy walked over to shake his hand. And then the students spontaneously implored Hobbie to pick up a basketball from a nearby rack of basketballs and try a midcourt shot. To the delight of the crowd, he agreed to do so.

Jerry Hobbie missed his first half-court shot attempt. The crowd groaned. Hobbie motioned for the ball to be passed back to him. He tried again—*and drained the half-court shot*! Bedlam in the Stanford student section! Hobbie was carried off the court on the shoulders of several Stanford students, as loud staccato chants of "*Hob-bie, Hob-bie*" reverberated inside Maples Pavilion. The Stanford Band took the cue and struck up a chorus of "All Right Now," the school's unofficial fight song, as an elevated Jerry Hobbie left the floor.

Not surprisingly, following the Stanford-North Carolina game, Jerry Hobbie was named to the six-man all-tournament team, along with North Carolina's Sam Perkins, Matt Doherty, and Buzz Peterson, and Stanford's Keith Jones and John Revelli. On a night when Hall of Fame Tar Heel coach Dean Smith won his 500th career game and his North Carolina team preserved its national #1 ranking with a tightly contested win over Stanford, the story was—and forever remains—a Fordham guard named Jerry Hobbie.

As far as Stanford Basketball's young men in 1983-84, the great 11-1 non-conference start did not lead to equal success as conference play began. Several narrow losses were part of a disappointing six-game Cardinal losing streak to begin the Pac-10 portion of the schedule. But immediately thereafter Stanford reeled off six straight conference wins heading into a Saturday, February 18, 1984, matinee at home against perennial power UCLA. Before a sellout crowd, and despite having inserted a freshman—football starting quarterback and two-sport athlete John Paye—into the starting lineup at point guard, the Cardinal prevailed against the Bruins, winning by the score of 75-64. Once again the fans flooded the floor in a raucous postgame celebration.

In their final game against UCLA that February 1984 Saturday afternoon, Keith Jones scored 23 points and John Revelli added 21 points to lead the way for Stanford. The Cardinal shot 54% for the game and went to the free-throw line an astounding 37 times, making 29. The national television audience on CBS saw the Cardinal win its 18th game of the 1983-84 campaign, against just 8 losses, by outscoring the Bruins by 12 points in the second half. The Dr. Tom playbook was in full effect in the victory over UCLA: Cardinal players moving the ball side to side on offense to put the defense on its heels, then either passing the ball inside for power buckets and free throws (typically Revelli or sophomores Earl Koberlein and Andy Fischer) or hitting the open outside jump shot (typically Jones or junior Steve Brown).

The possibility for Stanford Basketball to gain its first postseason berth in many years suddenly became very real immediately following the UCLA win. But the Cardinal could manage only a 1-4 record to close out the regular season. That tepid finish meant that—despite a very worthy 19-12 overall record—Stanford was denied an invitation not only to the NCAA Tournament but also to the postseason NIT.

The final two Tom Davis years are most remembered for the impressive recruiting haul that Davis and his assistants—Bruce Pearl, Gary Close, and Kermit Washington—turned in with regard to the incoming 1985-86 freshman class. The signees were Todd Lichti, Howard Wright, Terry Taylor, and Bryan McSweeney. Together with the prior year's freshman class, which featured Eric Reveno, Greg Butler, and Scott Meinert, the foundational pieces were in place for Stanford Basketball to at least approach, if not realize, its dream of returning to postseason play.

Head coach Tom Davis, however, was not around to see Stanford fulfill its goal of returning to the NCAA Tournament. Reportedly disappointed by Admissions Department decisions regarding Stanford Basketball recruiting targets—the most prominent of which involved a San Francisco prepster named Chris Munk—Davis left Stanford following the 1985-86 season for the University of Iowa, where he would guide the Hawkeyes to the NCAA Tournament Elite Eight in his first season and the Sweet 16 in his second.

Clearly, the Cardinal had lost a very good coach, one who recruited well, taught the game effectively, and maximized the available basketball talent on the roster. Could the Cardinal find that kind of teacher, that kind of exceptional fit, that kind of winning potential in a successor?

The answer was a resounding yes.

TOP LEFT: *Kimberly Belton, best player of the late 1970s;* TOP RIGHT: *John Revelli, four-year starter in the early 1980s;* ABOVE: *Keith Jones, two-time All-Pac-10 guard and one of the most gifted offensive players in school history.*

TOP: *Maples Pavilion, shown prior to its renovation in 2004, has been the home of Stanford Basketball since 1969;* ABOVE LEFT: *Dick DiBiaso's seven-year run as head coach featured multiple wins over top-ten-ranked UCLA teams;* ABOVE RIGHT: *Dr. Tom Davis (1982-86) brought pressure defense, high-percentage frontcourt offense, and rapid-fire player substitutions.*

VI. The Mike Montgomery Tenure Begins

Postseasons Aplenty and Glimpses of the College Basketball Summit

Even by lesser, mid-1980s-era media attention standards, Stanford's search for a new head basketball coach in the spring of 1986 was a quiet one. The football team had just been to its first bowl game in eight seasons. At that time, basketball was drawing less media attention than other corners of the Stanford Athletic Department. The baseball team would make a deep run in the NCAA playoffs. The first-year women's basketball coach had just signed a heralded recruiting class that four years later would bring a national championship to the Farm.

Quietly, 39-year-old Mike Montgomery was hired by Athletic Director Andy Geiger to take the men's basketball program reins. Young, competitive, and honest to a fault, the man nicknamed Monty already had had eight years of NCAA Division 1 head coaching experience at Montana, where he won two-thirds of his games, 154 in all, slightly more than 19 games per season on average.

The mid-1980s were a time when, happily, a "win-the-press-conference" (read: splashy) hire was not something athletic directors were yet thinking about or falling prey to. Instead, the common approach for an athletic director was simply to hire the best possible candidate, give the new coach some time to ripen his skills, and then wait a few years before later reevaluating if necessary. Geiger followed that playbook.

The ripening happened fast. In Montgomery's first year, 1986-87, the new coach had some pretty favorable tailwinds. The roster was more talented than most in college basketball knew. Todd Lichti and Howard Wright, who had had terrific freshman seasons as starters—with Lichti winning first-team All-Pac-10 honors—were already program cornerstones entering their sophomore seasons. Greg Butler in 1986-87 would be an upperclassman, a 6′ 10″ long-distance shooting forward who had the size and savvy to be a scoring threat inside as well. He started more than half the games he played in. Another big man poised to contribute was fellow junior Eric Reveno, a 6′ 8″ and 260-pound bruiser who could provide power in the paint.

The guards, senior Novian Whitsitt and sophomore Terry Taylor, were both 6′ 2″ and double-digit scoring threats. Whitsitt had herky-jerky quickness and was more of a scorer than a shooter. Taylor, by contrast, was a deadly deep threat with a quasi–set shot release and shooting range out to 25 feet.

Todd Lichti, too, was a deep shooting threat. So was Greg Butler. So were sophomore reserve guard Scott Meinert and sophomore reserve forward Bryan McSweeney. In short, new coach Mike Montgomery had inherited a team full of exceptional shooters. This was a significant positive, for 1986-87 was the season that the three-point field goal came to college basketball. And perhaps the best news for Mike Montgomery was this: Of his top eight players, only Novian Whitsitt was a senior.

The 1986-87 season is not remembered as the breakthrough year in the Montgomery coaching era. There were no splashy, UCLA-upset-at-Maples type wins in 1986-87. None of the players was—yet—spectacular. But with Montgomery establishing a sound, inside-out offensive philosophy, and with practices crisp and detailed, the team played smartly and efficiently. A final record of 15-13 belied some startling achievements. Stanford finished with a .500-or-better conference record (9-9) for the first time in 14 seasons. The team shot nearly 43% from three-point range in 1986-87, with the sophomores Lichti and Taylor producing impressive 48% and 47% shooting percentages, respectively, from three-point distance.

The 1986-87 season ended with the Cardinal bowing out of the inaugural Pac-10 postseason basketball tournament with a first-round loss to Washington. But, clearly, the pieces were in place—talent, experience, and coaching—for possible future NCAA or NIT postseasons bids. The wait would not be long.

As the 1987-88 season began, juniors-to-be Todd Lichti and Howard Wright were poised for even bigger achievements. Lichti was coming off his second straight first-team All-Pac-10 season, having averaged nearly 18 points per game. Wright had averaged 11 points and 7 rebounds per game, and had been on the cusp of earning first-team All-Conference honors. Both were entering their upperclassman years and ready to lead Stanford Basketball to plateaus of achievement not seen since the early 1940s.

The Cardinal opened up the 1987-88 season winning six of its first eight games. The two losses were by a combined total of four points. The conference season opened that year during Christmas week. The Cardinal destroyed USC, 88-62, in the conference opener at Maples Pavilion on Monday night, December 21, 1987. The win over USC was a mere prelude to the much-anticipated matchup, two nights later, of two very good 1987-88 Pac-10 teams: Stanford and UCLA. The Stanford-UCLA game of Wednesday, December 23, 1987, would join the ranks of the handful of memorable Stanford-UCLA games ever played at Maples Pavilion. The game also would serve notice to the nation that Stanford was ready to play with anyone, in any style, and on any stage.

Maples Pavilion was again packed to the ceiling. And the Cardinal got the crowd going early, taking the early lead and going into the locker room at halftime leading by the score of 41-36. Stanford came out on fire to start the second half, building the lead to 16 points after the first six minutes of the second half. But the Bruins came back and cut the Cardinal lead to single digits. Then, with 33 seconds remaining in the game, Bruin guard Pooh Richardson scored a basket to tie the game at 84. Stanford had the ball for the final possession but could not score, sending the game to overtime.

In the first overtime, UCLA came out firing and built a 98-92 lead late in the overtime period. But Howard Wright hit a free throw, and then on the next Stanford possession—with 18 seconds remaining in the overtime—freshman forward Andrew Vlahov hit a three-point basket to bring the Cardinal within two points. Stanford had to foul and did so, sending Bruin forward Trevor Wilson to the free-throw line. Wilson hit one of two free throws, making the score 99-96 in favor of UCLA. On Stanford's final possession, with two seconds remaining, Todd Lichti rose, released, and nailed a dramatic three-pointer to tie the game and send it to a second overtime. Fifteen points had been scored by each team in the first overtime—a very high number. And the shootout continued in the second overtime period.

The Cardinal, even more fired up now, took control of the game early in the second overtime. Lichti hit a basket and then Terry Taylor swished a three-pointer, offsetting a basket by Richardson and two Bruin free throws. The score stood at 104-103 in favor of Stanford, with less than three minutes to go in the second overtime. And then Stanford hit the gas pedal, figuratively speaking. Greg Butler scored a basket. Then Terry Taylor hit two free throws. Then Lichti hit two free throws. Then Bryan McSweeney hit two free throws. Suddenly the score was a 113-103 in

Stanford's favor with just 45 seconds left to play—too big a deficit for the visiting Bruins to overcome. The final score was 116-110 Stanford, in double overtime. It was the most points a UCLA team had ever surrendered in a basketball game.

Howard Wright scored a team-high 30 points for Stanford. Todd Lichti added 24 points, and Terry Taylor contributed 21 points and made 4 of his 5 three-point shot attempts. Three other Stanford players scored in double figures—Brian McSweeney with 16 points and each of Greg Butler and freshman Andrew Vlahov with ten points. Although outrebounded by ten rebounds, and although scoring six fewer field goals, the Cardinal more than compensated with a remarkable 40-of-56 performance from the free-throw line.

Following the win, Stanford was 2-0 in the conference race, while UCLA was 0-2. For the first time in a generation, the Cardinal program was on par with UCLA's. This was no upset win as were the 1970s and early 1980s Stanford wins over UCLA. Unlike the Cardinal squads in those years, this was a Stanford team good enough to beat any team in the Pac-10. And in fact, for the first time in its history of playing in the Pac-8 or Pac-10, Stanford would indeed beat each of the nine other conference teams at least once during the 1987-88 season.

In January the Cardinal stumbled, winning just three of its seven conference games and getting blown out in road losses at Arizona, Arizona State and Oregon. Exiting January of 1988, Stanford's overall won-loss record stood at 12-6, and its Pac-10 record was a modest 5-4. The calendar turned to February, and for the 21st time in its history, the Cardinal prepared to face the nation's top-ranked team. Stanford's all-time record against #1-ranked teams? 0-20.

The date was February 4, 1988. The opponent was top-ranked Arizona, brandishing a 20-1 won-loss record that included a perfect 9-0 mark in Pac-10 games. Arizona featured a big-name lineup of forwards Sean Elliott, Anthony Cook, and Tom Tolbert, together with guards Steve Kerr, Craig McMillan, and—coming off the bench—Kenny Lofton. All were upperclassmen. Four would play at least four seasons in the NBA, and a fifth—Lofton—would have a long major league baseball career.

It was an Arizona team, not surprisingly, that would reach the Final Four seven weeks later. But Arizona wasn't good enough to beat the Cardinal that night.

Before a capacity crowd of 7,500 at Maples, Stanford fell behind nine points in the first half. But the Cardinal did not allow itself to fall behind further. Trailing at the half, Stanford slowly cut into the Arizona lead. With just under six minutes remaining in the game, the Cardinal finally pulled even at 72-72. Thirty seconds later, Sean Elliott scored to put Arizona back on top by two points. Lichti answered with a midrange bank shot to tie the game at 74. After a spate of missed shots by both teams, Wright was fouled with 2:59 left to play in the game. He made the first free throw to give Stanford its first lead of the second half, 75-74.

Wright missed the second free throw, but Greg Butler swooped in, grabbed the rebound, and scored a putback basket, putting Stanford ahead 77-74. Three more points were scored by Stanford during the next two minutes of game action, without an answer from the Wildcats. Stanford was leading, 80-74, entering the game's final minute when two Todd Lichti free throws capped the scoring.

In all, it was a 10-0 Stanford scoring run over the final four minutes of the game that decided the outcome. Todd Lichti had possession of the ball at the end, slowly dribbling the ball near midcourt as the jubilant Stanford student section—loudly and as one—counted down the final seconds. As the final buzzer sounded, Lichti and his Stanford teammates were swallowed up by the fastest and most forceful postgame court rush in Maples Pavilion history. Lichti finished with 23 points, and Howard Wright added 22. Said Wright after the game, "If I could bottle this feeling, I would be a millionaire, this is so sweet."

The Cardinal went on to win five of its next eight games to finish the conference season with a won-loss record of 11-7. Stanford then went 1-1 at the Pac-10 Tournament, losing by 14 points in the semifinals to Arizona at the tournament's Tucson, AZ, venue. Following its Pac-10 Tournament exit, the Cardinal record stood at 20-11. Would it be good enough for an NCAA or an NIT invitation? Answer: the NIT, not the NCAA Tournament. Still, it was a big moment for Stanford Basketball. For the first time since the 1941-42 season, Stanford had advanced to a postseason tournament.

The first NIT game was at home, against Long Beach State on Friday evening, March 18, 1988. Todd Lichti was brilliant, scoring 34 points—making 12 of 13 shots—including the go-ahead basket with 33 seconds remaining in the game. In the final seconds, Scott Meinert's two free throws sealed the outcome in an 80-77 Cardinal victory.

The second-round NIT game was also at Stanford. The date was Tuesday, March 22, 1988; the opponent was Arkansas State. It was to be a painful ending to an otherwise positive season. Although Stanford led 59-56 with two minutes remaining, Arkansas State scored on a free throw and a rebound putback to tie the game, then—following a Cardinal missed shot with 35 seconds remaining—got the ball back for one last possession. A half-second before the final buzzer sounded, Howard Wright fouled Arkansas State's Rhon Johnson while the latter was shooting, and Johnson's ensuing free throw ended the game and, for Stanford, the 1987-88 season.

As painful as it was for the Cardinal players to leave Maples Pavilion that night, having lost an NIT game by one point at home, it was not to be the most painful loss that this great core of Stanford players would suffer—that loss would come the following season. Recapping the individual achievements in 1987-88, Todd Lichti and Howard Wright were named first-team All-Pac-10—Lichti for a school-record-tying third time. Lichti made 53% of this field-goal attempts and nearly 52% of his three-point field-goal attempts in 1987-88, and he also averaged more than 20 points per game. Wright averaged 16 points and 8 rebounds per game. Greg Butler made 56% of his field-goal attempts, averaging double digits in scoring for the first time in his career, and Terry Taylor made nearly 47% of this three-point attempts.

Stanford ended the 1987-88 season with a 21-12 record. It was heady stuff for Stanford Basketball—a 20-plus win season, a postseason berth for the first time in four decades, and a first-ever win over the nation's #1-ranked team. And the future looked even brighter: Seven of the top eight scorers, plus a healthy Eric Reveno—who missed all of 1987-88 due to injury—would return for the 1988-89 campaign. Six of those eight players would be seniors. For the fast-rising Stanford Basketball program, 1988-89 could not come fast enough.

For head coach Mike Montgomery, who had put together winning seasons in his first two years on the Farm—no Stanford coach had had back-to-back winning seasons in twenty years—non-conference scheduling was to be a carefully addressed issue in 1988-89. Monty knew he had a very talented and experienced roster, one capable of not only earning an NCAA Tournament berth but also making a deep NCAA run. So Monty wanted to toughen up the November-December portion of the schedule, the better to get his team ready for a run at the conference title and the possible NCAA bid.

And tough the non-conference portion of the 1988-89 schedule indeed proved to be, with road opponents that included Indiana (84-73 loss, Bobby Knight accusing the Cardinal of playing too physical) and North Carolina (11-point loss to Dean Smith's nationally ranked Tar Heels). Other formidable road foes that season included Vanderbilt, St. Mary's, and Florida, each of which the 1988-89 team defeated.

No Stanford Basketball team had ever played a higher percentage of non-conference games away from home than did the 1988-89 Cardinal, and none had ever faced a more difficult non-conference schedule.

The Cardinal won-loss record, partly as a result of this grueling early season schedule, was a good-but-not-great 8-3. But as the calendar turned to January 1989 and the beginning of the Pac-10 schedule, Stanford found itself in the Associated Press (AP) poll of ranked teams for the first time in decades. With a 1-1 conference record, it was time again for Stanford to play a highly ranked Arizona team. The date was Thursday, January 5, 1989. The venue was Maples Pavilion.

For the first time ever at Maples Pavilion, two top fifteen-ranked teams would do battle: #12-ranked Stanford versus #8-ranked Arizona. The college basketball world knew it would be a big-time game. ESPN—for the first time in Maples Pavilion history—would be there to televise it. The game would not disappoint the tens of thousands of nationwide viewers.

Arizona was the Pac-10 Media's preseason pick to win the conference, fresh off an appearance in the 1988 NCAA Final Four. Arizona had a 14-game Pac-10 winning streak going—the streak having begun the first game following Arizona's upset loss at Stanford eleven months earlier. The game started badly for Stanford. The Wildcats scored the first points of the game, and then scored again and again in the opening few minutes. Sean Elliott, the senior All-American forward for Arizona, scored eight early points as the Wildcats burst out to a 21-4 lead six minutes into the game. With Stanford down by so many points, Coach Montgomery—not one disposed to using timeouts early in a game—was forced to take a timeout to try to settle his players down.

The fast start was standard "Stanford" operating procedure for Arizona under Lute Olson, usually displayed in games against Stanford in Tucson. The strategy was simply to jump on the Cardinal early, build a big early lead, and make the first half deficit so great that Stanford could not come back. It had happened most recently in the 1988 Pac-10 Conference Tournament semifinal in Tucson just ten months earlier in March 1988, when UA burst out to a 16-2 lead in that game and the Cardinal never recovered, losing 97-83. But this 1989 Stanford-Arizona matchup was not to be that type of kill-Stanford-early game. Stanford slowly began to chip away at the early 17-point Arizona advantage. By halftime, Stanford was down by only single digits.

The second half featured one of the great individual duels in both Maples Pavilion and Pac-10 conference history. Arizona senior Sean

Elliott and Stanford senior Todd Lichti traded basket after basket on slashing drives and finishes, powerful pull-up jumpers, and high-arching three-point swishes. Each player's game scoring total eclipsed the 20-point mark early in the second half. Then, later in the second half, each passed the 30-point mark. After trailing the entire game, Stanford finally took the lead midway through the second half on a basket by Eric Reveno. Stanford built the lead to nine points later in the second half, 71-62, then had to withstand a furious Arizona rally in the final five minutes as the Wildcats cut the Stanford lead to eight…six…four…and then just two points.

With four seconds remaining in the game, with Stanford ahead by just two points, Arizona guard Harvey Mason was fouled by Eric Reveno while driving to the basket, giving Mason the opportunity to tie the game with two made free throws. Mason missed the first free throw, generating a huge roar of glee from the sellout and partisan Maples Pavilion crowd. Mason then tried to miss the second free throw, but he botched the effort, throwing the ball off of top of the backboard and out of bounds.

On the resulting Stanford inbound play, rather than go for the steal, Mason intentionally fouled Stanford's Bryan McSweeney. McSweeney made one of two free throws. Stanford was then awarded the ball due to the foul having been deemed intentional. The ball was inbounded to McSweeney, and McSweeney was intentionally fouled *again*. This time the senior forward made both free throws, clinching victory for the Cardinal, 83-78.

Emotionally and physically spent, Sean Elliott yelled angrily at Harvey Mason as the game ended. Mason's intentional foul of McSweeney in the final seconds had killed what little remaining chance Arizona had to win the game. As the final buzzer sounded, the Stanford students cascaded onto the floor, as they had one year earlier when Stanford had knocked off #1-ranked Arizona. For a fifth consecutive season, the Cardinal had beaten Arizona at Maples Pavilion.

The story of the game was not only the exciting battle of two nationally ranked teams, but also the great duel between the great Pac-10 and All-American seniors, Todd Lichti and Sean Elliott. Lichti finished with 35 points, scoring 27 in the second half. Lichti also made all 15 of his free-throw attempts. Elliot finished with 34 points and made all four of his three-point field-goal attempts in the game.

Of Lichti, Arizona coach Lute Olson said, "Lichti is as tough to handle as anyone I've seen." In its college basketball section the following week, *Sports Illustrated* hailed Lichti as the "toast of the [West] coast."[25]

And, just as Sean Elliott never lost a game in Tucson to Stanford, Todd Lichti and his fellow Cardinal seniors—Eric Reveno, Bryan McSweeney, Scott Meinert, Terry Taylor, Howard Wright—walked out of Maples Pavilion that January 1989 evening knowing that their Maples Pavilion won-loss record against powerhouse Arizona would always be an undefeated one.

And that ebullient feeling would continue beyond the Arizona game. The Cardinal powered through its next 15 games, winning 13. Stanford finished the Pac-10 schedule of games with a scintillating 15-3 record—not quite good enough to equal the record of eventual conference champion Arizona, which finished 17-1. The lone Arizona loss in Pac-10 play, of course, had come on that January night in Maples Pavilion.

Next up on the 1988-89 schedule was the Pac-10 Tournament at the Great Western Forum in Los Angeles. Stanford defeated USC and UCLA on successive days, before falling to Arizona in the conference tournament final. But the Cardinal, which had remained firmly positioned in the upper half of the weekly college basketball rankings since early January, knew that its record, 26-6, would be good enough to achieve a long-standing program goal—getting back to the NCAA Tournament. At the conclusion of the Sunday afternoon Pac-10 Tournament final loss to Arizona, the news came: The Cardinal had received a #3 seed in the East Region of the 1989 NCAA Tournament.

Stanford's first-round matchup would be against #14-seed Siena College, at the Greensboro Coliseum in Greensboro, NC, on Thursday afternoon, March 16, 1989. For all of the excitement surrounding Stanford's appearance in the 1989 NCAA Tournament, a harsh reality lay around the corner. The maiden Montgomery NCAA Tournament road would not to be a smooth one.

First came the travel trouble. A scheduled Tuesday, March 14, late afternoon flight from San Francisco to Chicago was delayed because of thunderstorms in the Windy City. The team got to the O'Hare Airport Hilton after midnight, four hours later than planned. With only five hours of sleep behind them, the players and coaches had to catch an early Wednesday morning flight to Greensboro, arriving there just 24 hours prior to tipoff of the Siena game. Upon landing in Greensboro, the team and players had to hurry from the airport to the arena to meet NCAA-mandated media obligations.

On paper, the Stanford-Siena matchup in the first-round game looked like it would be an easy double-digit Stanford victory. But Stanford had not been in the NCAA Tournament in a long time. It had no experience with what "playing as a heavy favorite" was like—or with the pressure and pitfalls that can come with that.

Siena was an unusual team. Experienced, significantly undersized but with a number of good three-point shooters, the Saints were accustomed to playing against bigger teams. Its offense was almost exclusively reliant on the three-point shot. Even on the fast break, a Saints player would routinely stop and hoist up a three. Another thing unusual about Siena was that, just two weeks earlier, Siena's campus had endured a measles outbreak, which had required the basketball team to play its games in a quarantined arena—meaning no fans and no crowd noise. For a variety of reasons, then, Siena would not be intimidated by its opponent's size or the unfamiliarity of the Greensboro arena.

From the start, the game was difficult for Stanford. The Cardinal fell behind by 16 points in the first half. Todd Lichti took a spill and banged his head hard on the floor. The contact would affect him the remainder of the game. But the Cardinal roared back and tied the game by halftime, 37-37.

Stanford moved out to a 43-40 early second half lead, but then the Saints went on an incredible 21-2 scoring run to go back up by 16 points, 61-45, with 12 minutes remaining in the game. Then it was Stanford's turn to go on a scoring binge. The Cardinal went on a 21-5 scoring surge during the next six minutes to tie the game, 66-66.

Siena then went up by five points, then Stanford tied it again, 76-76, with 1:46 remaining. Siena senior guard Marc Brown then hit a jumper to put the Saints up by two points, after which Stanford sixth-man Adam Keefe—only a freshman—answered with two free throws in a pressure-filled one-and-one situation. The score was now 78-78. Thirty-four seconds remained in the game.

Siena held the ball for one final shot. With no inside game, and with Marc Brown having already scored 30 points, the Cardinal believed that Brown would be the one to try the final shot for Siena. Stanford guessed correctly; it was Brown who attempted the shot. Unfortunately for Stanford, Marc Brown was fouled by Todd Lichti while Brown was shooting. Three seconds remained on the scoreboard clock. Brown made both free throws.

Against pressure, Stanford was able to inbound the ball successfully, but with so little time remaining that all Terry Taylor could do was heave a backcourt rainbow toward the hoop. His extremely low-percentage shot attempt did not come close to its target. Stanford, in its first NCAA Tournament game since World War II, was an upset victim. The final score: Siena 80 – Stanford 78.

With Todd Lichti compromised because of the head injury, it was the freshman Adam Keefe who led the Cardinal in scoring with 22 points. Keefe also scored Stanford's last ten points and 14 of its final 18 points. But that was no consolation in a Cardinal locker room full of accomplished seniors, who were as disconsolate as any Stanford team, in any sport, could possibly have ever been following a season-ending loss.

Todd Lichti finished his stellar Stanford Basketball career with a school-record 2,336 points, along with a Stanford and Pac-10 conference record *fourth* consecutive first-team All-Pac-10 citation. Howard Wright also garnered first-team All-Pac-10 honors, the second straight year he had made the All-Conference team. But each young man would have traded those honors for a do-over of the Siena game.

The next season, 1989-90, promised to be a letdown year for Stanford Basketball. Never had a Stanford team previously seen so much talent depart in a single year. The headline returnee was Adam Keefe. Other than Keefe and 6′ 7″ and 240-pound forward Andrew Vlahov, no other returning Stanford player had any appreciable playing experience. But the other new starters—6′ 7″ forward Deshon Wingate, 6′ 4″ junior point guard John Patrick, and 6′ 3″ junior off-guard Kenny Ammann—did not suffer for their inexperience in 1989-90. The Cardinal managed 18 wins overall and a 9-9 record in Pac-10 play in 1989-90. Included among those 18 wins was the first-ever Stanford win in UCLA's Pauley Pavilion, 70-69, on February 18, 1990. Not since 1952 had the Cardinal defeated a Bruin team in Los Angeles.

Because of its 18-win regular season accomplishment, the 1989-90 Cardinal was rewarded with a third straight postseason berth, earning a spot in the 1990 NIT. Stanford, however, had to travel to the University of Hawaii for a first-round matchup and fell to the Rainbows, 69-57, ending the 1989-90 Stanford Basketball season.

The 1990-91 season would be the opposite of the prior season as far as returning experience—all five starters returned, and each of them was now an upperclassman. The 1990-91 campaign got off to a promising start. The Cardinal put together a 7-3 won-loss record in November and December, which was even more impressive considering one of the three losses included an 11-point December 30th loss to #7-ranked North Carolina at a holiday tournament in Florida.

The conference season, on the other hand, was a disappointment. Other than another thrilling win at Pauley Pavilion on January 16, 1991—with the building heavily secured due to the outbreak that evening of U.S. military operations in Iraq—the Cardinal suffered its first nonwinning conference record (8-10) in Mike Montgomery's five years as Stanford's head coach. But five of the Pac-10 losses had been by single digits, including a heartbreaking 78-76 loss at Maples Pavilion to Arizona on January 24, 1991, when Arizona's Sean Rooks banked in a shot over Adam Keefe with one second remaining in the game. Another reason for the ten Pac-10 losses was that starting forward Andrew Vlahov had missed several conference games due to an ankle injury.

The regular season portion of the 1990-91 campaign ended with Stanford sporting a modest overall won-loss record of 15-13. That record contained no postseason conference tournament wins, as the Pac-10 Tournament had been eliminated from the schedule after a four-year run. Nevertheless, despite only fifteen regular season wins, the Cardinal won a spot in the 1991 NIT. Stanford Basketball fans will always remember what came next in March of 1991. For two weeks, a seemingly ordinary Stanford Basketball team suddenly became quite extraordinary—with a couple of well-scissored Madison Square Garden nets and a national championship trophy to prove it. What follows is a summary of the remarkable Stanford NIT run in 1991.

> First Round, March 13, 1991, Maples Pavilion, Stanford, CA: Stanford 93 – Houston 86. *The Cardinal got a big momentum boost when senior starting power forward Andrew Vlahov, who had missed several games at the end of the regular season due to the ankle injury, returned to action for the opening-round game against the Houston Cougars. Vlahov's stock-in-trade was physical toughness, and that toughness helped to successfully neutralize 7' 1" Houston center Alvaro Teheran as the Cardinal prevailed, 93-86. Senior starting off-guard Kenny Ammann scored a career-high 29 points, hitting on five three-pointers to lead Stanford in scoring. Junior Adam Keefe added 22 points in the win—Stanford's first postseason win since the first-round NIT win over Long Beach State three seasons earlier.*

> Second Round, March 18, 1991, Wisconsin Fieldhouse, Madison, WI: Stanford 80 – Wisconsin 72. *Stanford journeyed to the Midwest for its second-round game—a matchup with Wisconsin. The Cardinal took hold of the game from the start, making eight of its first nine shots and exploding to a 26-9 first-half lead. Wisconsin closed the deficit to 39-30 at the half, but Stanford*

opened the second half with an 8-0 scoring run, with senior small forward Deshon Wingate scoring six of those points. The Cardinal was never seriously threatened thereafter, winning the game by the score of 78-72. Keefe's career-high 33 points led the way for Stanford. Senior starting point guard John Patrick chipped in with a team-high eight assists.

Quarterfinal Round, March 21, 1991, SIU Arena, Carbondale, IL: Stanford 78 – Southern Illinois 68. *As at Wisconsin, Stanford started strong, building first half leads of 18-10 and 31-20 as the Cardinal converted on 13 of its first 19 shot attempts. Southern Illinois cut the Cardinal lead to five points at the half, but Stanford answered with second-half scoring runs of 7-0 and 23-11 to build a double-digit advantage midway through the second half. With reserve guard Marcus Lollie hitting several pressure free throws down the stretch, Stanford was able to maintain the lead and prevailed in the end, 78-68. Keefe's 24 points, Wingate's 16 points and Vlahov's 14 points spearheaded the victory that sent Stanford to the NIT Final Four at Madison Square Garden in New York City.*

Semifinal Game, March 25, 1991, Madison Square Garden, New York, NY: Stanford 73 – Massachusetts 71. *Yet again Stanford jumped out to a hot start, roaring to a 24-8 lead against the John Calipari-coached Minutemen. UMass clawed back, however, to trail at halftime by only four points. Stanford had another strong start in the second half, with Adam Keefe scoring eight of Stanford's first 11 points, but with five minutes remaining in the game the score was tied. But then John Patrick hit a three-pointer and Andrew Vlahov started hitting free throws—lots of them. With five seconds left, Vlahov hit two free throws—the second of which was his 12th made free throw in 12 attempts—which provided the decisive margin in a 73-71 semifinal game victory for Stanford. Keefe had 24 points, while Vlahov contributed 20 points, 11 rebounds, and eight assists.*

Championship Game, March 27, 1991, Madison Square Garden, New York, NY: Stanford 78 – Oklahoma 72. *Late in the first half of the title game, with the scored tied at 26, a key sequence occurred: Andrew Vlahov was fouled on a controversial play, in vocal opposition to which Oklahoma coach Billy Tubbs drew a double-technical, game-ejection whistle. Vlahov hit his two free throws, then John Patrick hit all four of the technical foul free throws, then—with Stanford awarded possession of the ball—Kenny Ammann hit a three-point basket to give Stanford a 35-26 lead. The Sooners scored the next 13 points, including the first two of the second half, to take a four-point lead. But Stanford stormed back to tie the game at 60 late in the second half, and then put together a 7-0 scoring run in the final minutes to secure its first-ever NIT championship trophy, 78-72.*

In the championship game victory, all five Stanford starters—junior Keefe (12 points) and the four seniors Ammann (22 points), Patrick (13 points), Deshon Wingate (13 points, 13 rebounds), and Vlahov (14 points, 11 rebounds)—tallied double figures. With the Oklahoma defense having clogged the paint to try to defend Keefe, Patrick and Ammann made a combined seven three-point baskets. Said Kenny Ammann after the game: "Oklahoma did a good job of keeping us from throwing it inside to Adam, but that allowed us to shoot from outside—John and I love zones."

Adam Keefe—who would conclude his magnificent Stanford career a year later as the No. 2 career scorer in Stanford Basketball history—scored 115 points during the five games and was named Most Outstanding Player of the 1991 NIT in the postgame ceremony on the Madison Square Garden floor. But Keefe's postgame comments in the Stanford locker room focused more on the team rather than on his individual achievement. "We won this game and this tournament because we came together as a unit," said Keefe. "People have said this wasn't much of a team and that it has just one player, but the way the scoring was spread around proved that that's not true."

Here is a summary of the arduous but unforgettable Stanford NIT story in March of 1991: five games, fifteen days, four different arenas, four different states—with final exams taken right in the middle of the tournament. The result of this landmark Stanford Basketball journey was twofold. The result for the team was that a 1991 NIT championship banner was added to the 1942 NCAA championship banner hanging in Stanford's Maples Pavilion rafters. The result for coach Mike Montgomery was achieving his 100th career Stanford win in the NIT championship game, completing his fifth year as Stanford Basketball's head coach with a fourth postseason trip and an NIT championship.

The next season, 1991-92, was another experience-to-inexperience pendulum swing. Four senior starters were gone; only the All-American Adam Keefe returned—Keefe having announced in May 1991 that he would *not* bypass his senior season to enter the 1991 NBA Draft. The new starters around Keefe for the 1991-92 campaign were as follows: 6′ 9″ senior center Paul Garrett, 6′ 7″ junior forward Brent Williams, 6′ 4″ junior guard Peter Dukes, and 6′ 0″ junior point guard Marcus Lollie—Lollie having been the key sixth man the previous season.

Although seemingly less talented than the 1990-91 NIT championship squad the year prior, the 1991-92 team exceeded the regular season achievement of its predecessor. An 8-2 non-conference record—with the only losses being at Michigan State by ten points and at Notre Dame by one point—preceded Stanford compiling a respectable and a better-than-expected 10-8 Pac-10 conference record in 1991-92.

And this Pac-10 record and national profile would have been even better had the Cardinal not suffered another heartbreaking home loss to #7-ranked Arizona on February 6, 1992. Stanford had stayed close to the heavy-favorite Wildcats the entire game, and had a chance to tie with five seconds remaining as Adam Keefe went to the free-throw line with five seconds remaining and the Cardinal trailing by just one point.

Keefe made the first free throw to tie the game 70-70, but was denied a second free-throw attempt due to a Stanford lane violation. Arizona then inbounded the ball to guard Khalid Reeves, who sped downcourt and scored a layup as time ran out to win the game for the Wildcats, 72-70.

Nevertheless, with an overall won-loss record of 18-10, including 10-8 in the Pac-10, the Cardinal was able to secure one of the last spots in the 1992 NCAA Tournament. Stanford, as the #12 seed in the Southeast Regional, was slated to meet the #5-seed Alabama Crimson Tide at the Riverfront Coliseum in Cincinnati on Thursday, March 19, 1992. Alabama had a roster featuring four future NBA players: Robert Horry, Latrell Sprewell, James "Hollywood" Robinson, and Jason Caffey. Yet the Cardinal that afternoon in Cincinnati put forth a tremendous "team" performance against the talented Crimson Tide squad. With senior forward Brent Williams hitting shots from everywhere, and the entire Stanford team making three-pointers at a rate of 50%, the Cardinal hung tough with the favored Tide for the full 40 minutes.

The Cardinal trailed by only four points at halftime, and—except for one interruption—led Alabama from the 17-minute mark in the second half until the 5-minute mark. At that point, Crimson Tide forward Latrell Sprewell scored eight straight points to enable Alabama reclaim the lead, 69-64. Although the Cardinal was able to whittle that lead to just two points with just under three minutes remaining in the game, Alabama was able to hold on for the win, 80-75.

The game marked the 125th and final game of Adam Keefe's brilliant Stanford Basketball career. Keefe earned All-America honors in 1992 and finished with a career total of 2,319 points, #2 on the all-time Stanford list and just 17 points behind all-time leader Todd Lichti. Without Adam Keefe the next season, the Cardinal was set up for a "down" year, and that's what happened. Without Keefe, and plagued by injuries such as a season-ending injury to sophomore forward Andy Poppink, Stanford Basketball in 1992-93 struggled all season, finishing with just 7 wins against 23 losses. It was Mike Montgomery's first losing season in fifteen years as an NCAA Division 1 head coach. One bright spot in 1992-93 was the play of 6′ 2″ freshman guard Dion Cross, who, with his brilliant outside shooting touch, became a starter late in the season and would finish the year averaging nearly eleven points per game.

Stanford fans wondered whether Cardinal Basketball was heading into a "dark night" period, as far as a metaphor for the program's near-term future prospects. As things would turn out, while the *night* metaphor turned out to be phonetically correct, it would carry a far different and far more positive image going forward. For, beginning in 1993-94, a little-known freshman named *Knight* would radically change the program's direction—not only back to winning seasons, but to levels of achievement long unseen on the Farm.

ABOVE, CLOCKWISE FROM TOP LEFT: *Howard Wright, two-time All-Pac-10 selection; Todd Lichti, four-time All-Pac-10 selection; Adam Keefe, three-time All-Pac-10 selection; Coach Mike Montgomery and starting forward Andrew Vlahov following Stanford's 1991 NIT championship game victory.*
RIGHT: *The Stanford student section rushes the court as the final buzzer sounds following Stanford's 82-74 victory over #1-ranked Arizona on 2/4/88.*

STANFORD
STANFORD WINS
HOME
0:00
VISITORS
82
PERIOD 2
74
TEAM FOULS
PLAYER FOULS
TEAM FOULS
7
11 2
7
PEPSI
MEN
ZA
Giant
ICE CREAM

VII. Mid-1990s Monty

NCAA Tournament Breakthroughs and a Program-Changer Named Brevin

He was recruited by only two NCAA Division 1 schools, Stanford and Manhattan. He won a New Jersey Player of the Year award. He went to Seton Hall Prep in New Jersey and led his team to three state tournament championship games during a three-year period in which his teams went 83-6, yet nearby and affiliated Seton Hall University somehow decided not to recruit him.

He stood only 5′ 10″. Few on the West Coast, other than Mike Montgomery and his staff, had heard of him when he arrived on campus in the fall of 1993. It wasn't even clear that he was the best point guard in the incoming Stanford class—a junior-college point guard named Frank Harris had been recruited as well.

His name was Brevin Knight. Before December of 1993 had come and gone, three events announced to the world that freshman Brevin Knight was in command of the Stanford Basketball team, and that his command would be something special.

The *first* sign of Knight dominance was the early season scrimmages. Mike Montgomery, always attentive to even the smallest details at practice, noticed that Knight's teams almost always won the five-on-five scrimmages. He noticed how demanding Knight was that Knight's team win each scrimmage game. He noticed that Knight was not only the quickest player that he had ever coached, but also that he had ever seen—lethal on defense as a long-armed, cat-quick threat to steal the ball from a ball-handler at any time. Mike Montgomery knew, before Brevin Knight had even played one game, that he had a four-year starter and big-time leader in his stable.

The *second* sign of Brevin Knight dominance was the Stanford–Santa Clara game of December 11, 1993, just the fourth game of Brevin

Knight's college career. No one knew it at the time, but the matchup of starting point guards in this game—freshman Brevin Knight for Stanford and sophomore Steve Nash for Santa Clara—would be one of two future multidecade NBA players. The prior season, as a freshman, Nash had come from nowhere to become the West Coast Conference Tournament MVP and help the Broncos to an NCAA Tournament bid and a memorable first-round upset of #2-seed Arizona.

At one point during the Stanford–Santa Clara game, with Steve Nash dominating on offense, Santa Clara led by 15 points. But the Cardinal climbed back into the game on the back of young Brevin Knight, finally evening the score at 68-68 at the end of regulation. And in the overtime, the Brevin Knight-versus-Steve Nash duel *really* swung in the Stanford freshman's favor. Although the Broncos scored the first basket of the overtime, Stanford proceeded to reel off the next—and final—fourteen points of the overtime period, with Knight scoring the majority of those points in late-shot-clock, one-on-one dribble penetration situations, knifing past Nash several times and repeatedly producing baskets for Stanford.

On the defensive end, Knight simply would not allow Nash to set up for a three-point shot in the overtime, and on Nash's drives to the basket, Knight harassed the taller Nash just enough that the Bronco guard could not score when he got into the paint or near the rim. The final score was 82-70 in favor of Stanford, but what has been remembered more than the final score is the Knight-Nash duel, as Nash finished with a game-high 24 points and Knight countered with a career-high 23 points and 8 assists.

The *third* sign of Brevin Knight dominance was the departure of the other "new" point guard on the Cardinal roster. Shortly after the Santa Clara game, when the fall academic quarter had ended, point guard Frank Harris—who had come to Stanford just three months earlier in the group of new players that included fellow newcomer and fellow point guard Brevin Knight—announced he was leaving school immediately to transfer.

Knight's reputation as a firecracker competitor, a defensive terror, and an as-need-be clutch scorer only rose as Pac-10 conference play began. Twice during the 18-game conference schedule, the freshman hit a game-winning basket as time ran out to win a game for Stanford. In the conference opener at Maples Pavilion on January 6, 1994, Knight's 15-foot jump shot at the buzzer secured a 67-65 Stanford victory over Washington. On February 3, 1994, at Oregon, Knight's runner in the paint in the final seconds enabled Stanford to edge the Ducks by the score of 69-67.

With both Brevin Knight and his sweet-shooting backcourt mate, sophomore Dion Cross, each averaging double figures in scoring, Stanford managed another better-than-.500 won-loss record in conference play, finishing 10-8 in the Pac-10 and 17-10 overall when the regular season ended. That performance was good enough to earn another NIT bid for Stanford, Montgomery's sixth trip to the postseason in eight seasons as the Stanford Basketball head coach.

It is an axiom of college basketball that freshmen—not being used to the length and intensity of a full college season—often "hit the wall" starting in mid-March of that first college season. Unfortunately for Stanford, Brevin Knight encountered that proverbial wall in the 1994 NIT first-round game, at Maples Pavilion, against Gonzaga. The Pac-10 Freshman of the Year was held scoreless, missing all six of his field-goal attempts.

Stanford trailed by 12 points at halftime. Still, the Cardinal was able to make up for Knight's empty scoring night, was able to get back into the game, and was able to draw to within two points of the Zags in the final minute. With 21 seconds left to play in the game, Stanford junior forward Andy Poppink stole the ball from the Zags, but with six seconds remaining Poppink was called for an offensive foul. That call ended Stanford's hopes, and with it the 1993-94 season as the Cardinal fell to Gonzaga by the score of 80-76.

In the game, sophomore guard Dion Cross scored 25 points and senior forward Brent Williams, in his final college game, added 24 points. Among the uniformed Stanford seniors exhausting their eligibility that evening was three-sport Stanford athlete and future Stanford head football coach David Shaw, a reserve guard on the 1993-94 Cardinal squad.

In the gloom of the emptying Maples Pavilion that March evening in 1994, no one had any inkling that Stanford would not play in the postseason NIT again for more than a decade. The reason? Beginning the very next season, Stanford Basketball was destined to play in the better postseason event—the NCAA Tournament—every year for a long, long time.

As the 1994-95 season began, it was clear what Brevin Knight and the Stanford team had its sights set on: a Stanford return to the NCAA Tournament. Coach Montgomery figured that his team had finished just a couple of wins short of that goal in 1993-94. And it was clear, right from the very first game in 1994-95, that the Cardinal was determined not to waste any opportunity to win any game on its 1994-95 schedule. Narrow losses were not to be tolerated, not with Knight as a late-game "closer" either scoring or passing, not with Dion Cross on the wing ready to shoot the Cardinal into the lead or net a game-winning basket.

One theme in 1994-95 showed up early—increased toughness. A player who, in addition to Brevin Knight, embodied that toughness was 6′ 3″ redshirt junior David Harbour. A Southern California native who had been the sixth man in 1993-94, averaging seven points per game, Harbour had an inspiring—and toughness-breeding—story to share.

David Harbour had lost most of the thumb on his right hand—his non-shooting hand but nonetheless a potentially career-ending injury—in a water-skiing injury in the summer of 1992. He underwent a radical surgical procedure, in which another part of his body was excised and attached to his right hand to become a "replacement" thumb, and then understandably took a redshirt year of rehabilitation in 1992-93. The year-long rehab brought Harbour back, in his comeback 1993-94 season, to his pre-injury performance profile as a significant in-game contributor for Stanford. Harbour played in all 28 games in 1993-94 as the Cardinal's sixth man, averaging 7 points and 3 rebounds per game.

In 1994-95, though still slated to be the sixth man, David Harbour was ready to be the face of the "no-back-down" Cardinal, even more so than Brevin Knight. If Knight was the guy who might get under an opponent's skin with a bit of trash talk—and then further infuriate the guy by backing it up with superior basketball play—Harbour was the guy on the Stanford Basketball roster who would not take any guff, physical or verbal. The 1994-95 team thus had a couple of tough guys on its roster, though their physical traits would not have suggested this at first glance.

This toughness was evident in the opening two months of the 1994-95 season. The Cardinal had dispatched Colgate—with future longtime NBA forward Adonal Foyle at center—as well as St. Peter's, San Jose State, Cal Poly, and USF with relative ease to open the season with a 5-0 record. Next came the first road trip of the season, a two-game road swing to both American University in Washington DC and Virginia in Charlottesville, VA. Stanford swept past American U, 97-71, on Monday night, December 19, 1994. What followed the next three days might best be described as toughness in the face of fire for a Stanford Basketball team and program on the cusp of new breakthroughs of achievement.

On Tuesday morning, December 20, 1994, the Stanford Basketball program was invited to a private tour of the White House. Arranged by an FBI official who was an uncle of former Cardinal Basketball player Earl Koberlein, the team began its tour at 10:00 A.M. By 10:30 the tour had taken the guests to the half-circle driveway in front of the north side of the White House. Suddenly, from the direction of Lafayette Square adjacent to the White House on the north side, a gunshot rang out. Players, coaches and other members of the traveling party spontaneously dived to the ground, unsure of the shooter and whether further shots were coming.

After a very tense couple of minutes, it became clear that the shooter had in fact been a federal police officer who had seen a man brandishing a knife by the fence in front of the White House. The officer had demanded that the man drop the knife and then had fired when the request was not complied with. The traveling party, relieved upon learning the news, collectively dusted itself off and resumed the tour in full.

The next day, Wednesday, December 21, 1994, the team practiced at University Hall in Charlottesville, home of the Virginia Cavaliers. Perhaps from the prior days' tension, perhaps from travel-related irritation, tempers were short on the practice court. At one point, Mike Montgomery barked a coaching point at David Harbour. Harbour, displeased, barked back. Montgomery—always and forever an "old-school coach"—then reacted to Harbour's insubordination by launching *even more* verbal fire in Harbour's direction. Tempers on all sides cooled, but it was clear Stanford was antsy and ready for action.

The Cardinal's opponent was formidable. Virginia was the #22-ranked team in the country, had a future NBA player in guard Cory Alexander, and had physically imposing talents Junior Burrough and Harold Deane playing alongside Alexander in the Cavalier lineup. And the first three quarters of the game certainly reflected the Cavalier toughness. The Cardinal trailed at the half, and was trailing by single digits in the second half when Brevin Knight took an elbow from Alexander with 7:42 remaining and had to leave the game. It was an ominous sign for Stanford.

But then Stanford's newfound toughness kicked in. Knight returned to the game, hit a go-ahead three-point shot with 3:42 remaining and the Cardinal withstood a spirited Cavalier comeback attempt in the final two minutes to win the game, 64-60. Knight had 20 points to lead the Cardinal to the landmark road win, Stanford's first-ever win at longtime ACC-title-contender Virginia. Dion Cross added 12 points while junior starting forward Darren Allaway—a 6′ 8″ and 240-pound physical presence down low—did enough banging in the paint against Burrough to keep the burly Cavalier forward from getting rebounds and putbacks during the crucial final minutes of the game.

Stanford's won-loss record was now 7-0. A week later, with home wins over both Cornell and a Wisconsin team led by future NBA All-Star Michael Finley, the Cardinal had improved its non-conference record to

9-0. Stanford's pre-conference record in 1994-95 was its best in nearly four decades. A "bank account" of wins, so vital to earning a spot in the NCAA Tournament, had been built up. Unfortunately, the Pac-10 schedule would somewhat drain that bank account. As it had the prior year, the Cardinal produced a 10-8 Pac-10 record. Among the eight conference losses, two were particularly galling.

On January 14, 1995, Stanford fell to No. 13 Arizona at Maples for a fifth consecutive season, 89-83 in overtime. Wildcat guard Damon Stoudamire torched Stanford for a Maples Pavilion-record 45 points, including eight of Arizona's thirteen points during the overtime period. The Cardinal had blown a golden opportunity to win the game; Stanford had an 11-point lead midway through the second half. Despite losing the lead and falling behind by seven points, Stanford fought back to tie the game by the end of regulation prior to ultimately succumbing in the overtime period.

Twelve nights later, at #4-ranked UCLA, Stanford had another opportunity for a road win against a ranked opponent. The Ed O'Bannon–led Bruins, who three months later would win the NCAA title, had Stanford down by 14 points in the first half. Brevin Knight, in foul trouble, played just 11 minutes in the first half. Neither Knight nor freshman center Tim Young—who was becoming an increasingly potent scoring threat for Stanford—scored in the first half.

Once again, however, Cardinal toughness propelled a big second half comeback. Stanford sliced into the Bruin lead, and the Cardinal went ahead by one point on a three-pointer by Dion Cross with just over one minute left in the game. But then UCLA senior center George Zidek got Tim Young to commit a foul, and Zidek converted the two free throws to put the Bruins up one point. David Harbour then was called for a charging foul with 32 seconds remaining in the game. UCLA was fouled on the ensuing two possessions, hit two of four free-throw attempts, and escaped with a 77-74 victory.

Following the loss to UCLA, Stanford's won-loss record in 1994-95 stood at a still-respectable 11-3. Confidence remained high. Team members believed, as Montgomery repeatedly reminded them, that the narrow losses to Top 25-ranked Arizona and UCLA and the win over Top 25-ranked Virginia on the road meant something. Team members and their coach believed that Stanford could compete with any team in any venue—even in a big arena, even in March against an NCAA Tournament foe.

With a record of 19-8 at the end of the regular season, Stanford thought it had done enough to get an NCAA bid, and indeed it had. The Cardinal received a #10 seed in the East Region of the 1995 NCAA Tournament, and was bracketed to face #7-seed UNC Charlotte (UNCC) in a first-round game to be played nearly 3,000 miles from Palo Alto, in Albany, NY. Adversity, then toughness, then smiles—this sequence had been a theme of the Washington-Virginia road swing in December, and it would be a theme of Stanford's NCAA trip to Albany in mid-March of 1995.

Stanford had not won a first-round NCAA Tournament game under Mike Montgomery in two previous tries. A determination to correct that record was evident right from the opening tip-in the first-round game against UNCC. The Cardinal played solid basketball in the first half and led by four points, 30-26, at halftime. But the 49ers hung on, came back, and took a five-point lead, 63-58, with 4:46 remaining in the game. Adversity, and another possible first-round exit, hovered ominously over the Cardinal.

But the Cardinal sucked it up, rather than sucked over the final four minutes. An ensuing 9-3 scoring run suddenly put Stanford in front by one point, 67-66, with one minute remaining in the game. UNCC guard Roderick Howard then missed a jump shot, whereupon Brevin Knight rebounded, sped downcourt, and fed Stanford senior center Bart Lammersen for a fast-break-finishing layup that gave the Cardinal a 69-66 advantage with 43 seconds remaining in the game.

With the score 70-68 a bit later, UNCC had one final possession to tie the game. However, a three-point jump shot attempt by the 49ers missed. Stanford, at last, had its first NCAA Tournament win since 1942. Montgomery's emphatic series of fist pumps—directed toward the Cardinal rooting section immediately following the game while standing at midcourt awaiting a CBS Television postgame interview—said it all. Stanford had toughed this one out.

The Cardinal would be blown out by #1-seed UMass two days later in Albany, 75-53. The more talented team won that game. But Stanford clearly was a comer in the NCAA Tournament world—it would have its entire starting lineup returning in 1995-96. And with point guard Brevin Knight likely to shine even more in his upcoming upperclassman years, the prospects of going even deeper in the NCAA Tournament seemed very realistic.

As far as the just-concluded 1994-95 campaign, Brevin Knight and Dion Cross were named first-team All-Pac-10, each for the first time. Each averaged nearly 17 points per game. Knight averaged over six assists per game, and Cross made 48% of his three-point attempts. Stanford finished 1994-95 with an overall won-loss record of 20-9.

As the 1995-96 season began, to a man, Stanford players believed they could eclipse the previous year's 20-game win total. That optimism was tested early. First, the Cardinal surprised many by losing two of its first five games in November and early December—one to an undermanned University of San Francisco team. Second, after the fifth of those five games to open the season, it was learned that sophomore center Tim Young, who had averaged 12 points and nearly 9 rebounds as the starting center the previous year, would be lost for the season due to back problems.

Without Tim Young, Stanford needed a new starter in the lineup. The hustler, scrapper and on-court tough guy, David Harbour, was promoted from his sixth-man slot into the starting lineup. Stanford had traded a seven-foot starter for a 6′ 3″ starter. With less size, the importance of Brevin Knight and Dion Cross became even more magnified, even though the Stanford Basketball toughness factor clearly would be ratcheted up with the increased presence of Harbour on the court.

Stanford finished the non-conference portion of the 1995-96 schedule with a 7-2 record. It was not as good as the previous year's 9-0 non-conference mark, although it was still very good. Nonetheless, given the 7-2 pre-conference record, Stanford would need, it seemed, at least 12 wins in Pac-10 play to be assured of another NCAA berth.

After the first half of the 18-game Pac-10 schedule, Stanford's conference record stood at 6-3, but after 16 games the conference mark was a less impressive 10-6. Overall, the Cardinal record stood at 17-8 as the calendar turned to March 1996. Without a big-name win on the schedule, it seemed clear that the Cardinal needed wins at Arizona and Arizona State in the next two games—the final two games on the 1995-96 regular season schedule—to be assured of another NCAA bid.

With regard to a possible upset Stanford win at Arizona, there was a problem: Stanford had not won at the McKale Center in over a decade. None of the Todd Lichti and Adam Keefe–led teams had ever won in Tucson, and, in fact, those teams had never come close to winning there. Arizona had the bigger team, Arizona possessed the added swagger of a #11 national ranking, and Arizona had the benefit of the oppressively loud McKale Center crowd. Once again, a Stanford Basketball team seemed destined for a wilting in the Tucson desert, metaphorically speaking.

What happened in Tucson, AZ, on March 5, 1996? Instead of an expected wilting, those in McKale that night saw chest-protruding Cardinal toughness. And it saw a Stanford Basketball swagger—and an outcome—not seen at McKale in a long time. Stanford fell behind early in the game, trailing by as many as 12 points in the first half before rallying to cut the deficit to two points at halftime, significantly aided by Dion Cross's 15 first half points. Then came 20 minutes for the ages, if one is a Cardinal fan.

A 7-0 Cardinal scoring run to open the second half put Stanford on top by five points. The Stanford lead was tenuous, however, and the Cardinal lost the lead when Arizona went up 51-50 just before the halfway point of the second half. Stanford's offense had stagnated, as Wildcat stalwarts Miles Simon and Reggie Geary took turns defending Dion Cross in an effort to try to hold the Stanford guard in check. As the game progressed, that Arizona defensive strategy worked less and less well.

Stanford suddenly turned on the jets, outscoring Arizona 19-9 to take a 69-60 lead, with David Harbour and Brevin Knight hitting some key shots. The Wildcats then stormed back to tie the score at 71-71 with just under four minutes to play in the game. But the Cardinal immediately retook the lead, 74-71, and three minutes later—with the score 74-73 in favor of the Cardinal—Cross hit a key three-point basket to put the Cardinal up 77-73 with less than one minute remaining. Following the Cross three-pointer, Knight and Harbour did a leaping chest bump at mid-court, right on the Arizona logo. The Wildcats were done; the final score was Stanford 85 – Arizona 79. It was Stanford's first win at the McKale Center since the 1983-84 season.

Stanford's three-guard lineup of Brevin Knight, David Harbour, and Dion Cross got the job done. As further and final proof of its team-wide mental focus and toughness, the Cardinal made 8 of 10 free throws in the final 41 seconds to snuff out any hope of a Wildcat comeback. Knight finished with 14 points and 11 assists, and he committed only three turn-overs against tough Wildcat defensive pressure defense. Harbour added 19 points, 15 of them in the second half. And Cross was, well, a revelation.

The Dion Cross stat line that March evening in hostile McKale Center was as follows: 9-for-9 in field-goal shooting. Of those nine baskets, seven were from three-point range, thereby setting a Pac-10 record for single-game three-point shooting proficiency. Throw in a 2-for-2 free-throw performance, and you get a 27-point scoring night that really can be called a "perfect game," if that baseball-centric moniker can be applied to basketball. And Dion Cross's perfect-shooting night was all the more remarkable because it was accomplished not at home against a low-level D1 opponent, but rather on the road in one of the toughest venues—McKale—and against one of the most difficult-to-score-against defensive teams—Arizona—in all of college basketball.

Dion was "on" that night in Tucson. Yet after the game, with his characteristic modesty, Cross politely deflected the praise back to his three-year backcourt mate Brevin Knight. Said Cross of his night—or his Knight, if you will—"I was getting great screens all night, and Brevin was good at getting the ball to me." It would not be the last time that 1995-96 season that these Stanford guards would make significant noise against a college basketball Goliath.

Stanford finished the regular season with 12 wins in Pac-10 conference play—its highest number of conference wins in seven seasons. With a 19-8 end-of-regular season record, thoughts turned to where, with what seed, and against whom the Cardinal's 1996 NCAA Tournament journey would begin. Going east to play in the 1995 NCAA Tournament the prior year had been tough, having had to play UMass in Albany, NY—relatively near the Minutemen's campus location in Amherst, MA—had been tough. So now, one year later in 1996, the Cardinal hoped that its better overall record, its higher national profile following the recent road win at Arizona, and the emerging national reputation of its brilliant junior point guard Brevin Knight would make for a better Stanford seeding in the 1996 NCAA Tournament than in 1995.

Unfortunately, those hopes were not fulfilled. Again Stanford was sent to the East Region. Again Stanford was sent to an East Coast city—Providence, RI. Again Stanford was bracketed to face UMass, which again was a #1 seed, in a potential second-round game. Again Stanford was assigned a twelve-noon tipoff time in its first-round matchup—the equivalent of a 9:00 A.M. start for Stanford players likely to have not yet fully adjusted from being on West Coast "body" time. The Cardinal's first-round opponent would be Bradley University in a March 14, 1996, first-round game.

So again, adversity stared Stanford Basketball in the face. No matter. The nation would see, that weekend, what Tucson, AZ, had seen one week earlier. This was a fearless set of Stanford hoopsters, ready to take on whatever opponent and whatever logistical difficulty presented itself. The Cardinal took care of Bradley, 66-58, in the first-round game. Despite Bradley guard Anthony Parker's 34 points, Stanford trailed only once—when the score was 2-0 in favor of the Braves—and with the help of a splendid 26-point effort from Brevin Knight, the Cardinal was able to hold off a late Bradley surge.

For Stanford in the NCAA second-round game, it would be NCAA déjà vu. Or more appropriately, déjà "*U*," as in "*UMass*." The East Region's #1 seed—and the #1 overall ranked team in the United States in the final regular season poll—UMass would be playing less than 100 miles from its campus. This wasn't a happy thought for Stanford fans.

The Stanford and UMass starting lineups were little changed from the prior year's second-round NCAA Tournament matchup between the two schools. The Minutemen had one of the nation's two most prominent centers, 6′ 11″ Marcus Camby—an enormous defensive and shot-blocking force destined for a multidecade NBA career. The UMass forwards were skilled and physical; the veteran UMass guards Edgar Padilla and Carmelo Travieso were an interchangeably quick and good-shooting pair.

The game tipped off at 12:10 P.M. EST—the only NCAA Tournament game being played in that two-hour time slot anywhere in the country. In other words, 100% of college basketball television watchers in the United States would be watching what almost everyone expected would be another UMass blowout of Stanford. The expectations turned out to be wrong. Two hours after the opening tip, respect for Stanford Basketball would be elevated to a new and higher place.

The first half was one of turf-establishing. Camby blocked a Brevin Knight layup attempt early in the game and smiled dismissively at Knight. Knight immediately threw a defiant "I'll be coming at you again" smile right back at Camby. Several officials' calls in the first half went against Stanford, drawing the ire of Mike Montgomery. Perhaps because of the accumulated frustration of the difficult travel and bracketing, and maybe also to fire up his team, Montgomery during one first half timeout walked along the scorer's table to where the NCAA Tournament Committee member was sitting and gave him a ten-second earful.

Despite the frustration and adversity, the Cardinal was not being dominated by UMass in the game, far from it. The Minutemen lead at halftime was just two points, 33-31. Millions of television watchers nationwide perked up.

The second half began, and both teams revved up the offense. First it was UMass. After building up its early second-half lead to mid-single digits, the Minutemen went on a mid-second half scoring run and led 66-53 with approximately eight minutes remaining. Stanford was teetering—and then suddenly got very sturdy. With Brevin Knight blowing past anyone who tried to guard him, and with freshman reserve Peter Sauer hitting multiple shots from the outside, the Cardinal went on an 18-7 run over the next six minutes to cut the deficit to two points, 73-71, with just under two minutes left to play. Stanford was on the cusp of an historic upset. Every possession counted.

Marcus Camby then scored to put UMass up by four points, 75-71.

Dion Cross answered—late in the shot clock—with a three-point basket to bring the Cardinal to within one point, 75-74. One minute remained in the game. The heavily pro-UMass crowd at the Providence Civic Center rose as the Minutemen worked the ball upcourt on the game's next possession. The crowd knew that UMass needed to score, lest Stanford have the chance to win the game with a score in its final possession. Late in the UMass possession, forward Donta Bright hit a clutch mid-range jump shot. The score was now 77-74 in favor of UMass. Thirty-one seconds remained in the game. Stanford would get a final possession, but it needed a three-point basket to tie.

The ball was inbounded to Brevin Knight, who dribbled for a few seconds, then attacked, then was cut off by two defenders, then passed to a wide-open Peter Sauer on the left wing outside the three-point arc. Sauer had hit five of his six field-goal attempts in the game. He did not hesitate to launch the potential game-tying three-point shot attempt. Sixteen seconds remained in the game. Sauer's shot missed. Marcus Camby rebounded, was fouled, and hit two free throws to make it 79-74, UMass.

Brevin Knight sped downcourt, right at the rim. There was contact; Knight's wild shot attempt in the paint missed. Knight exploded verbally at the officials, but time then ran out. Stanford had been eliminated from the 1996 NCAA Tournament.

A minute later, Knight cooled down. He and Marcus Camby—who stood over a foot taller than Knight—embraced in a show of mutual postgame respect a couple minutes after the final buzzer sounded, after the teams had concluded the ritual postgame handshake line. Five UMass players had scored in double figures, led by Camby's 20 points. For Stanford, Knight finished with 27 points and 9 assists, and Dion Cross added 16 points in what was his final college game. The freshman Peter Sauer chipped in with 11 points.

Five minutes later, the Arkansas basketball team took the court for pregame layup drills in advance of its NCAA Tournament game against Penn State. As the warm-up drill began, Arkansas All-American forward Corliss Williamson stopped, stepped out of his layup line, walked away from his team and toward where former Arkansas AAU teammate Dion Cross was being interviewed postgame by Stanford's radio broadcasters. Williamson gave Cross a warm embrace.

Twenty minutes later, this postgame quote came from Mike Montgomery concerning Sauer's attempt to tie the game in the final seconds: "It's not easy to pick your shots against UMass. The way the game was played, Peter had hit five of his previous six shots, so he wasn't a bad guy to take it." Ten minutes after Montgomery's postgame words, this quote came from UMass head coach John Calipari, regarding Brevin Knight's performance: "We had no answers for him. He was fabulous, unbelievable. The scary thing about this tournament is it's one and done, and one guy can carry a team. That's what almost happened."

Forty-five minutes after the game's conclusion, as the Arkansas-Penn State game was underway but in a television timeout, Brevin Knight—in civilian clothes—emerged from the participants' tunnel. He walked behind one of the baskets and began walking up one of the aisles in the arena. Immediately hundreds of fans in that section of the Providence Civic Center arena—virtually all UMass fans, by the way—rose as one and applauded the Stanford guard who had almost single-handedly played and willed his underdog and undersized Stanford team to victory 3,000 miles from home.

UMass would go on to play two weeks later in the Final Four. Stanford had been beaten by UMass again, but just barely. Stanford's significant ascent in the college basketball world, already visible to Stanford's Pac-10 opponents and fans in the three seasons since Brevin Knight had become the point man of the Cardinal program, immediately had become evident to a nation of NCAA Tournament television watchers on that mid-March weekend afternoon in 1996. And that ascent would continue.

The 1996-97 Stanford Basketball season couldn't arrive fast enough for Stanford fans. Brevin Knight, already an All-American, was back for his senior year. Seven-foot center Tim Young, a redshirt sophomore, was healthy again. Sophomore Peter Sauer, along with promising sophomore guards Kris Weems and Arthur Lee, were contenders for starting jobs. Two talented and energetic freshmen, Mark Madsen and David Moseley, were good enough to warrant playing time immediately.

The 1996-97 Stanford Basketball schedule was ambitious. It included a week in Alaska in the high-profile Great Alaska Shootout, as well as another East Coast non-conference road trip. Stanford and Kentucky—the defending NCAA champion—were the headliners in the Thanksgiving Week Great Alaska Shootout event. College basketball fans expected the two teams to face off in the tournament final. However, the Cardinal was upended by a very good College of Charleston team, 82-78, in the tournament semifinal. So, there would be no Stanford-versus-Kentucky in the championship game of the Great Alaska Shootout. ESPN probably wasn't happy that its project marquee matchup didn't happen.

But that Stanford loss to the College of Charleston was Stanford's only stumble during November and December, as the Cardinal fashioned a 7-1 record through the end of December 1996. When the calendar turned to January, Stanford was back among the nationally ranked teams, with a #21 AP ranking the first week of January 1997. Pac-10 conference play began that first January weekend, with the Cardinal on the road in the state of Arizona. Stanford knocked off Arizona State in the conference opener, and next up was #9-ranked Arizona in Tucson. Senior guard Miles Simon was out with injury, but the Wildcats had a strong lineup of guards Jason Terry, Mike Bibby, and Michael Dickerson, along with forwards Bennett Davison and A.J. Bramlett. It was, to the minds of many knowledgeable college basketball observers, an Arizona team good enough to win it all in April of 1997.

In the game against Arizona in Tucson, Stanford trailed at halftime by nine points, and was down 63-50 with nine minutes remaining. But then the Stanford defense picked up, and the Cardinal offense got some timely contributions from the bench. Over the next seven minutes, Stanford went on a 25-9 scoring run to take a 75-72 lead, with reserve forward Rich Jackson and starting center Tim Young hitting back-to-back baskets to cap the scoring run. The Cardinal was on the cusp of a second straight win in the McKale Center. One minute and fifty seconds remained on the scoreboard clock.

Bennett Davison's tip-in of a Wildcat missed shot, one minute later, cut the Stanford lead to 75-74. On Stanford's next possession, Brevin Knight was fouled. He missed the front end of a one-and-one free-throw opportunity, and Arizona rebounded and set up for its final possession. Again an Arizona player missed a shot, but again Davison was there to tip in the rebound. The Wildcats had the lead, 76-75, with six seconds left. On Stanford's final possession, Knight got a clean look at the basket, but his midrange jump shot missed and the Wildcats secured the rebound as the final buzzer sounded. Arizona had escaped with a one-point victory. Stanford had to wait until early March, when the Wildcats would play in Palo Alto, for a chance to avenge the loss.

One might say, however, that a manner of avenging took place in the very next Stanford game on the schedule. The next Cardinal game was on Thursday night, January 9, 1997, in Maples Pavilion—Stanford vs. UCLA. It was a game that will forever have a name attached to it, at least among Stanford fans: Massacre at Maples.

Final score: Stanford 109 – UCLA 61. It was like something John

Wooden teams used to do to Stanford Basketball teams in Maples Pavilion a generation earlier. The old order had not only changed, it had been flipped. Bruin interim head coach Steve Lavin watched helplessly as the Cardinal set a school record for three-point baskets with 15, in just 31 attempts. Stanford exploded to an early 17-1 lead, led by 31 points at halftime, shot 57% from the field for the game, and outrebounded the Bruins by 19. Brevin Knight had 25 points; Tim Young had 14 points and 10 rebounds in what was—and remains—the most lopsided loss in UCLA basketball history.

Over the next eleven Pac-10 games, the Cardinal would be perfect at home (6-0) but would struggle on the road, losing five of seven games. In the penultimate game of that losing stretch of games, Mike Montgomery made a change in the starting lineup, adding sophomore guard Arthur Lee to join Brevin Knight, Tim Young, Peter Sauer, and Kris Weems in the Cardinal starting five. In his very first game as a starter, Lee instantly justified Montgomery's lineup move, scoring a career-high 26 points in an 84-81 loss at USC.

The final weekend of the regular season found Stanford hosting Arizona and Arizona State. The Cardinal had a solid 18-7 won-loss record, probably already enough wins to get Stanford into the NCAA Tournament. But merely getting into the Big Dance wasn't the main objective of the weekend for Stanford. The objective was to get two more wins and get a good *seeding* in the Big Dance. Also significant was the fact that these were to be Brevin Knight's final two games at Maples Pavilion; he and forward Rich Jackson were the lone seniors on the 1996-97 Stanford Basketball roster.

On Thursday, March 6, 1997, #12-ranked Arizona came to Maples Pavilion. Despite dismissive rhetoric from Mike Montgomery and the players, the Cardinal deeply wanted to avenge the painful one-point loss in Tucson two months earlier. The game was a back-and-forth contest. Arizona raced out to a 21-10 lead. Then a 29-8 Cardinal scoring run put Stanford on top 39-29 late in the first half. Then the Wildcats got hot, closed the half with a 14-2 spurt and led by two points at halftime.

Arizona, for the most part, maintained the lead in the second half, and led by five points, 73-68, with six minutes to play in the game. But Stanford came charging back with an 8-2 run, capped by two Knight free throws, and suddenly the Cardinal led 76-75. Then Miles Simon hit one and Jason Terry two free throws, followed by a tip-in by Bennett Davison—all sandwiched around a lone Cardinal free throw—putting the Wildcats back on top, 80-77, with just over one minute remaining.

On Stanford's next possession, Brevin Knight drove and then fed Tim Young for a dunk with 56 seconds remaining, reducing Stanford's deficit to 80-79. On its ensuing possession, Arizona worked the shot clock down but Miles Simon misfired on a field-goal attempt, giving the Cardinal the ball back one final time. Knight ran the clock down while dribbling in the top-of-the-key area, then drove down the middle of the lane, then suddenly flipped a pass to an open Peter Sauer on the left baseline.

Sauer caught the ball and hit an eight-foot jump shot to put Stanford up, 81-80, with six seconds remaining. In a final minute that was almost exactly the reverse of what had happened in Tucson nine weeks earlier, Wildcat guard Mike Bibby had a final chance to win the game for Arizona, but his jump shot missed. Stanford had its revenge, its 19th overall win and—for sure—had removed what little doubt had previously existed that it would be receiving a berth in the 1997 NCAA Tournament.

Stanford won its regular season finale against ASU, and learned the next day that it had received a #6 seed in the West Region, that it would play in Tucson, AZ, and that it would play #11-seed Oklahoma in its first-round game. For the first time in its last four NCAA Tournament appearances, Stanford did not have to travel to the Eastern time zone for its initial NCAA games.

The Cardinal made quick work of Oklahoma, 80-67, in its NCAA first-round game on Friday, March 14, 1997. Kris Weems led the way with 20 points, while Brevin Knight and Tim Young added 18 and 15 points, respectively. The win advanced the Cardinal to the NCAA Tournament second-round for a third consecutive season. In its second-round game, Stanford once again would be facing a better-seeded team—a team that, like the UMass teams of Stanford's prior two NCAA Tournament second-round games, had an All-American center on its roster. It had been Marcus Camby of UMass each of the past two years in round two, and this year it would be Wake Forest's Tim Duncan that Stanford would be facing in the second-round as the opposition's big man and primary on-court threat.

How could Stanford, and particularly Tim Young, defend the NCAA Player of the Year Tim Duncan? Mike Montgomery gave it some thought, and came up with an interesting gameplan—have four different players, starter Tim Young and reserve big men Mark Madsen, Mark Seaton, and Pete Van Elswyk—take turns covering Wake's All-American center. The strategy would not only ensure a fresh body on Duncan at all times but would also mean no defender was likely to get into foul trouble, at least early in the game. Monty's rotation scheme meant the Cardinal had 20 fouls to play with in defending Tim Duncan.

It wasn't exactly a "Hack-a-Duncan" approach, but the Cardinal big men played physical-style defense against the Wake Forest star. The strategy helped Stanford build and maintain a first half lead. The score was 25-19 Cardinal at the end of the first half. Surprisingly, the Cardinal's defense in the first half was even more effective on the other Wake players than it was on Tim Duncan. Whereas Tim Duncan was 4 of 6 in first half shooting; the rest of the Wake team was just 2 of 14.

Predictably, this NCAA second-round game would come down to the final minutes. Perhaps from toughness gained through its NCAA Tournament battles against UMass the prior two seasons, the Cardinal did not wilt. Late in the game Peter Sauer hit back-to-back jump shots—the second of which put the Cardinal up by five points with 1:10 left. With just under a minute to play, with Stanford ahead by just four points, Sauer fired another jump shot from the left side, missed, but Arthur Lee had darted into the rim area as Sauer's shot was released and was there to tip in the miss. Stanford was now up 68-62, and two clutch free throws by Brevin Knight a short while later sealed the upset win for the Cardinal, 72-66.

Brevin Knight and Tim Duncan, teammates on the under-21 USA national team the prior summer, embraced at midcourt at game's end. Duncan's decorated college career was over; the four-man rotating Stanford defensive scheme on Duncan had held the Wake Forest center and National Player of the Year to just 18 points, three points below his season average.

Brevin Knight led the way for Stanford with 19 points, five assists and four steals. Peter Sauer finished with 14 points and seven rebounds. Arthur Lee and Kris Weems chipped in with 14 and 13 points, respectively. Stanford had won two games in an NCAA Tournament for the first time since 1942. Perhaps even better than that—at least emotionally, for Stanford fans—the Sweet 16 destination for the Cardinal was San Jose, California, just fifteen miles south of campus.

Stanford's Sweet 16 game was set. The date and venue: Thursday, March 20, 1997, San Jose Arena. The matchup: #6-seed Stanford versus #2-seed Utah, West Region semifinal, tipoff at 4:55 P.M. Every seat in the downtown San Jose Arena would be filled. The largely pro-Stanford crowd arrived early. CBS Television commentator Bill Raftery, who had coached Brevin Knight's father Mel Knight at Seton Hall a quarter-century earlier, enjoyed a pleasant on-court conversation with the Stanford All-American just before the game's tipoff.

The beginning of the game was, however, anything but pleasant for the Stanford Basketball team. The Utes, featuring a starting lineup that included future NBA players Andre Miller, Keith Van Horn, and Michael Doleac, surged ahead and led by fourteen points at halftime, 35-21. Stanford, though, toughened up after the intermission. A 10-2 Stanford scoring run to open the second half brought the Cardinal to within six points, 37-31. But then Brevin Knight picked up two quick fouls in succession, saddling him with four fouls with thirteen minutes to play in the game. Mike Montgomery wasted no time in making his decision—Knight would stay in the game with the four fouls.

Utah looked to be in control in the final minutes, leading by seven points, 63-56, with 1:55 to play. But a Stanford scoring flurry followed: a made free throw by Kris Weems, then a tip-in by Mark Madsen, then two free throws by Brevin Knight, then a basket plus an "and one" free throw by Knight—all sandwiched around a lone Utah basket. The flurry brought Stanford to within one point, 65-64, with 26 seconds remaining.

Stanford fouled the Utah center Michael Doleac on the inbound pass that followed Knight's free throw, and Doleac made both free throws to put the Utes back on top by three points. Stanford had one last chance. Brevin Knight's 15-foot runner seconds later was an air ball, but Keith Van Horn could not corral the rebound and the ball went out of bounds, possession awarded to Stanford, with ten seconds remaining in the game. There was still one more chance for Stanford.

What happened next was another magical Brevin Knight moment. The inbound pass went to Knight, who caught the ball in the left corner, beyond the three-point arc, with a defender chasing him. In one motion, Knight flung a long jump shot toward the basket as he was floating in the air sideways. Knight looked to have been fouled on the shot. No whistle was blown, but no matter—THE SHOT WENT IN! Tie score, 67-67, seven seconds remaining!

Utah fumbled the ball on the ensuing inbounds play, recovered the ball but was unable to get a good shot off before the final buzzer sounded. Overtime in the Sweet 16 game! Brevin Knight had scored eight points in the final minute, including the game-tying three-point basket.

In the overtime period, Keith Van Horn fouled out within the first 35 seconds, buoying Stanford's hopes. Brevin Knight's two free throws, following the Van Horn foul, gave Stanford the lead, 68-67. But that was the last time Stanford would have the lead in the game. Michael

Doleac scored, then Andre Miller hit two free throws, then a short time later Knight picked his fifth and disqualifying foul. Stanford had battled valiantly, but it could not overcome Utah's poise in the final two minutes of overtime. Final score: Utah 82 – Stanford 77.

Brevin Knight finished with the same stat line that he had finished with in the prior year's season-ending NCAA Tournament loss to UMass: 27 points and 9 assists. Tim Young added 15 points and 12 rebounds. Stanford's Achilles heel had been its field-goal shooting, just 32% for the game.

The great Stanford career of Brevin Knight had come to an end. The year before he matriculated at the Farm, Stanford won only seven games and had finished with a won-loss record that was 16 games under .500. By his final year, Stanford had won 22 games—with a won-loss 14 games above .500—and had made it to its third consecutive NCAA Tournament.

And it wasn't just the won-loss record and NCAA Tournament profile that had been raised. Maples Pavilion attendance was at all-time highs. The caliber of Stanford Basketball's recruits was now reaching the McDonalds All-America level: twins Jason and Jarron Collins, McDonalds All-Americans as high-school players in Southern California, would sign national letters of intent to come to Stanford beginning with the 1997-98 season.

Only graduating seniors Brevin Knight and Rich Jackson were departing the program—though Knight the All-American, three-time All-Pac-10 selection and firebrand competitor would be impossible to replace. Nevertheless, the collective size, shooting ability, depth, and experience—not to mention the hard-won NCAA Tournament game experience—of the returning roster players was exceptional. The notion of a Stanford team going even further than the Sweet 16 in future years seemed a realistic possibility.

1997-1998 would prove the point, dramatically.

OPPOSITE: *Brevin Knight was a first-team All-American (1997) honoree, a three-time All-Pac-10 selection, and almost single-handedly propelled the program to new heights.*

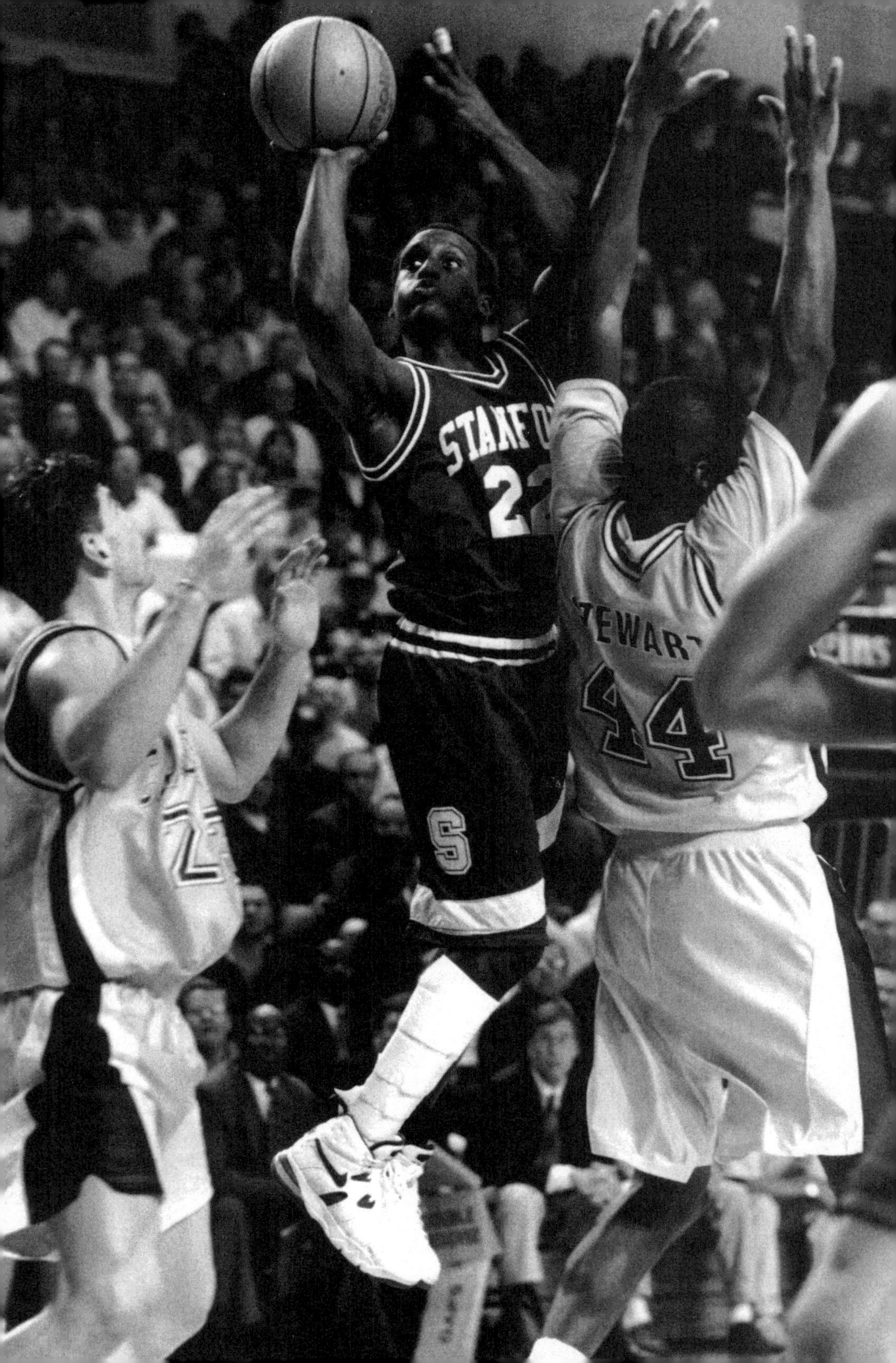
44
S

VIII. The Final Four Season

After a Knight Departs, an Arthur Reigns

One of the hallmarks of the Mike Montgomery era was that each season tended to feature a new accomplishment or a new success level achieved, beyond that which had been accomplished or achieved in the prior season. Even given that the 1996-97 season had established several new program milestones, including a postseason push into the NCAA Tournament Sweet 16, the Montgomery–era axiom would hold true the following season, 1997-98. Right from the start, the 1997-98 Stanford Basketball team pushed—and blew past—prior standards of program success.

Only three times prior to 1997-98 in Stanford Basketball history had a Stanford team gone undefeated during the pre-conference portion of the schedule. It would happen for a fourth time in 1997-98. Among Stanford's November-December victories were these: three wins and a championship at the eight-team Big Island Invitational in Hawaii, a victory over Georgia at the Honda Center in Anaheim, and wins over both Rhode Island and Santa Clara on successive nights in the Cable Car Classic in San Jose. Stanford also won five other games, making its pre-conference record 11-0 as the Pac-10 schedule began in January 1998.

Besides the undefeated won-loss record, Stanford carried a #10 national ranking into the opening weekend of conference play in January. Yet Stanford was not even the highest-ranked team in the conference, that honor belonging to #4-ranked Arizona. The Wildcats were the preseason favorite to win the Pac-10, although no one was counting out Stanford as a serious contender for the Pac-10 crown in 1997-98.

Stanford won each of its first seven conference games in January 1998 by double-digit margins. Not even the great 1988-89 Stanford team, with its 15-3 Pac-10 record, had won its conference games by such consistently large margins. Kris Weems scored 34 points in the second game of Pac-

10 play, a 22-point win over Oregon at McArthur Court in Eugene, OR. It was Stanford's largest margin of victory ever in that historic building.

Two weeks later, the Cardinal notched a home win over #8-ranked UCLA, 93-80, as Peter Sauer tied a career-high with 19 points and the Cardinal netted 14 of 26 three-point baskets. It was Stanford's 16th consecutive win to open the 1997-98 season, the longest winning streak ever to begin a Stanford Basketball season. Win #17 came five nights later in the next game at Pullman, WA, a ten-point triumph over WSU.

The next game, against Washington in Seattle, figured to be a difficult one. Washington was 12-3 overall, 5-1 in the Pac-10. The Huskies had very good talent in center Todd McCullough, forward Deon Luton and guard Donald Watts—good enough talent, in fact, to reach the NCAA Tournament Sweet 16 later that season. Stanford led at the half, 37-34. Stanford used a 15-6 scoring run to take a 52-40 lead with 16 minutes remaining in the second half, but the Huskies answered with a 22-9 surge to claim the lead, 62-61, with just over five minutes left. The Stanford 17-game winning streak was definitely in jeopardy.

Back-and-forth the lead changed in the final minutes. With five seconds remaining, Donald Watts hit a six-foot baseline jumper to give the Huskies a 72-71 lead. Mike Montgomery called timeout. On the ensuing backcourt sideline inbound play, Peter Sauer passed the ball to Kris Weems well into the backcourt. Weems caught the ball, sped forward, pulled up at the top of the key (behind the arc) and let fly. The ball swished through the net as the final buzzer sounded. The Cardinal team engulfed Weems on the court. Consecutive win #18 was in the bank for Stanford, 74-72. Two days later, in the weekly AP Poll, Stanford's ranking had been bumped up from #5 to #4, its highest national ranking ever.

A new success level achieved, indeed. But Stanford was not a perfect team, and the imperfections soon surfaced. Stanford, at home for its next game against #6-ranked Arizona in a first-ever Maples Pavilion matchup of top-ten-ranked teams, saw its winning streak end in humbling fashion, 93-75. Two days later, the Cardinal lost at home to Arizona State by three points in an overtime game, then three days later won at Cal by just two points.

Two days after the squeaker win over Cal, the team traveled to Storrs, CT, for a weekend non-conference game with the Connecticut Huskies. That game, like the Arizona game, was a blowout loss, the Cardinal succumbing by twenty points, 76-56. Just two weeks after having been ranked #4 in the nation, Stanford's ranking dropped to #14 in the weekly AP Poll.

The losing streak stopped five nights later, with a tough 84-81 win over

#9-ranked UCLA at Pauley Pavilion. Stanford led by 15 points with eight minutes left to play in the game, but the Bruins clawed back and the game was tied at 78 with 33 seconds remaining. The Cardinal regrouped, however, as Arthur Lee and Kris Weems collectively hit 6-of-6 free throws in the final half-minute to enable the Cardinal to pull away for the victory. It was just the second time since 1942 that Stanford had swept a UCLA team in the season series.

Its record 19-4 overall and 9-2 in Pac-10, the Cardinal had seven conference games remaining on the 1997-98 regular season schedule. It won six of them, each by a double-digit margin except an eight-point Senior Night win over Oregon State. The one loss was a doozy—a 90-58 pratfall in Tucson against #2-ranked Arizona on February 26, 1998. A potentially troubling fact regarding the feasibility of a deep NCAA run in 1997-98 was this: Stanford's two losses to Arizona had been by a combined total of 50 points.

The NCAA seeding announcement represented another new achievement by the Stanford Basketball program—a #3 seed, its highest seed ever in an NCAA Tournament. The Cardinal was placed in the Midwest Region, where the #1 seed was Kansas and the #2 seed was Purdue. It seemed like a reasonably favorable draw for Stanford, given the style of play of the #1 and #2 seeds in the other regions that the Cardinal might have had to face. Stanford's initial weekend of NCAA play would be played in Chicago's United Center. If the Cardinal could win two games, it would advance to the Kiel Center in St. Louis for the Sweet 16 game and the possible Elite Eight game to follow.

Stanford's first-round NCAA opponent was a familiar one—one it had faced the year prior in the Great Alaska Shootout tournament, the College of Charleston (CoC) Cougars. Stanford lost that year-earlier game to CoC in Anchorage, so there was no chance that the Cardinal would take the #14-seed Cougars lightly in the NCAA Tournament first-round game.

Nevertheless, despite Stanford's focus, the CoC-Stanford first-round game was a battle. The Cougars had the lead, 52-48 with 6:51 remaining in the second half. After a Mark Madsen tip-in, a Stanford free throw, and an exchange of baskets between the two teams, junior forward Ryan Mendez—Stanford's deadeye deep shooter off the bench—nailed a three-point basket from the left side to put Stanford up by two points. CoC promptly tied the score moments later with a basket, but Mendez then hit an even longer-distance three-pointer to give Stanford a three-point lead. An 8-1 Cardinal run thereafter ensured that Stanford would advance to its fourth consecutive second-round appearance in the NCAA Tournament.

Stanford caught a big break in the second round. #11-seed Western Michigan upset #6-seed Clemson, so it was the Cardinal versus the WMU Broncos in an NCAA second-round game on Sunday, March 15, 1998, in Chicago. Stanford capitalized on the opportunity, dominating the second half and winning by a comfortable margin, 83-65.

The turning point in the Western Michigan game came with twelve minutes remaining in the second half. Bronco guard Rashod Johnson—the team's second leading scorer and who had scored a team-high 32 points in WMU's NCAA first-round upset win over Clemson—drew his fifth foul, and then drew a technical foul for complaining about the foul call. From that point forward the Broncos never could escape a double-digit deficit. Arthur Lee led the way for Stanford with 24 points, including a 10-of-10 performance from the free-throw line, and he added seven assists. Tim Young and Mark Madsen dominated the play inside, with Young producing 19 points and 13 rebounds and Madsen contributing 19 points and 10 rebounds.

Meanwhile, elsewhere around the Midwest Region, multiple upsets had eliminated several of the teams on the higher-seeded side of the bracket, including #1-seed Kansas, which fell to #8-seed Rhode Island. Also gone were #7-seed St. Johns and #4-seeded Mississippi, the latter gone thanks to the famous last-second shot by Valparaiso's Bryce Drew. The four teams advancing to the Midwest Region Sweet 16 in St. Louis were the following: #2-seed Purdue, #3-seed Stanford, #8-seed Rhode Island, and #13-Valparaiso. For Stanford and the other three surviving teams in the Midwest Region, a golden opportunity to reach the Final Four lay ahead in the Gateway Arch city.

The Sweet 16 matchup for Stanford was Purdue, the Big 10 champion whose playing style mirrored Stanford's—an emphasis on "get-the-ball-inside" offense and on disciplined man-to-man defense. Stanford experienced adversity early in the game. The Cardinal trailed, 24-20, with five minutes remaining in the first half. Tim Young was on the bench with three fouls. But with Mark Madsen playing well and freshman Jarron Collins helping mightily off the bench in Young's absence—with each providing significant scoring punch in the paint—the Cardinal ended the first half with a 17-2 scoring run and was ahead of the Boilermakers by 11 points, 37-26, at halftime. Collins had ten points in the first half.

The second half was as close to a football game as an NCAA Tournament game could be permitted to be. Purdue center Brad Miller twice had to have his chin stitched up due to contact with a Stanford player. But a Gene Keady–coached team doesn't back down, and the Boilermakers didn't. Madsen was whistled for his fourth foul midway through the second half, and drew his disqualifying fifth foul with 1:30 remaining when he fouled Purdue's Brian Cardinal as Cardinal was scoring a basket. Cardinal made the "and one" free throw and Purdue was within three points.

Perhaps the most important Stanford possession came next. The Cardinal ran its half-court offense deliberately and patiently. With the shot clock under five seconds, reserve guard David Moseley—in possession of the ball near the top of the key—knew he had to hoist a shot up quickly. Fortunately for Stanford, Moseley's three-point field-goal attempt was splashed through the net, doubling the Cardinal lead to six points with one minute remaining in the game.

That Moseley three-pointer was the back-breaker. Arthur Lee made sure Stanford would not relinquish the lead, hitting all four of his free throws in the final minute when Purdue had to foul and hope the Stanford missed free throws. As time expired, the Sweet 16 scoreboard was indeed sweet for the Cardinal: Stanford 67 – Purdue 59.

The final stats reflected a balanced scoring game for Stanford: Mark Madsen led with 15 points, while Arthur Lee, Jarron Collins and David Moseley added 13, 12 and 10 points respectively. The key for the Cardinal was its physical dominance and defensive excellence; Stanford out-rebounded Purdue, 51-39, and held the Boilermakers to just 31% shooting for the game.

Another new and higher success level for the Cardinal indeed had been reached. For the first time since 1942, Stanford had advanced to the NCAA Tournament's quarterfinal, or Elite Eight, round. A win over #8-seed Rhode Island, to be played on Sunday, March 22, 1998, was all that separated Stanford from the Midwest Region championship and—more importantly—a ticket to San Antonio and a berth in the 1998 NCAA Tournament Final Four.

The two teams were certainly familiar with one another. Jim Harrick, the UCLA coach from 1988 to 1996, was in his first year as the head coach at Rhode Island. And the two teams had faced each other earlier in the season, in San Jose at the Cable Car Classic tournament. The December 29 matchup had been tightly contested: The final score was Stanford 70 – Rhode Island 69. Despite URI's relatively low seeding, the Cardinal coaches knew it would be a tough game. Just one week earlier, Rhode Island had upset #1-seed Kansas, 80-75, in its second-round game. The Rams had talent, experience, and toughness.

The first half of the game bore that truth out. The halftime score was

Stanford 38 – Rhode Island 38. In the second half, the Rams seized control of the game, or so it seemed. With 8:40 remaining, the Rams led by eleven points. With 2:13 left to play in the game, Rhode Island still led by six points, 66-60. With 59 seconds remaining, despite a three-point basket and a two-point basket by Lee in the intervening 74 seconds, it was still a six-point game, with the Rams seemingly comfortably ahead by the score of 71-65.

But then Art Lee made a three-point basket. Then, following a Rhode Island free throw, Lee made a brilliant pass leading to a Madsen layup. Stanford suddenly was down by only two points. Then, after two Rhode Island free throws by Preston Murphy, Lee drove the length of the court for a basket and was fouled. He made the free throw. Stanford was now down just one point, 74-73, with 32 seconds remaining.

On the ensuing Rhode Island backcourt inbound pass, Arthur Lee deflected the ball away from a Ram dribbler and into the hands of Mark Madsen, who secured the ball, took a big step toward the basket, and dunked the ball with two hands. And he was fouled on the play! Madsen made the free throw and with 26 seconds left Stanford was suddenly—incredibly—*ahead* by two points.

Rhode Island's Antonio Reynolds-Dean then committed an unforced turnover in the URI frontcourt. Fourteen seconds were now left in the game. Kris Weems was fouled on the ensuing inbound pass. He made one of two free throws; Stanford was now ahead, 77-74. Thirteen seconds remained.

The Rams hurried into the frontcourt. Point guard Tyson Wheeler dribbled the ball to a spot outside the arc on the right wing, suddenly fired up a three-point shot attempt, and in so doing was fouled by Arthur Lee—the last thing Stanford needed at that point. Rhode Island had a chance to tie, if Wheeler could make all three free throws. Wheeler was a 65% free-throw shooter. Five seconds were left on the clock.

Wheeler missed the first free throw.

Wheeler missed the second free throw.

Trying at this point to miss the third free throw intentionally, Wheeler missed the third free show with a hard fling of the ball off of the rim. The Rams, trying for the rebound, knocked the ball out of bounds. Ryan Mendez inbounded the ball to Arthur Lee, who was immediately fouled. Two seconds were left on the clock. Lee made both free throws, his 25th and 26th made free throws in 26 attempts in his four 1998 NCAA Tournament games. The score was now 79-74 in favor of Stanford, and it was "game over" for Rhode Island.

The Rams' Cuttino Mobley hit a meaningless half-court shot at the buzzer, making the final score Stanford 79 – Rhode Island 77. For Stanford, dream had become reality. The colossal Cardinal celebration began—beginning with Lee being hoisted onto the shoulders of teammates and being paraded around the court.

Stanford was going to the Final Four!

Arthur Lee had scored *thirteen* points in the final two minutes. He finished with 26 points overall to lead the Cardinal in scoring, making nine of his fifteen shots overall and all four of his field-goal attempts in the final two minutes. He had dished out a game-high seven assists as well. Little wonder he was named Most Outstanding Player of the 1998 Midwest Region.

Mark Madsen contributed 15 points, while Tim Young added 14 points and 12 rebounds in the historic Cardinal win. And one fact, not captured on the stat sheet, certainly helped the Cardinal comeback: Coach Mike Montgomery had saved all of his timeouts and used them following each Stanford basket or made free throw in the final minute, which allowed the Cardinal to set up its defense and receive instruction about which Rhode Island player to foul. The Lee steal, which led to Madsen's decisive dunk, likely would not have happened had Monty not used a time-out with which to set up a full-court-press defense.

On the happy charter flight from St. Louis back to the Bay Area, Mike Montgomery and assistant coaches Doug Oliver, Trent Johnson, and Eric Reveno were talking about securing game tapes of Kentucky and preparing scouting reports, with Kentucky looming ahead as Stanford's opponent in the national semifinal in San Antonio. Further back in the plane, Cardinal players celebrated with cheerleaders, members of the band, and with each other.

About the only player subdued, at least initially, was Arthur Lee. He was busy composing a letter of apology regarding a "choke sign" made by him as Wheeler was missing his three free throws near the end of the game. "So many things had me hyped up at that moment, I wasn't really aware of what I was doing, but there definitely is no excuse for what I did," Lee later told a Stanford radio broadcaster, "I had to apologize, it's the right thing to do given what I did."

Doing the right thing—and doing the "Knight" thing, too. Arthur Lee certainly had played like Brevin Knight in the regional final, perhaps even a bit better than Brevin Knight had done in his greatest NCAA performances. The frustration of being in Knight's shadow was gone, once and for all. And a Final Four berth for Lee and for Stanford was the reward. Lessons had been learned, new plateaus had indeed been achieved.

"I felt no pressure," said Lee. "I just had to be Arthur Lee. I love Brevin, but I think I am an OK player." Given his "KO" of Rhode Island, Stanford fans would certainly agree with that assessment.

So it was on to San Antonio and the Saturday, March 28, 1998, date with Kentucky in the national semifinal matchup. Forty thousand fans would be on hand at the Alamodome. In the days leading up to traveling with his team to San Antonio, Mike Montgomery worried privately whether they would be a bit too awed by the grandness of the stage, the week-long hoopla, the Kentucky name. Once he and his team got on the floor at the Friday open practice at the Alamodome, one day before the game, Montgomery's concerns were allayed. "Right then," said Montgomery, "I knew we would be fine."

If the start of the national semifinal was any indication, Stanford would be more than fine. The Cardinal raced out to an 8-0 lead—with Lee hitting two three-pointers and scoring all eight points—before Kentucky scored its first point. And the Cardinal would keep that lead for a long time.

Stanford led 13-3 early in the first half. Stanford led 37-32 at halftime. Stanford led 46-36 early in the second half. Stanford was handling Kentucky's pressure defense successfully. But each time Stanford built a lead, Kentucky always would come back, four times reducing the Stanford lead to one point during the game's first 30 minutes. Finally, with 10:04 remaining in the second half, Kentucky got *its* first lead, as forward Scott Padgett hit a pair of free throws.

Kentucky was accustomed to playing in Final Fours, having played in the most recent two. The Wildcats knew what a third weekend of NCAA play was like, particularly in the second half of games when pace and stamina were important issues. Stanford did not have a previous Final Four experience to draw upon, and in the second half things started to catch up with the Cardinal.

Eleven of Stanford's thirteen turnovers in the game were committed after halftime. In addition, Stanford's defense on Wildcat center Nazr Mohammad weakened somewhat in the second half, with Mohammed scoring 17 of his 18 points after halftime. And Kris Weems could not find his shooting legs, either before or after the halftime break. Stanford's All-Pac-10 guard Weems was just 6 of 23 in field-goal shooting for the game.

But the Cardinal hung with the Wildcats down the stretch in the second half. Back-and-forth the lead changes went. Neither team had more than a three-point lead between the ten-minute mark and the two-minute mark of the second half. Kentucky upped its lead to 72-68 with two minutes remaining, on a three-point basket by guard Jeff Sheppard.

But a Mark Madsen putback basket made the score 72-70 Wildcats, and after Kentucky's Wayne Turner made one of two free throws to make it 73-70, Arthur Lee—who else?—hit yet another three-point basket for Stanford to tie the game at 73-73 with 25 seconds left. Turner's runner in the final seconds rimmed out, and the national semifinal game went to overtime.

The game continued to be an uphill battle for the Cardinal in the overtime period, particularly on defense. The Wildcats scored on each possession in the first three minutes of overtime, building a 78-73 advantage with three minutes left. Less than a minute later, the score was 79-78 in favor of Kentucky when Scott Padgett tried to dunk after driving to the basket from the right wing, with Mark Madsen going airborne in an effort to block it. The dunk hit the back of the rim and ricocheted 30 feet behind Padgett, landing out of bounds along the right sideline.

Somehow, the officials ruled that the missed Padgett dunk was last touched by Madsen, not by the would-be dunker Padgett. The ball was awarded to Kentucky, and following the inbound pass Jeff Sheppard drilled a top-of-the-key three-point basket to boost the Wildcats' lead to 82-78. As things would turn out, the sequence of the out-of-bounds ruling followed by the ensuing Sheppard three-pointer was enormously pivotal to the game's outcome.

Nevertheless, Stanford continued to fight the uphill fight. Jarron Collins hit a free throw and Ryan Mendez hit a three, sandwiched within four UK-converted free throws over a 90 second period. The score was 86-82 Kentucky when, in the final seconds, Peter Sauer drilled a 27-foot three-point basket. It was now 86-85 Wildcats, with just nine seconds remaining. Seconds later, Jarron Collins was able to tie up a Kentucky player for a "held ball" call in the backcourt. However, under the then-in-effect alternate possession rule, the Wildcats kept the ball. That was the Cardinal's last gasp. The final score was 86-85, in favor of Kentucky.

Stanford's historic 1997-98 season was over. There was disappointment in the Cardinal camp, but many were the reasons to celebrate the historic Final Four game and entire 1997-98 season. Stanford's final won-loss record was a sterling 30-5. The thirty wins constituted the most wins in a season in Stanford Basketball history. In the Final Four loss to Kentucky, Arthur Lee once again led Stanford in scoring with 26 points, including 5-of-8 shooting from three-point range and a 9-of-9 performance from the free-throw line. Kris Weems scored 17 points,

Mark Madsen contributed 11 points and 16 rebounds, and Tim Young added ten points and seven rebounds.

Arthur Lee was named to the All-Final Four team, his second award in the 1998 NCAA Tournament after having earlier been named Midwest Region Most Outstanding Player. Lee averaged 21 points and six assists in the five NCAA Tournament games in 1998, and shot nearly fifty percent from three-point range (making 20 threes in all). And in free-throw shooting, Lee made 35-of-35 free throws, an all-time NCAA Tournament record for free-throw shooting marksmanship in a single NCAA tournament—and a record, like Joe DiMaggio's 56-game hitting streak, so incredibly difficult to achieve that it may never be exceeded.

Left: Mark Madsen, perpetually inspirational frontcourt player whose famous "dunk and dance" play propelled Stanford to a spot in the 1998 Final Four; Right: Kris Weems, All-Pac-10 guard on the Final Four team.

1997-98 Stanford Basketball Radio-Television Roster

3 Kris Weems
Guard

4 Michael McDonald
Guard

5 Peter Sauer
Forward

11 Arthur Lee
Guard

15 Dave Bennion
Guard

20 Alex Gelbard
Guard

21 David Moseley
Guard/Forward

30 Johannes Burge
Guard

31 Jarron Collins
Forward

32 Ryan Mendez
Forward/Guard

33 Jason Collins
Center

35 Kamba Tshionyi
Guard

40 Pete Van Elswyk
Forward

44 Mark Seaton
Forward

45 Mark Madsen
Forward

55 Tim Young
Center

Mike Montgomery
Head Coach

Doug Oliver
Assistant Coach

Trent Johnson
Assistant Coach

Eric Reveno
Assistant Coach

Mark Thompson
Undergrad. Asst. Coach

Jeff Roberts
Trainer

Scott Swanson
Strength Coach

ABOVE: *The roster of the 1998 team, which won a school-record 30 games and reached the Final Four.*
OPPOSITE: *Arthur Lee's incredible 1998 NCAA Tournament line: 103 points scored, a perfect 35-of-35 in free-throw shooting, and 13 points scored in the final two minutes of the historic 79-77 comeback win over Rhode Island in the regional final.*

STANFORD
11

IX. The Full Monty

Conference Championships, #1 National Poll Rankings, and #1 Seeds in NCAA Tournaments

A few weeks after the Final Four, the 1997-98 team end-of-season banquet was held. Fittingly, it was held in the very structure—the 76-year-old Stanford Pavilion—that had served as the team's home arena from the early 1920s through the late 1960s, including the 1942 NCAA championship season. The symbolism was obvious: the program's second-ever Final Four team, dining on the very floor where the first Final Four team had practiced and played.

As each player was celebrated at that April 1998 event, as the highlight videos rolled, banquet attendees could not help think two things: (i) each of the program's top eleven scorers and rebounders would be returning for the 1998-99 season, an unusually high percentage of returnees, and (ii) since virtually every player would be returning from a team that had come within one point of reaching the NCAA title game, would next year's banquet be celebrating a Stanford Basketball national title?

When it came time for Mike Montgomery to wrap up the evening, in the midst of his praise of the team's effort and accomplishments, he noted a couple of things about the next season's goals and schedule. Monty said that the non-conference schedule would be the toughest yet, with more travel than usual and more high-profile games—the better to prepare the team for possible championships. And then he said "that's championships, PLURAL." Monty then said that while he understood all of the dreaming about a national title, and that it's fine for everyone to have that as a goal, the primary championship that the Stanford Basketball team needed to focus on was the PAC-10 CHAMPIONSHIP. After all, Monty said matter-of-factly, Stanford hadn't won one in decades.

Predictably, the preseason media hype surrounding the 1998-99 Stanford Basketball team was off the charts. Numerous sports and basketball-themed magazines featured a Stanford player, usually Arthur Lee, on the cover in the fall of 1998. More than one national preseason poll picked the Cardinal not only to return to the Final Four but to win the NCAA title in April 1999.

So great was fan interest in the upcoming season that, for the first and only time in program history, a "midnight madness" event was held to kick off the 1998-99 season. It was not Mike Montgomery's preferred way to begin a season; in fact, he thought it might put a bit of undue pressure on his team. As practices got underway in October of 1998, Montgomery found himself constantly reminding media members covering the team of this truth: Even though the Stanford team was a veteran squad, the Cardinal players were still just young people aged 18-22, and even mature and smart youngsters can struggle under the weight of expectations.

Arthur Lee, Kris Weems, Tim Young, Mark Madsen, and Peter Sauer, of course, were all back as starters, so the high expectations for the 1998-99 campaign certainly were not ill-founded. All had averaged double figures in scoring the prior year. All had significant and pressure-tested NCAA experience. All were now seniors except Madsen, who was now a junior.

The Cardinal opened the 1998-99 season with three blowout wins at home, each by a victory margin of 25-or-more points. Then began the travel, starting with two games in the Preseason NIT "Final Four" at Madison Square Garden in New York on November 25 and 27, 1998. The semifinal game was against #23-ranked St. John's, a New York City borough school. Monty wasn't kidding about the tough scheduling—if the Cardinal could get by St. John's, perennial power and 1998 Final Four participant North Carolina likely would be next.

The Cardinal got its first taste of being a big target that an opponent had circled on its schedule and was fired up to play. An unusually large Thanksgiving Eve crowd showed up at Madison Square Garden, nearly 15,000 fans in all, for the Stanford–St. John's matchup. The large MSG crowd revealed this truth: Many folks with no ties to the Stanford Basketball program wanted to come out and see a Final Four–caliber team.

St. John's threw the first punches, figuratively speaking. With forward Ron Artest providing the spark on offense, the Red Storm led by three points at halftime, and then by ten points with just under six minutes remaining in the game. The pro-St. John's crowd lustily and loudly sensed an upset.

But the Cardinal responded. A 12-3 Stanford scoring run, keyed by two Arthur Lee baskets and a three-point basket by Peter Sauer, allowed the Cardinal to seize the lead, 52-51. With the score tied at 53, with 15 seconds remaining in the game, Ron Artest missed a free throw, and then Artest fouled Arthur Lee who had received the outlet pass following the ensuing Stanford rebound. Lee reprised his NCAA Tournament free-throw prowess of eight months earlier, calmly hitting both free throws to provide Stanford with the margin of victory in a 55-53 win.

In the Preseason NIT title game two nights later against #9-ranked North Carolina, the Cardinal did not fare so well down the stretch. Again Stanford trailed at halftime, this time by the score of 32-23. Again Stanford fought back, cutting the deficit to three points with two minutes remaining. But Tar Heel point guard Ed Cota hit several free throws in the final two minutes—negating yet another Stanford comeback surge fueled by Arthur Lee, who hit two three-point baskets in the final two minutes—to preserve the lead and secure the victory for North Carolina, 57-49.

The Cardinal returned to Palo Alto from New York City on Saturday, November 28, 1998, and six days later the team was back on a plane to the East Coast—specifically, to Washington, DC, to play in the BB&T Classic. Next up for Stanford was the highest-ranked team it had yet faced, #5-ranked Maryland. Maryland's lofty ranking was based in part on a new player, a much-hyped junior-college transfer guard named Steve Francis. Francis lived up to his billing, scoring 24 points in a narrow 62-60 Terrapin victory over Stanford on Sunday, December 6, 1988. For a second straight game, a team with a "visibly motivated-to-play Stanford" guard had just enough juice to overcome the powerhouse Cardinal.

It was the last loss Stanford would suffer prior to the start of Pac-10 play. In the six Stanford games following the Maryland loss and prior to the start of conference play—four of them away from Maples Pavilion—the Cardinal won all six by an average margin of victory of 24 points. Stanford's won-loss record in 1998-99 stood at 10 wins and 2 losses as the calendar turned to January 1999 and the beginning of Pac-10 play.

If there was a dominant theme in Mike Montgomery's messaging to his 1998-99 team—a team that did not need much motivational messaging—it was one thing: Let's win the Pac-10, we haven't done that yet. Great teams, Monty kept saying, won their conference championship. There certainly would be formidable competition for that elusive Pac-10 title. At the start of Pac-10 play in 1999, three Pac-10 teams were ranked among the AP's top-ten-ranked teams: #5 Stanford, #6 Arizona, and #10 UCLA.

The fight for the conference crown began with three consecutive home games—all wins for the Cardinal, over the Oregon schools and Cal. Next came a road win at USC, Stanford's tenth-consecutive victory since the Maryland loss. With a 4-0 Pac-10 record, the Cardinal next faced its first big test—a January 16 date at UCLA.

Stanford led the Bruins at halftime 33-27, but found itself down by five points midway through the second half. Pauley Pavilion was sold out and loud, and Mike Montgomery sensed his team was out of rhythm and needed something. So Montgomery did something he didn't often do—he changed the defense to a zone defense. And that was the difference. The Cardinal went on a 30-12 scoring run during the final 12 minutes of the game and won by the score of 72-59. All five Stanford starters scored in double figures. Said Bruin guard Baron Davis of the Stanford zone: "They made us take shots we didn't want to take."

Following a home sweep of the Washington schools, Stanford ventured out on the road to face its other chief rival for the conference crown: Arizona. The Cardinal was leading the league race with 7-0 won-loss record, but Arizona was right behind in the standings at 6-1. A Stanford win would be a huge step forward in its quest for the Pac-10 championship.

Twice during the 1990s the Cardinal lost a game to Arizona on an Arizona basket in the final seconds, and unfortunately for Stanford it happened again on January 28, 1999. Wildcat guard Jason Terry hit a spinning ten-foot jump shot with three seconds remaining to give the Wildcats a 78-76 victory over the Cardinal. Such had been Stanford's rise to college basketball prominence that when a home team knocked off a visiting Stanford team, the win often would trigger an end-of-game celebratory court rush by the fans. It happened that night at the McKale Center in Tucson—a place where court rushes by fans following wins had hardly *ever* happened.

Following a bounce-back win at Arizona State and a win at Cal in its next two games, the Cardinal did a one-game detour away from the Pac-10. As Mike Montgomery had promised, the schedule had been purposely crafted to prepare the team for a deep NCAA Tournament run. So it was time for one last non-conference test—a home matchup against the #1-ranked Connecticut Huskies.

So many sportswriters—including a couple of dozen from Connecticut alone—had requested credentials for the Stanford-UConn game that a separate media workroom had to be set up in a building adjacent to Maples Pavilion. CBS Television was on hand for a national television broadcast of the game. Maples Pavilion was packed. Since neither Arizona nor UCLA had yet visited Maples, this was the first big home game on the 1998-99 schedule. It was also the first time two top-five-ranked teams had ever squared off at Maples, as the Cardinal carried a #4 national ranking into the matchup against the top-ranked Huskies.

Like North Carolina, like Maryland, and like Arizona, Connecticut featured an exceptional point guard, 5′ 10″ Khalid El Amin, and a suffocating, pressure-based half-court defense. UConn had beaten Stanford by 20 points the year prior in Storrs, CT. And given that UConn was a No. 1 team used to playing big-name opponents in hostile arenas in the Big East conference and elsewhere, most believed that UConn would not be fazed by the Maples Pavilion noise or the reputations of Arthur Lee and Mark Madsen and the rest of Stanford's veteran lineup.

UConn's good play in the first half evidenced all of that. Early scoreboard snippets in the first half were as follows: 17-4 UConn, 22-6 UConn, 26-8 UConn. Not only was Stanford rattled in its field-goal shooting the entire afternoon, it was affected at the free-throw line as well, making only 12 of its 24 free-throw attempts. Meanwhile, El Amin was leading the way for UConn on offense with 23 points and five assists, to go along with five steals on the defensive end. The game wasn't as close as the final UConn victory margin suggested: UConn 70 – Stanford 59.

Arthur Lee summed up what a lot of Cardinal fans were thinking: "We've just got to keep going. It's a loss. We've got to get ready for the tournament." Even though its coach was repeatedly emphasizing the conference championship goal, Stanford players still had Final Fours—past and future—intruding on their minds. And the loss to UConn, clearly a potential Cardinal obstacle in the upcoming NCAA Tournament, showed that the Stanford team needed to improve if it had designs on returning to the Final Four in late March of 1999.

Stanford returned to Pac-10 play five nights later to face yet another biggie: UCLA at Maples Pavilion. It was the *seventh* time, in 1998-99, that the Cardinal would be squaring off against a Top 25-ranked team. The Cardinal trailed UCLA by two points at halftime, and by five points early in the second half, but a 16-6 scoring run put Stanford up by eleven points midway through the second half. Despite making only one field goal in the final six minutes, Stanford's rebounding strength and free-throw shooting proficiency—19 of 21 down the stretch—were the difference in a 77-73 win over the Bruins. Arthur Lee had 17 points, Tim Young added 12 points, and Mark Madsen chipped in with 11 points and 12 rebounds, offsetting Baron Davis's 23 points and JaRon Rush's 20 points for UCLA.

Said Rush after the game, "We thought Stanford was vulnerable." Nevertheless, the Cardinal got the win and thereby maintained a two-game lead over Arizona at the top of the Pac-10 standings. Mike Montgomery's goal of a Pac-10 championship was within sight.

During the next two weeks, Stanford and Arizona each lost one Pac-10 game: Stanford at home to USC (in overtime), and Arizona to Cal at Cal. With three games to go in the Pac-10 race, Stanford's Pac-10 record was 13-2, while Arizona's was 11-4. Next up for Stanford was its final home game, on Saturday, February 27, 1999. It was Senior Night—the final home game for seniors Arthur Lee, Peter Sauer, Mark Seaton, Kris Weems, and Tim Young. The opponent was #7-ranked Arizona. If Stanford won, it would clinch its first-ever Pac-10 championship.

Stanford was ready for its moment.

Despite an abundance of physical play early—nine fouls were called in the first three minutes alone—the Cardinal got hot and burst out to a 20-point lead midway through the first half. Kris Weems had five three-point baskets in the first half alone. Arizona managed to whittle the deficit to nine points by halftime, but that was as close as the Wildcats would get.

Stanford was even hotter in the second half, making 58% of its field-goal attempts, and midway through the second half the Cardinal lead grew to more than twenty points. Arthur Lee, who a few days earlier had been named first-team All-Pac-10, was hitting basket after basket en route to a career-high 29 point scoring night. Once again, Lee was coming up big in a big Stanford game—the story of his Stanford career.

The unexpectedly lopsided final score was Stanford 98 – Arizona 83. Thirty-six years of waiting had come to an end. Stanford Basketball had secured its first conference championship, either outright or shared, since the 1962-63 season.

The celebration went far beyond fans flooding the Maples Pavilion court, which, as one prominent media outlet put it, "pitched and rolled as if an earthquake were rumbling across the Stanford campus." Each player and each of the coaches climbed a ladder positioned under the north basket and took a turn clipping the net as the band played an endless loop of "All Right Now." The final person to cut the net, and the one to remove it, was Mike Montgomery, who twirled it emphatically and forcefully several times as the camera flashes popped all around him. The level of program achievement he had most sought since arriving on the Farm—a conference title—had finally been attained.

Stanford's record at the end of the 1998-99 regular season stood at 25-6 overall. Most seasoned college basketball observers believed that the Cardinal would receive a #2 seed in the 1999 NCAA Tournament, and that's what Stanford received—a #2 seed in the West Region. For Stanford, that meant a first, and a potential second, round of tournament games in Seattle, WA.

Two "bad facts" accompanied the Cardinal into the 1999 NCAA Tournament, however. In the penultimate regular season game, at Oregon on March 4, 1999, Jarron Collins suffered a high-ankle sprain. Stanford won the Oregon game, but it would not have Jarron Collins for the regular season finale at Oregon State two days later. That Collins was injured and unable to play was very likely a factor—in addition to the general letdown accompanying a team that had a week earlier clinched the conference championship—that explained a 59-49 loss to a struggling Oregon State team on March 6, 1999, a loss that may have cost the Cardinal a #1 seed in the NCAA Tournament.

The other bad fact: Once the 1999 NCAA Tournament brackets came out, Stanford found out that its possible second-round opponent was Gonzaga, a dangerously under-seeded #10 seed and one that the Cardinal would have to play in the Zags' home state in the event both teams advanced to the NCAA second-round game in Seattle. The Gonzaga that would become a basketball power in the first decade of the 2000s was not yet recognized as such a program, but in March 1999 the talent was in place for the Zags to make a big move in that direction.

In the first round of the 1999 NCAA Tournament, Stanford took care of Alcorn State, 69-57. On the same day, Gonzaga knocked off a better-seeded team, #7-seed Minnesota, 75-63. So the stage was set: Stanford vs. Gonzaga, March 13, 1998, Key Arena in Seattle. There would be no doubt as to who the vast majority of the 15,187 fans would be cheering for in this game—the Cardinal was booed loudly as it came on to the court for pregame warm-ups. The NCAA did Stanford no favors in seeding in the 1999 NCAA Tournament; the Seattle site hardly felt like a neutral one.

Stanford took a 1-0 lead on a free throw and then fell behind—by a lot. The score was 23-10 in favor of Gonzaga midway through the first half. Gonzaga was hurting Stanford with its three-point shooting prowess, hitting five threes in the first twelve minutes of the game.

Stanford narrowed the deficit to four points by halftime and managed to tie the score at 49 with eleven minutes remaining. But Gonzaga then regained the lead and built it back up to ten points. The Cardinal starters were not hitting their shots with their usual proficiency. And without Jarron Collins, whose ankle injury had been a season-ending one, Stanford had one less weapon off the bench to provide help.

Ironically, with just one minute left in the game Stanford was down by six points—just as it had been in the Rhode Island game a year earlier. At that point Arthur Lee hit two free throws to bring the Cardinal to within four points. But Stanford got no closer. Gonzaga had been making—and was continuing to make—its free throws, making 13 of 16 over the final two minutes. The largely pro-Gonzaga Key Arena crowd was loud and proud as the final seconds ticked away. The final score was Gonzaga 82 – Stanford 74.

Not since the Siena game a decade earlier had a Stanford team suffered an NCAA upset loss as big. Stanford was the first high seed to fall in the 1999 NCAA Tournament. Arthur Lee finished with a game-high 24 points in his final Stanford Basketball appearance, but he made just 6 of 18 of his field-goal attempts. For Gonzaga, the star was senior guard Matt Santangelo, a one-time Cardinal recruit who dazzled with 22 points, 6 assists, and 6 rebounds.

Thus ended the run of the deepest and most accomplished class in Stanford Basketball history: Arthur Lee, Kris Weems, Tim Young, Peter Sauer, and Mark Seaton had been part of the first post–World War II Stanford team to reach the NCAA Tournament Sweet 16, and then one year later were the core members of the first postwar team to go a couple of steps further and reach the Final Four. As seniors, these five also were the pillars of the first Cardinal team to win a conference championship in 36 years. It seemed as though the loss of these five young men, talented and accomplished as they were as a group, would set the program back a few steps.

Yet despite the painful loss to Gonzaga in the 1999 NCAA Tournament, and despite the reality that a great senior class was moving on, there was no doubt that Stanford Basketball was now among the nation's elite college basketball programs. Three times in less than a decade, the program had not only survived the departure of an all-time great—Todd Lichti in 1989, Adam Keefe in 1992, and Brevin Knight in 1997—it had also flourished. Throughout the mid and late 1990s, it seemed that new great players materialized on the roster just as great ones were departing.

Certainly the five-man freshman group that joined the Stanford Basketball team in the fall of 1999 was a case study in the program's ability to replenish elite talent. It was, based on collective accolades earned during their high-school years, the most talented class of freshmen that the program had ever recruited to the Farm. Headlined by 6′ 6″ guard Casey Jacobsen, one of the top five scorers in California high-school history as a prep player at Glendora High School in Southern California, the class also featured seven-foot center Curtis Borchardt, 6′ 1″ guard Julius Barnes, 6′ 8″ forward Justin Davis, and 6′ 10″ center Joe Kirchofer.

The freshman would be put to the test right away. The opening game of the 1999-2000 season was slated for Madison Square Garden. The date was November 11, 1999. The event was the four-team, high-profile Coaches vs. Cancer Tournament. The opponent for Stanford in the tournament's opening night game was Duke University. It would be the first time the two programs had ever met.

There was no mistaking the similarities of the two programs at the end of the 20th century. Both Stanford and Duke were recruiting the same elite high-school players. Both regularly were ranked among the top teams in the weekly national college basketball polls. Even the coaches were very similar—both were named Mike, both had even been born within two weeks of each other in 1947.

Duke's lineup that November 1999 evening was daunting; its starters included Shane Battier, Carlos Boozer, Jason Williams, and Mike Dunleavy. The Cardinal led at halftime by two points in a back-and-forth game played in front of an A-list celebrity crowd that included actor Bill Murray. But late in the game, a bad event occurred on the Stanford side—senior Mark Madsen injured his hamstring and had to leave the game.

In part because of Madsen's absence, Duke was in a great position to win the game in regulation, leading 66-60 with 39 seconds remaining. But in those final 33 seconds, sandwiched around two Duke free throws, Ryan Mendez and David Moseley hit clutch three-point baskets to pull the Cardinal to within two points. Then, with three seconds remaining in the second half, Jarron Collins's layup tied the game 68-68, sending the game to overtime.

In the overtime period, Stanford exploded. Following two free throws by Duke's Chris Carrawell 33 seconds into the extra session, the Cardinal went on a 10-0 scoring run. Two three-point baskets by Stanford's new starting point guard, junior Michael McDonald, were followed by a David Moseley layup and a dunk by Jason Collins. Collins, a 6′ 11″ center and the twin of Jarron Collins, had missed the prior two seasons due to injury. With 2:03 remaining, the Cardinal was ahead on the scoreboard, 78-70.

Duke then went on a 9-2 scoring run, but—thanks to a missed 25-foot jump shot attempt by Nate James—the Blue Devil rally fell just short. Final score: Stanford 80 – Duke 79. Senior David Moseley's 20 points led the way for Stanford, but a big story in the game was the Cardinal defense, which held Duke to just 28% field-goal shooting. A memorable play in the game was produced by Stanford's seven-foot freshman center

Curtis Borchardt, who demonstrated his considerable shot-blocking prowess by swatting a Jason Williams layup attempt into the first row of seats at Madison Square Garden.

The next evening, in the Coaches vs. Cancer championship game, the Cardinal dispatched Iowa to win the crown. Jason Collins, starting in place of the injured Madsen and starting for the first time at Stanford alongside his brother Jarron, had 18 points and 12 rebounds. Jarron, not to be outdone, had 17 points and 10 rebounds. The game was also a coming-out party for the frosh phenom Casey Jacobsen, who tallied 17 points and made four of his five field-goal attempts from three-point range.

The remainder of Stanford's 1999-2000 non-conference portion of the schedule played out in much the same way as it had the two prior seasons: a lot of wins, with several of the games played away from home in big, NBA-style arenas of the sort in which NCAA games were typically played in March. First came two wins at Maples Pavilion, including a game in which an opponent, Cal State Bakersfield, was held to 31 points for the entire game by a robust Cardinal defense that included center Curtis Borchardt breaking Kent Seymour's 15-year single-game shot block record. Next came a Saturday, November 27, 1999, win over Auburn in Anaheim, CA—a game in which Borchardt had a key three-point jump shot late in the game to seal the win. The following Monday, Stanford achieved its highest-ever ranking, #3, in the weekly AP college basketball poll.

A week later came a December 4, 2000, overtime win over Georgia Tech at the Phillips Arena in Atlanta—a tense game in which Jason Collins's defense of a last-second Jason Collier layup attempt preserved the Cardinal win. In the AP Poll the following Monday, Stanford—with its 6-0 record—was up to #2 in the rankings, behind only Cincinnati. Five more Cardinal non-conference wins followed, each by an average victory margin of 31 points. And in the middle of that two-week, late-December 1999 string of wins came Stanford's first-ever #1 ranking in the AP Poll.

The top-ten-ranked teams, according to the December 21, 1999, AP College Basketball Poll, were these, in order of ranking: Stanford, UConn, Arizona, Cincinnati, Michigan State, North Carolina, Auburn, Florida, Syracuse, and Duke. Not only was Stanford standing atop the world of college basketball, it had also already beaten Duke and Auburn—two schools on that list of top-ten-ranked teams—earlier in the season. It would play two others on that list before the season was over. It was an impressive new level of achievement for Mike Montgomery and the Stanford Basketball program.

Stanford carried a perfect 11-0 record into the first weekend of Pac-10 play, an early January weekend homestand against the Arizona schools. There was good news for the Cardinal going into that weekend of play: After missing several weeks following his season-opening-game hamstring injury, Mark Madsen would be back in the Stanford starting lineup. After a 19-point win in the conference opener against Arizona State, next up for the Cardinal was #5-ranked Arizona—only the second time two top-five-ranked teams had ever squared off in a game at Maples Pavilion.

Despite losing star forward Richard Jefferson to a broken foot in the game's opening minutes, the Cardinal was able to manage only a two-point halftime lead. Then came a disastrous scoring drought for Stanford: In the opening eight minutes of the second half, Arizona outscored Stanford 18-4 to take a 47-35 lead. Although Stanford would close that deficit to six points with nine minutes remaining, it would get no closer until the final, meaningless seconds of the game. For the second time in three seasons, Arizona had ended a long season-opening Cardinal winning streak with a win at Maples Pavilion, by a score of 68-65.

Stanford was now 12-1, 1-1 in the Pac-10. The following Monday, Stanford's national ranking fell to #3. But for the next thirteen games, Stanford played like a #1 team as it mowed down one Pac-10 opponent after another. Thirteen consecutive Pac-10 wins ensued, a new Mike Montgomery–era standard of accomplishment, given that it was a school record for consecutive conference game wins. Seven of those wins had come without the contribution of Curtis Borchardt, who suffered a season-ending foot injury in a mid-conference-season road loss at USC.

None of those thirteen consecutive wins had a margin of victory of less than double digits. One of those wins included a 51-point pasting of Cal on Saturday, February 19, 2000. The following week, the Cardinal had regained a #1 national ranking in the weekly AP Poll. Going into game #16 of the 18-game Pac-10 schedule—Stanford's home finale—the Cardinal record was a gaudy 25-1. UCLA would be the opponent on Senior Day, Saturday, March 4, 2000. It would be the final Maples Pavilion appearance for Cardinal seniors Mark Madsen, David Moseley and walk-on Alex Gelbard.

It was a wild game with a wild finish. Stanford had early leads of 12-0 and 18-4 in front of the boisterous Senior Day crowd. But Stanford's defense, which was leading the nation statistically in allowing opponents only 34% field-goal shooting, was not strong on this day; UCLA was on its way to making 55% of its field-goal attempts, including 12 of 23 from three-point distance. A Mike McDonald three-point basket put Stanford up by two points, 80-78, with 17 seconds left in regulation, but UCLA center Jerome Moiso hit a short turnaround jumper at the buzzer to send the game into overtime. In the overtime period, Stanford led by four points with 54 seconds remaining, but JaRon Rush hit a three-point basket for UCLA with 42 seconds left, slicing the Cardinal lead to 93-92.

After the Rush basket, Stanford could not get the ball inbounds within five seconds, thereby turning the ball back over to UCLA. The Bruins ran the clock down and took a shot with seven seconds remaining—after, it appeared, the shot clock had expired. In the ensuing scrum for the loose ball, JaRon Rush came up with it along the left baseline and fired a corkscrew ten-foot jump shot toward the basket as time ran out. The shot went in, the official replay review confirmed it, and the Bruins had themselves a 94-93 upset victory over top-ranked Stanford at Maples Pavilion.

Stanford's overall 1999-2000 won-loss record now stood at 25-2, with its Pac-10 record at 14-2. Arizona was in second place in the Pac-10 with a 13-3 conference mark. The two teams faced each other in the next game each played, March 9, 2000, at the McKale Center in Tucson.

Arizona led by two points at halftime and by fifteen points with just 6:23 to play. Then David Moseley almost single-handedly brought Stanford all the way back. He scored fourteen consecutive points in the ensuing minutes, pulling the Cardinal to as close as three points, but the deficit was too much to overcome as Stanford fell to the Wildcats, 86-81.

Following the game, both teams were tied atop the Pac-10 standings with identical 14-3 conference records, with one game for each to play. On the last day of the Pac-10 season, both teams won, Stanford at ASU (65-57) and Arizona at home over Cal (70-61), thus resulting in a sharing of the regular season Pac-10 title. Nonetheless, the Cardinal had earned a share of a second straight conference championship.

There was good news regarding Stanford's 2000 NCAA Tournament bracket situation: For the first time in program history, the Cardinal received a #1 seed. There was also some bad news: Stanford was being sent to Birmingham, AL and the Southeastern Region, where #8-seed North Carolina was looming, potentially, in a second-round matchup.

Having made the cross-country trip to Birmingham, AL, via connecting flights and having gotten itself acclimated to the game site, Stanford had no problem in its first-round game against South Carolina State on Friday, March 17, 2000, winning by the score of 84-65. But, predictably, North Carolina took care of Missouri, 84-70. Thus, for the ninth time in history, Stanford and UNC would square off in a basketball game.

Stanford's record in its previous eight games against UNC was not a good one: 0-8, including the Tar Heels's win over Stanford in the 1998 Preseason NIT championship game sixteen months earlier at Madison Square Garden. The Tar Heels had underachieved during the 1999-2000 regular season, producing an uncharacteristically pedestrian 18-13 regular season record. Like Gonzaga had been a year earlier, North Carolina was a massively under-seeded team in the 2000 NCAA Tournament.

The game was tense, with Stanford emerging with an eight-point lead late in the first half, but then North Carolina went on a 14-0 scoring run spanning the end of the first half and the start of the second half, putting the Tar Heels up by six points. The Cardinal then retook the lead by four points, 47-43, with nine minutes remaining. And then the Tar Heels took off.

First came a hook shot by seven-foot center Brendan Haywood. Then came a driving layup by freshman shooting guard Joseph Forte. This was followed by back-to-back three-point baskets by Forte. Suddenly, the score was 53-47 in favor North Carolina. With point guard Ed Cota hitting late free throws and power forward Julius Peppers—later to have a long NFL career as a defensive lineman—denying Stanford its bread-and-butter offensive rebounds, the Cardinal could not regain the lead. A breakaway Forte slam dunk sealed Stanford's fate: The final score was North Carolina 60 – Stanford 53.

For a second straight season, Stanford as a #1 or #2 seed had been eliminated in the second-round of the NCAA Tournament. No one was more distraught, postgame, than freshman Casey Jacobsen, who struggled through a 2-for-12 shooting game as part of an uncharacteristically low five-point scoring afternoon. Said Jacobsen, "This team was special and it tears my heart out that I will never get the chance to play with Madsen, Moseley, and the rest of the seniors again."

The 1999-2000 team finished with a fabulous 27-4 overall record, the best Stanford season won-loss mark in 63 years. At season's end, both Casey Jacobsen and Mark Madsen were named to the All-Pac-10 basketball team, Madsen for a second consecutive year. Jacobsen led Stanford in scoring with a 14.5 points-per-game average. He had made 50.8% of his field goals and 43.5% of his three-point shots in his maiden Stanford Basketball season. Yet because of the disappointing NCAA Tournament ending in Birmingham, Casey Jacobsen and the other nine returning Cardinal players were determined to produce a better outcome in 2000-01, at least in the March portion of the season.

Going into the 2000-01 season, Coach Montgomery knew his new team would have to make up for the losses of the inspirational—not to mention highly productive—Mark Madsen and David Moseley. The Stanford defense clearly would suffer a bit in their absence. But certainly the Cardinal offense in 2000-01 figured to be even better than its 79 points-per-game average in 1999-2000, which was among the 20 highest-scoring offenses (out of 330 teams) in NCAA Division 1 college basketball.

The starting lineup was set. The four LA-area guys—sophomore Casey Jacobsen (Glendora), fourth-year players Jarron and Jason Collins (North Hollywood), and fellow senior Mike McDonald (Long Beach) returned as starters. The fifth starter in 2000-01 was Texas-native, sharpshooter deluxe and fifth-year senior Ryan Mendez. To beat this veteran and offensive-minded Stanford squad in 2000-01, an opponent probably would have to put up a big number on the scoreboard.

Oh, and if the Cardinal needed defense, several guys were ready to come off the bench and provide it. Not only did Stanford have the sensational shot-blocking sophomore Curtis Borchardt as the first big man off the bench, it also had a couple of freshman backups to help on the defensive end. Six-foot-eight forward Justin Davis—an exceptional natural defender and rebounder—provided defensive help in the paint. Six-foot-five wing Teyo Johnson, a football-basketball "combo" player, was capable of defending opponents both inside and on the perimeter.

Only once in Stanford's eleven non-conference games in 2000-01 did the Cardinal score fewer than 78 points. Again the Cardinal traveled far and wide in November and December: Over the Thanksgiving Break it ventured to Puerto Rico for a three-game tournament, which it won handily with a 3-0 record in games that included wins over Memphis and Georgia. But the non-conference game everyone remembers—and will always remember—was Stanford's December 21, 2000, game at the Oakland Coliseum against #1-ranked Duke.

The largest crowd ever to attend a college basketball game in California was on hand, 19,804 persons in all, to witness the matchup. Celebrities came out in force: Secretary of State nominee and Stanford professor Condoleeza Rice, Jim Plunkett, Jerry West, Tiger Woods, Dusty Baker, Tony LaRussa, Brent Jones, and future Golden State Warriors owner Joe Lacob were just some of the luminaries on hand. Both teams were undefeated going into the game. Duke was eager to avenge the one-point loss to Stanford thirteen months earlier at Madison Square Garden. Casey Jacobsen, for his part, was eager to show the national television audience that his most recent big-stage game—his forgettable effort against North

Carolina in the prior year's NCAA Tournament—was not representative of the real Casey Jacobsen.

Almost from the jump, the Cardinal was behind and playing catch-up. Stanford trailed by as many as sixteen points in the first half, and it might have been more had not Jacobsen ended a Duke first-half scoring run with a spectacular 28-foot jump shot from the right wing. Still, the Cardinal deficit at halftime was 13 points, 43-30. The second half was the same story—at least the first sixteen minutes of the second half. Stanford trailed by 15 points with seven minutes remaining, and trailed by 11 points, 77-66, with four minutes remaining.

The Cardinal defense then stiffened. Guard Julius Barnes—who would prove himself perhaps the greatest leaper in Stanford program history—blocked a Duke slam dunk attempt by the five-inches-taller Nate James to get the Stanford team, and the pro-Cardinal crowd, fired up. On offense, Stanford followed Barnes's defensive gem by scoring four quick points, then got a clutch three-point basket from McDonald with two minutes remaining to cut the deficit to four points, 77-73.

The Cardinal then scored six of the game's next seven points over the next 50 seconds, tying the score at 79 on a Julius Barnes layup. Twenty seconds later, however, Mike Dunleavy's leaner broke the tie and gave Duke the lead, 81-79. Stanford answered with a free throw. Then each of Duke's Chris Duhon and Stanford's Jason Collins hit two free throws. The Blue Devils still had the lead, 83-82, with fourteen seconds remaining in the game.

At that point, with Stanford desperate to get the ball back, Duke's Mike Dunleavy was fouled by a Cardinal player. Incredibly, Dunleavy missed *both* free throws. Stanford rebounded, dribbled the ball into the frontcourt, and called a timeout with seven seconds remaining to set up a final play.

The ball was to be inbounded on the frontcourt sideline, right in front of the Stanford bench. The five Cardinal players on the court moved, screened, and cut. Jacobsen received the inbound pass well outside the arc on the right side of the court, about 25 feet from the basket. He rapidly dribbled to his left, across the free-throw line area and into the left wing mid-post area. The sophomore then suddenly stepped back and softly wristed a ten-foot bank shot toward the basket. Good! Among the courtside celebrities leaping skyward on the sidelines at that moment was a *very airborne* Tiger Woods, a former member of the Stanford Golf team.

Just 3.6 seconds remained in the game. No timeout was available for use by Duke. The ball was quickly inbounded to Duke point guard Jason Williams. Williams raced down court and looked as though he might get a game-winning layup. However, rules-compliant harassment in the rim area by Stanford's Jason Collins, coupled with the Duke guard being a bit out of control in his haste to get the shot off, resulted in Williams's running bank shot missing its mark.

The game was over. For the second time in its history, Stanford had knocked off the nation's #1-ranked team.

It had been a classic. Shane Battier and Jason Williams each scored 26 points for the Blue Devils. Casey Jacobsen set a new personal Stanford career-high with 26 points of his own, making 11 of 19 shots. Ryan Mendez and Jarron Collins added 14 points apiece. Jason Collins had 10 points and 15 rebounds, and he helped hold powerful Duke forward Carlos Boozer to just four points. Julius Barnes scored nine of Stanford's 15 total points from the bench.

Following its triumph over Duke, Stanford was 9-0 and was the nation's #2-ranked team, behind only top-ranked and defending national champion Michigan State. The Cardinal improved that record to 11-0 a week later with two late-December wins at the Cable Car Classic over Fordham and Santa Clara. Stanford thus was able to maintain its #2 national ranking as the schedule turned to conference play in January 2001.

The wins just kept coming for Stanford as Pac-10 play began. The Cardinal reeled off eight wins in eight Pac-10 games in January. The January 27, 2001, win at Washington State was Stanford's 19th consecutive win to begin the season, breaking the record of 18 wins to begin a season set three seasons earlier, in 1997-98. Another new Stanford success level had been reached.

Another win came February 1 at home against USC, by the score of 77-71. Little did anyone know that the Trojans would be one of three Pac-10 teams to reach the Elite Eight a few weeks later. But an unfortunate event occurred in the USC win—for the second consecutive season, backup center Curtis Borchardt suffered a broken right foot in the game in Maples Pavilion and, as was the case the previous year, would miss the remainder of the season. The absence of Borchardt, particularly his defensive contributions as a backup to Jason Collins, would become a negative factor for the Cardinal as the season progressed, particularly in March postseason games.

Stanford, however, was a perfect 20-0 following the USC win and remained the nation's lone unbeaten team. Next up for Stanford was a February 3, 2000, Saturday afternoon home date with UCLA. Coach Steve Lavin decided to employ a pressure defense against Stanford and the strategy was successful, slowing down Jacobsen and forcing Stanford into eight first-half turnovers. The Bruins led by three points, 40-37, at halftime after having led by as many as nine points earlier in the half.

The Cardinal struggles continued in the second half. With Jason Collins slowed by effects of the flu, UCLA was able to score inside more easily than it had in recent games with Stanford. UCLA led by 11 points with eight minutes remaining and by nine points with just under three minutes remaining. The Cardinal got no closer than three points as the final three minutes elapsed, suffering its first loss of the 2000-01 season by the final score of 79-73.

UCLA shot 50% for the game and outrebounded the Cardinal by three. Casey Jacobsen struggled through a 4-for-18 shooting afternoon, though he did lead the Cardinal in scoring with 17 points. Stanford's "perfect season" bubble had been burst.

Apparently unfazed by the home loss to UCLA, Stanford's winning trend resumed and its hold on first place in the Pac-10 solidified. In the weeks following the loss to the Bruins, Stanford would build a two-game lead on Arizona in the race for the conference title, winning its next seven games while Arizona won only six of its seven during the same stretch. In one of those wins, a 99-79 pasting of Washington at Maples Pavilion, Jason Collins hit his first 13 shots of the game, including an incredible 4 of 4 from three-point distance. Late in the game, to the mock groans of Cardinal fans, Collins launched a 14th field-goal attempt—from three-point territory—which missed, ending his perfect shooting stat line. But Collins still finished with a career-high 33 points, one-third of Stanford's scoring total that evening.

In another of the wins during the Cardinal seven-game winning streak, at UCLA in game #16 of the Pac-10 schedule, Stanford avenged its lone loss of the 2000-01 season. Four of Stanford's five starters—Jason Collins, Jarron Collins, Casey Jacobsen, and Ryan Mendez—each scored 16 points to lead the Cardinal to victory. The win meant Stanford needed only one win in the final weekend's two games—both home games—against the Arizona schools to clinch a third consecutive Pac-10 crown.

On Thursday, March 8, 2001, Stanford hosted Arizona. The Cardinal had beaten the Wildcats in Tucson in early January, just the second time the Cardinal had won at the McKale Center in 17 games there since 1985. In the rematch at Palo Alto, for the third time in eleven seasons, Stanford was victimized by an Arizona basket in the final seconds. Arizona forward Michael Wright's layup with three seconds remaining gave the Wildcats a 76-75 win. It was just Stanford's second defeat of the season.

Nonetheless, the Cardinal needed only a win on Saturday, March 10, 2000, against Arizona State, to secure the Pac-10 championship. On Senior Night for Jason and Jarron Collins, as well as for Michael McDonald and Ryan Mendez, Stanford players made sure the seniors would get a victory—and with it another Pac-10 championship—in their final Maples Pavilion game. All five Cardinal starters scored in double figures in the 99-75 home finale win over the Sun Devils: Jacobsen had 21 points, Mendez 19, Jarron Collins 15, McDonald 12, and Jason Collins 10.

And in a fitting signature Senior Day performance, Ryan Mendez extended his consecutive-free-throws-made streak to 49, making 6-of-6 free throws before missing on his seventh attempt. Nevertheless, Mendez had established both school—going past Todd Lichti's record of 41—and Pac-10 records for consecutive free throws made. Mendez closed his career, and remains, statistically one of the most proficient free throw and three-point shooters in Stanford Basketball history.

In the final regular season poll, Stanford finished with a #2 ranking, placing the Cardinal right behind #1-ranked Duke. At two different times during the 2000-01 season, the Cardinal had held the weekly #1 ranking for multiple consecutive weeks. After mid-December, the Cardinal never held a ranking lower than #3.

There was, of course, no question that Stanford would receive a #1 seed in the West Region of the 2001 NCAA Tournament. The first and second-rounds for the Cardinal would be played in San Diego; the regional semifinals and final, a week later, would take place in Anaheim. It presented as a very favorable path to the Final Four for Stanford Basketball.

At the Cox Arena in San Diego, Stanford had no trouble with its first-round opponent, UNC Greensboro, winning by the score of 89-60. Jason Collins scored 25 points to lead the way for the Cardinal. The second-round NCAA Tournament game, however, would be a different story.

St. Joseph's had a gunner, a guard named Marvin O'Conner, and his marksmanship was otherworldly in the March 17, 2001, second-round game between Stanford and St. Joseph's. O'Conner scored 37 points and, given the additional contribution of fellow Hawk guard Jameer Nelson, who added 14 points, 9 rebounds and 9 assists, the Atlantic 10 school had the Cardinal on the ropes at multiple junctures during the second half.

The Hawks led the game 67-62 with just over eight minutes remaining, despite the fact that Stanford had led by nine points at halftime and by ten points with 17 minutes left. A 21-6 St. Joe's scoring run, which exactly coincided with Michael McDonald being on the bench with four fouls for a nine-minute stretch during the middle portion of the second half, was responsible for the five-point Hawks lead.

However, McDonald soon reentered the game and helped Stanford reclaim the lead, and the Cardinal increased that advantage to four points, 80-76, on a Julius Barnes's dunk with two minutes remaining in the game. With under two minutes remaining and St. Joseph's down by four points, Marvin O'Conner scored on a drive and then again with a jumper to tie the game at 80—the latter basket accounting for his 25th and 26th points *of the second half.*

What would save the Cardinal in this game was its free-throw shooting and its defense. Stanford hit 13 of its final 13 free-throw attempts in the game, including all ten in the final minute, to seize back the lead from St. Joseph's and keep hold of it. And in the final 90 seconds, the only St. Joseph's score was a lone three-point goal by—who else?—Marvin O'Conner. The final score was Stanford 90 – St. Joseph's 83.

O'Conner, disconsolate, nevertheless left the floor to appreciative, crowd-wide chants of "*Marvin, Marvin, Marvin.*" Stanford coach Mike Montgomery, following the game, simply said, "I'm relieved." After two years of second-round stumbles, the Cardinal this year was back in the Sweet 16 and would next face #5-seed Cincinnati in Anaheim.

The matchup with Cincinnati essentially boiled down to Stanford's size versus Cincinnati's quickness. In the first half, the Bearcats used that quickness to reel off a 21-10 late first-half scoring run to turn a 24-17 deficit into a 38-34 halftime lead. But with the Collins twins dominating the Bearcats inside, and with the Cardinal team continuing to make shots at a rate well over 50%, Stanford was able to reclaim the lead early in the second half, and followed that up by going on a 15-4 scoring run that gave the Cardinal a commanding 62-50 advantage with eight minutes to play. With the Cardinal defense holding the Bearcats to 39% shooting and operating with a big size advantage against the Bearcats in the rebounding department, Cincinnati did not have the ability to mount a comeback.

The final score of Stanford's second-ever Sweet 16 game: Stanford 78 – Cincinnati 65. Playing in the same arena where his Glendora high-school team had won a California Interscholastic Federation (CIF) championship, Jacobsen netted a career-high 27 points for the Cardinal in the Sweet 16–game victory. Ryan Mendez scored 16 points, Jason Collins added 15 points, and Jarron Collins tallied 14 points. Stanford recorded its 31st victory with the win, a Stanford single-season record for games won.

For the second time in four years, Stanford had earned a ticket to the

ABOVE: *Hank Luisetti was a three-time consensus All-American (1936, 1937, and 1938 seasons), a two-time national player of the year, and is the only men's basketball player to have had his uniform number (#7) retired by Stanford University.* OVERLEAF: *The 1942 NCAA championship Stanford Basketball team: starters Bill Cowden, Howie Dallmar, Ed Voss, Jim Pollard, and Don Burness, along with head coach Everett Dean.*

STANFORD
6

STANFORD
17
STANFORD
8

ABOVE: *Claude Terry (1970-72), three-year starting guard and still the program's all-time leader in career points per game (20.6) in an era that did not have the three-point field goal;* OPPOSITE: *Rich Kelley, first-team All-Pac-8 in each of his three varsity seasons (1973-75) and still the program leader in career rebounds per game (12.4).*

STANFORD
53
42

TOP LEFT: *Todd Lichti, the only four-time first-team all-conference player in program history;* TOP RIGHT: *Adam Keefe, three-time all-conference selection and 1991 NIT Most Outstanding Player;* ABOVE: *the 1991 NIT champions;* OPPOSITE: *Mark Madsen, a Midwest Regional all-tournament selection, and Midwest Regional MVP Arthur Lee celebrate Madsen's tie-breaking dunk with 26 seconds remaining in the 1998 NCAA Tournament Midwest Regional Final—a dunk that was set up by Lee's backcourt steal and ended up being the decisive basket that propelled the Cardinal into the 1998 Final Four.*

STANFORD
45
LEE
11

STANFORD
23

OPPOSITE: *Casey Jacobsen was a three-time first team All-Pac-10 selection and a scoring machine who had 49 and 41 point games against Pac-10 opposition eight days apart in 2002;* TOP: *Jarron Collins played a key role in the dramatic 84-83 win over top-ranked Duke on 12/21/00;* ABOVE: *The Stanford bench erupts in celebration following the Duke win.*

TOP: *The historic 2003-04 team, champions of the Pac-10 regular season and conference tournament, #1-ranked nationally for multiple weeks, and a #1 seed in the 2004 NCAA Tournament;* ABOVE: *Coach Mike Montgomery led Stanford to ten consecutive NCAA Tournament appearances from 1995-2004;* OPPOSITE: *Nick Robinson launches the most famous shot in Stanford history—a 35-foot runner at the buzzer on 2/7/04 that upended #12-ranked Arizona 80-77, a shot that extended the Cardinal's undefeated season record and helped lift Stanford to a #1 national ranking.*

21
CATS

STANFORD
11

OPPOSITE: *Brook Lopez converts a baseline leaner with 1.3 seconds remaining in overtime against Marquette in a 2008 NCAA Tournament thriller won by Stanford by a score of 82-81;* TOP LEFT: *Landry Fields is one of only three Stanford players to lead the conference in scoring since the Pac 8/10/12 was founded;* TOP RIGHT: *Josh Huestis sets the school record for career blocks with this block against USC on 2/16/14;* ABOVE: *Dwight Powell, two-time All-Pac-12 forward, scores a layup in the 2012 NIT championship game win.*

TOP: *The 2012 NIT champions celebrate following their 75-51 victory over Minnesota at Madison Square Garden;* ABOVE: *Chasson Randle converts a free throw—late in the first half of Stanford's 2015 NIT semifinal win over Old Dominion—for his 2,337th career point to become the program's all-time leading scorer;* OPPOSITE: *Randle scores a layup over Kansas All-American Andrew Wiggins in Stanford's 2014 NCAA Tournament second-round victory over the Jayhawks.*

KANSAS
22

Brevin Knight leads all Stanford Basketball players in career assists and career steals by a wide margin, earned first-team All American (1997) and all Pac-10 (1995-97) recognition, and was the first player in program history to play in as many as three NCAA Tournaments.

regional final, otherwise known as the Elite Eight. The opponent would be a somewhat familiar one, at least to some of the Cardinal players: #3-seed Maryland. The teams had played two years prior in Washington, DC, a game won by the Terrapins by two points. Maryland no longer had All-American guard Steve Francis, who had hurt the Cardinal in the regular season Stanford-Maryland game two years earlier, but it did have a number of players with good offensive statistics: guards Juan Dixon and Steve Blake, center Lonny Baxter, and forward Terence Morris.

On Saturday, March 24, 2001, the Maryland offense wasn't merely good—it was great. Seemingly every Maryland player was hitting shots in the first half—even low-scoring reserve Terrapin center Tajh Holden was contributing with, of all things, *multiple* three-point baskets. Maryland's first-half torching of the Anaheim Pond arena nets produced a ten-point halftime advantage over the Cardinal.

The onslaught didn't let up in the second half. Lonny Baxter was able to score on whatever Collins twin was covering him—he finished with a game-high 24 points. By game's end, Juan Dixon had scored 17 points and Steve Blake had added 13 points; together, they made 5 of 6 three-point attempts in the game. Tajh Holden finished with 14 points, ten above his per-game average. The final Maryland shooting totals: 58% from the field, 69% from three (9 of 13), and 14 of 21 from the free-throw line. The final score wasn't particularly close: Maryland 87 – Stanford 73. Stanford's spectacular 2000-01 season ended one game shy of the Final Four.

Though the Cardinal final won-loss record in 2000-01 was a shiny 31-3, the spirits of the Cardinal players following the game were anything but glittering.

Jason Collins, Jarron Collins, Ryan Mendez, and Michael McDonald had played their final games for Stanford. The Cardinal won-loss record during their four years was 114-19, the best consecutive four-year record in Stanford Basketball history. This senior group had also won nine NCAA Tournament games, won or shared three Pac-10 championships, and had a cumulative conference won-loss record of 61-11. Theirs remains the four-year gold standard in Stanford Basketball history. And they had come within one game of the Final Four—a fact that is a permanent reason to celebrate the great 2000-01 Stanford Basketball team and that at the same time remains a permanent source of bitter disappointment to the players and coaches on that Stanford squad.

Each of the Collins twins earned All-Pac-10 honors in 2000-01, Jarron for a second time. Casey Jacobsen earned not only first-team All-Pac-10 honors but also first-team All-American honors from four organizations—AP, The Sporting News, John Wooden, and the US Basketball Writers Association. Jacobsen thus became Stanford's first consensus first-team All-American since Hank Luisetti in the late 1930s.

Jacobsen averaged 18 points per game in 2000-01, shot better than 50% from the field for a second consecutive season, and his three-point shooting percentage was 47.2%—among the very best single-season three-point shooting marks in Stanford Basketball history. Jason Collins made 61% of his field-goal attempts, among the top single-season field-goal-shooting performances in Cardinal history, and his brother Jarron made nearly 56% of his field goal tries. The two averaged 14.5 and 12.8 points per game, respectively. But they, along with McDonald and Mendez, would no longer—due to graduation in June of 2001—be furnishing those gaudy numbers in furtherance of Stanford Basketball wins.

ABOVE: *Curtis Borchardt, exceptionally athletic though injury-plagued center who helped the 2000-02 teams reach the NCAA Tournament;* OPPOSITE: *Jason Collins, along with his twin brother, Jarron, achieved All-American status during a four-year run that was the most successful in program history as measured by winning percentage (.857) and number of weeks as the nation's #1-ranked team.*

STANFORD
34
DUKE
34
STANFORD
32
DUKE
14

X. The Final Montgomery Years

The Pinnacles and Perils of Being Number One

As the 2001-02 season approached, Mike Montgomery faced a couple of difficult realities. Not only was the prior season's stunningly successful senior class—with its record-shattering 114-19 won-loss record—no longer at his service, Montgomery's starting lineup had also been gutted. For just the second time in ten seasons, as few as just one starter would be returning from the previous season.

Granted, that one returnee was Casey Jacobsen, a first-team All-American with 1,065 points scored through his freshman and sophomore seasons combined, a Stanford record. Most believed that Jacobsen's junior campaign in 2001-02—assuming an injury-free and customary high-scoring season by Casey—would be his last at Stanford and that he would opt to make himself available for the NBA Draft in the spring of 2002. Who would the four starters be alongside Jacobsen? The answer: it varied.

During the first handful of games in 2001-02, the starters were junior Curtis Borchardt at center, junior Julius Barnes and senior Tony Giovacchini at the guard positions (alongside Jacobsen to form a three-guard starting lineup), and freshman McDonald's High School All-American Josh Childress at forward. Childress, in particular, had solid performances in his first four games, scoring 21 points at Purdue in his third college game and averaging 13 points and shooting better than 50% from the floor in each of the four games. But in games #5 and #6 Childress struggled, scoring only five points against each of Long Beach State and Belmont, and his rebounding average through his first six college games was less than five per game.

Mike Montgomery, a coach who generally favored—with a couple of notable exceptions being Brevin Knight and Casey Jacobsen—not starting freshmen to give them time to acclimate to the college game, made a change in the starting lineup in the seventh game of the 2001-02 campaign that involved the freshman Childress. Maintaining his three-guard lineup, Montgomery elected to sacrifice scoring (Childress) for additional rebounding, moving 6′ 8″ redshirt sophomore Justin Davis into the starting lineup. In his first start, against BYU, Davis scored 19 points and grabbed 10 rebounds. Davis would start all but four of the remaining 23 games in 2001-02, providing—along with the shot-blocker Borchardt at center—two excellent defenders in the paint for the Cardinal, in addition to the rebounding skill that each player possessed in abundance.

Stanford finished the non-conference portion of the 2001-02 schedule with an 8-2 record, which included neutral court losses to Texas and BYU, but which also included a win over #13-ranked Michigan State in Oakland at the Pete Newell Challenge. In that game, Curtis Borchardt broke through for a career-high 27 points while also grabbing ten rebounds and blocking six shots. It was becoming clear that Borchardt would, more often than not, be the Cardinal's second-best scoring option—particularly against the better teams—after Casey Jacobsen.

The conference season for Stanford figured to be a step or two down from the prior four Pac-10 campaigns, in which the Cardinal had won no fewer than 15 conference games in each of those seasons. Through the first eight games of the 2001-02 Pac-10 schedule, Stanford's won-loss record was 5-3. In none of the games did Stanford have a margin of victory—or defeat, for that matter—of less than eight points. There was no particular drama in any of those games.

The next three games would change that. Game #9 of the 2001-02 Pac-10 slate was a home game against Arizona State, Thursday night, January 31, 2002. Stanford trailed at halftime 44-39. Casey Jacobsen had scored 18 of Stanford's first half points. In the second half, Jacobsen would do something no Stanford player had done in 22 seasons, and he nearly did something no Stanford player had ever done.

In those twenty second-half minutes against the Sun Devils, Casey Jacobsen scored 31 points—giving him 49 points for the game—in what became a 90-81 Cardinal victory. Jacobsen missed—by one point—tying Hank Luisetti's all-time single-game scoring record of 50 points set in 1938. It was the first time in 22 seasons that a Stanford player had scored 40 or more points in game.

"This doesn't happen too often," said Jacobsen. "When it does happen you have to ride it as long as you can. When I realized this could be a good night, I was looking to shoot it every time the ball came my way." The junior guard certainly made a high percentage of his shot attempts, making 14 of 22 field-goal attempts during the game. Jacobsen was also 6 of 10 from the three-point range and 15 of 17 from the free-throw line.

The next game—yet another Stanford and Arizona thriller at Maples Pavilion—featured more team drama than individual drama. Stanford led by 15 points in the second half, but gave up all of that lead and nearly lost the game in regulation, only winning a reprieve when Arizona guard Jason Gardner missed a jump shot at the buzzer that would have won the game for the Wildcats at the end of the 40-minute regulation period. The game went to overtime; however, despite Casey Jacobsen's 24 points and Curtis Borchardt's 25 points and 21 rebounds, Stanford fell to Lute Olson's Wildcats in the extra period, with the final score being 88-82 in favor of Arizona.

The next Stanford game was also at home, February 7, 2002, against Oregon. The most recent two games at Maples had provided the thrill of both individual player brilliance and dramatic game endings. Would the next Cardinal game bring either of those features? The answer: it would bring both.

Oregon came into the Stanford game as the first-place team in Pac-10 standings with a record of 9-2, and the Ducks held a #13 national ranking in the weekly AP Poll. The game was tied at halftime, 34-34. After halftime, Casey Jacobsen reprised his ASU magic from a week earlier, scoring 26 points after the intermission. But Stanford trailed by three points with four seconds remaining in the game.

Stanford had the ball on an inbound play in the frontcourt. The Cardinal tried to get the ball to Casey Jacobsen. Jacobsen, however, was blanketed by multiple Oregon defenders. So the inbound pass came to senior guard Tony Giovacchini 28 feet from the basket, along the sideline in front of the Stanford bench. Giovacchini let fly. Swish! Tie game!

Oregon could not get a shot off as time ran out in regulation, and in overtime the Cardinal seized—and maintained throughout the overtime—the lead, defeating the Ducks, 90-87. Casey Jacobsen finished with 41 points. He had scored 114 points in three consecutive Stanford games. No Cardinal player in Stanford Basketball history had ever come close to that amount of scoring over a consecutive three-game period.

Stanford would win its next three Pac-10 games—and five of its final seven Pac-10 games—to finish the 2001-02 regular season with an overall won-loss mark of 18-9, including a 12-6 record in the Pac-10. During that four-week stretch Stanford for a time earned a spot in the weekly AP Top 25 rankings. A landmark win during that span of Pac-10 games came at Arizona in early March, a game in which Curtis Borchardt scored 28 points and made 11 of 11 free throws—including 6 of 6 during the last 15 seconds—to preserve a Stanford upset victory over the Wildcats.

After a disappointing loss to disappointing USC at the newly reborn Pac-10 postseason tournament, Stanford learned it had earned a bid as a #8 seed in the Midwest Region of the 2002 NCAA Tournament. The Cardinal was sent to St. Louis—not to the Kiel Arena, where it had won the 1998 regional amid Arthur Lee's late-game heroics, but to the much-larger-in-size Edward Jones Dome.

Stanford was matched against Western Kentucky in the first round. For the eighth straight season, the Cardinal won its first-round NCAA Tournament game. For a seventh consecutive year, the score in the first-round game was not close: Stanford 84 – Western Kentucky 68. Curtis Borchardt scored 19 points and grabbed 12 rebounds, while Casey Jacobsen chipped in with 17 points despite making just 4 of his 12 field-goal attempts.

Stanford's reward for advancing to the second round was a date against the Midwest Region's top seed, Kansas. The Cardinal knew Jayhawk starting guard Kirk Hinrich was suffering from an ankle sprain suffered in Kansas's first-round game, and that he might not play. The Cardinal hoped it could take advantage, have some things break right, and upset KU in its own backyard.

The game began. Hinrich was able to play. Nothing went right for Stanford.

Stanford trailed 6-0, then 10-0, then 12-0. The Kansas fans in the Edward Jones Dome were roaring louder, seemingly, with each successive KU score. The Cardinal needed a timeout to regroup. Mike Montgomery, who liked to save his timeouts until a game's final minutes or seconds—and had done it brilliantly in St. Louis four years earlier against Rhode Island to help Stanford get to the Final Four—resisted the impulse initially. But finally, with the early score 15-0 in favor of Kansas, the Cardinal coach had to give in. Timeout, Stanford.

Unfortunately, it didn't help much. Kansas—with Hinrich playing in pain but nonetheless playing well—continued to dominate the action, leading by 22 points at the half and by as many as 31 points and at two different junctures in the second half. The final score was Kansas 86 – Stanford 63. Casey Jacobsen led the Cardinal with 24 points. It would turn out to be the final Stanford game for the juniors Casey Jacobsen and Curtis Borchardt. Both submitted their names into the 2002 NBA Draft, and both ended up being selected in the first round, Jacobsen by the Phoenix Suns and Borchardt by the Utah Jazz.

Stanford ended the 2001-02 campaign with its eighth consecutive season of at least twenty wins, producing a final overall won-loss record of 20-10. The Cardinal had finished in a four-way tie for second place in the Pac-10 race with a 12-6 mark, behind first-place (14-4) Oregon. What was the prognostication for the 2002-03 campaign? With the loss of the program's third-highest career point scorer Casey Jacobsen, as well as the productive Curtis Borchardt at the important center position, and with two new starters in the lineup who had played only sparingly the prior season, it seemed as though the 2002-03 Cardinal might have trouble keeping alive the program's consecutive season streak of 20-or-more-wins.

Stanford quashed that thought within the first two weeks of the 2002-03 campaign. In the second game of the season—a second-round game of the Preseason NIT—Stanford upset #11-ranked Xavier at Maples Pavilion by one point, 63-62. Montgomery used a "one three hybrid zone" defense to help neutralize Xavier All-American forward David West. The zone certainly befuddled Musketeer coach Thad Matta, who asked after the game, "was that a zone?"

With the win, the Cardinal earned an unexpected trip to New York and a spot in the Preseason NIT Final Four along with powerhouses Florida, Kansas, and North Carolina. So unanticipated was Stanford's presence at Madison Square that ESPN columnist Andy Katz had written that the Cardinal was a party crasher in New York, implying that Mike Montgomery's team wasn't of the caliber as the other three teams. At the shoot-around prior to Stanford's Preseason NIT semifinal game against #7-ranked Florida, Montgomery got in some good-natured ribbing with Katz, who was present at the shootaround. "Party crashers at your service" said a saucy Montgomery to Katz, or something to that effect. Katz took the jab with a smile. It wasn't the first time a good-naturedly sarcastic Monty salvo was sent a media member's way.

Montgomery was doubly satisfied when his Cardinal continued the party crasher theme, knocking off the Gators 69-65 at Madison Square Garden on Wednesday, November 27, 2002. The new starters figured prominently in the Stanford win. New starting center, sophomore Rob Little, scored a team-high 18 points and new starting guard Matt Lottich, a junior, hit two key three-baskets late in the game to fuel a late-game Cardinal comeback and the win.

Although the Cardinal fell the next night to Raymond Felton–led North Carolina, 74-57, Stanford in that 2002 Thanksgiving Week had continued a remarkable historical string of good performances at Madison Square

Garden. Including its 1-1 record at MSG in the 2002 Preseason NIT, and dating back to its first appearance at MSG in the 1930s, Stanford's all-time record at the famous arena stood at an impressive 10 wins and 3 losses.

With its starting lineup firmly established—as had not been the case the prior year—the 2002-03 Stanford Basketball team finished the non-conference portion of the schedule with 9 wins and 3 losses. Also unlike the prior year, which featured two dominant scorers in Jacobsen and Borchardt, balance was the byword as far as scoring on the 2002-03 team. The starters—forwards Justin Davis and Josh Childress, center Rob Little, and guards Matt Lottich and Julius Barnes—each had scoring averages above, or right around, ten points per game through the November-December stretch of games.

The Cardinal won five of its first seven Pac-10 games in 2002-03, with four of the five wins being by single digits. Game #8 on the Pac-10 slate was a big one—a date with #1-ranked Arizona in Tucson on January 30, 2003. The game marked the 27th time in its history that Stanford squared off against a #1-ranked team. The only prior wins against a #1-ranked opponent had been against Arizona at Maples Pavilion in 1988, and the "Jacobsen-game-winner-in-the-final-seconds" game versus Duke in 2001 at the Oakland Coliseum.

Despite its relative lack of experience in the starting lineup compared to the veteran Arizona squad, the Cardinal on that January evening in Tucson dialed up the same unexpected grit displayed two months earlier in the upset wins over No. 11 Xavier and No. 7 Florida. First-year starter Matt Lottich was again in the middle of things, making numerous clutch baskets. His three-point basket in the final minute, together with two clutch free throws by Julius Barnes, sealed a huge upset win for Stanford, 82-77. Lottich, or "Lotty" as he was known to teammates, had 23 points to lead the Cardinal.

Another theme of the 2002-03 Stanford team, besides the clutch jump shots late in games, was on display in the upset win over #1-ranked Arizona. The Stanford guards, Lottich and Barnes, had held the talented UA guard duo of Jason Gardner and Salim Stoudamire to just 4 of 15 shooting from three-point-range. With starting forward Justin Davis and reserve forward Nick Robinson also displaying consistently solid defense inside, the 2002-03 Cardinal was beginning to win games as much because of its defense as because its offense.

Following its win over Arizona, Stanford was 6-2 in the Pac-10 race, just one game behind the first-place Wildcats. The winning continued, with the Cardinal claiming seven of its next eight Pac-10 games. Stanford's national ranking in the February 23, 2003, weekly AP Poll was #19—its highest ranking of the season.

It's rare that a Stanford team plays a #1-ranked team once in a season, let alone twice. But that occurred in 2002-03. On March 1, 2003, Arizona came calling at Maples Pavilion, again as the #1-ranked team in the United States. The Cardinal trailed by three points at halftime, despite having made only 29% of its shot attempts in the first half. The reason was that the Stanford defense was playing well once again, throttling an Arizona team whose roster featured future NBA players Andre Igoudola, Channing Frye and Luke Walton, in addition to the All-Conference caliber guard tandem of Jason Gardner and Salim Stoudamire.

Stanford tied the game midway through the second half, but could not pull ahead. Despite a three-point goal by Josh Childress in the final minute that pulled the Cardinal to within one point, Stanford ultimately fell to the Wildcats, 72-69. A season-long trend had shown up again; in Stanford's losses in 2002-03 against the better teams, it seemed as though a high-scoring guard on the opposing team was usually the reason for the loss. In this game, it was the scoring of Arizona guard Salim Stoudamire, who had a team-high 18 points.

The Cardinal would have to settle for second place in the Pac-10 race. Still, it was an unexpectedly high achievement for this particular Cardinal squad. With a second straight first-round exit in the Pac-10 Tournament—again via a loss to USC—the Cardinal took a 23-8 record into the 2003 NCAA Tournament. The Cardinal received a #4 seed in the South Region. For the second time in five seasons, the Cardinal's first and second-round destination was in the state of Washington, this time in Spokane.

Round One of the 2003 NCAA Tournament was another Stanford win. Twenty-four hours after war, with U.S. involvement, had broken out in Iraq, the Cardinal outlasted the University of San Diego (USD) Toreros, 77-69. Once again, a clutch three-point basket by Matt Lottich in the final minute helped ensure victory for Stanford. The Stanford Pep Band, perhaps in sympathy with France's protestation of the war's outbreak, wore berets—to the cheers of some and the disapproval of others. Josh Childress finished with a team-high 22 points and 11 rebounds, while Julius Barnes added 18 points and Lottich 17 points in the win over USD.

The win over USD was the Cardinal's ninth consecutive first-round win in the NCAA Tournament. But, again, a large second-round hurdle loomed. Fifth-seeded UConn was the matchup for Stanford in the second-round game on March 22, 2003. The Huskies' lineup featured two of the college game's most talented and prominent players, center Emeka Okafor and guard Ben Gordon.

Stanford led at halftime, 44-39, as Julius Barnes converted four three-point goals in the first half. Stanford also led 54-51 early in the second half. But UConn at that point went on a 14-4 scoring run, and thereafter the Cardinal spent the rest of the game playing catch-up. With guard Ben Gordon scoring a game-high 29 points—yet another high-scoring guard that Stanford could not contain—and with center Emeka Okafor collecting 18 points and 15 rebounds, UConn prevailed in the end by the score of 85-74.

Stanford finished the season with 24 wins and 9 losses, a better record than what was initially expected for the 2002-03 team. Senior Julius Barnes was Stanford's lone All-Pac-10 selection in 2002-03, having averaged 16 points per game. His 33 points in a Cardinal win at Oregon State on February 8, 2003, represented a personal single-game career high for points scored, and his eight three-pointers in the game tied Terry Taylor's Stanford Basketball single-game record for three-point baskets.

Coming off the 24-win season in 2002-03, with four starters returning and key reserve Nick Robinson returning as well, the 2003-04 Stanford Basketball season promised to be one that would rival Cardinal achievements during the glorious four-year period between 1997-98 and 2000-01. The AP Poll was a bit less sanguine, tagging the Cardinal with a #19 preseason ranking, but that did not dampen the enthusiasm of Stanford fans going into the 2003-04 campaign. Added to the optimism generated by the returning players was the buzz around a player that had missed virtually all of the prior season due to injury—6′ 2″ redshirt sophomore point guard Chris Hernandez. A hustling floor general with the ability to hit three-point baskets consistently, Hernandez stepped into the starting lineup vacancy created by the graduation of Julius Barnes.

Hernandez's on-court contribution would be felt almost immediately. In the fourth game of the 2003-04 campaign, on December 6, 2003, Stanford ventured south to Anaheim to play unbeaten and #1-ranked Kansas in the John Wooden Classic. Playing without an injured Josh Childress, the Cardinal got off to a great start, building a first-half lead of 27-15 and a halftime advantage of 36-29. Predictably, the powerful Jayhawks came back to cut the Stanford lead to just one point, 56-55, with four minutes remaining in the game.

Matt Lottich then hit a big three-point basket. Then Chris Hernandez hit four clutch free throws in four pressure-filled attempts. Justin Davis also added a free throw during that stretch, which put Stanford up 64-55 and gave the Cardinal enough of a late-game lead to prevail over the Jayhawks in the end, 64-58—Stanford's fourth-ever victory over a #1-ranked team.

Besides the returning roster experience and the impact of Chris Hernandez's addition to the starting lineup, two additional characteristics of the 2003-04 Stanford Basketball came to the fore in that Kansas win: defense and depth. Stanford had held Kansas to just 37% shooting—the fourth straight game to open the season that a Cardinal opponent was held to under 40% shooting. As for the Stanford role players in the Kansas win—besides the effective play of Nick Robinson as a replacement starter for the injured Childress—redshirt sophomore and reserve center Joe Kirchofer was a difference-maker against Kansas, scoring ten points off the bench to equal his career high for points scored in a game.

The win over Kansas improved Stanford's record to 4-0 and its national ranking to #13 in the AP Poll the following week. And Josh Childress, Stanford's junior forward and All-American candidate, hadn't even played a minute yet due to a stress reaction in his left foot.

Childress wouldn't see action until the beginning of Pac-10 play in January. But the deep and defense-minded Cardinal didn't need him the remainder of December; the team won all five games, including a win over #13-ranked Gonzaga in Oakland at the Pete Newell Classic. For the fourth time in the Mike Montgomery era, the Cardinal entered conference play with an undefeated record, sporting a 9-0 won-loss mark going into the January 2, 2004, opener against Washington State at Maples Pavilion. Stanford's national ranking was a lofty #4.

Stanford won both games at home against the Washington schools, with Childress returning to action in a reserve role. He would be needed the following weekend, as Stanford faced two tough road games in Arizona. In the first of those road games, in Tempe, AZ, against ASU, Childress scored a rebound basket with nine seconds remaining to give the Cardinal a one-point lead, 58-57, and the Stanford defense denied ASU game-tying or game-winning points on the final Sun Devil possession.

Next up on the Cardinal schedule was a big one: Saturday, January 10, 2004, #4-ranked Stanford against #3-ranked Arizona. Tipoff was scheduled for twelve noon at the McKale Center in Tucson. It was to be one of the most remarkable Cardinal road games ever played.

Let's begin with the halftime score: 33-20 in favor of Stanford. Stanford held Arizona to just *six* first-half baskets and just 19% shooting

(6 of 31)—the worst such offensive numbers ever produced by an Arizona team in one half at the McKale Center during the Lute Olson–coaching era. And things didn't get much better for the Wildcats in the second half. The Stanford defense continued to be stingy and the Cardinal offense continued to be efficient. The score was 68-48 Cardinal with four minutes remaining in the game, and at that point many among the sellout crowd at McKale headed for the exits.

Only a meaningless 24-14 scoring run by the Wildcats in the final four minutes—with Mike Montgomery having inserted his backups into the game—made the final score respectable. All five Stanford starters scored in double figures in the 82-72 win at Arizona, reflecting the balance and efficiency of the 2003-04 Cardinal team. Josh Childress finished with a game-high 19 points, Matt Lottich had 17 points, Rob Little had 13 points, Justin Davis contributed 10 points and 10 rebounds, and Chris Hernandez added 11 points and 9 assists.

The win at Arizona was another landmark Stanford Basketball victory—for a couple of reasons. It was a Stanford road win over the clear-cut favorite to win the Pac-10 title in 2003-04, and it was also the fourth year in a row that Stanford had won a game over Arizona at the McKale Center. No non-Arizona program had ever won more than two games in a row at McKale in the Lute Olson coaching era. And for Matt Lottich, a unique distinction was achieved that afternoon in Tucson. Lottich became—and remains—the only Stanford player ever to play four games in four seasons at the McKale Center and never lose a game.

Stanford's won-loss record was now 13-0, 4-0 in the Pac-10. Stanford moved up one spot in the January 13, 2004, AP Poll, to #3 in the national ranking, behind only UConn and Duke. The winning in 2003-04 continued. Three straight home wins followed the historic road win at Arizona. First came home wins over Cal, USC, and UCLA, then came a road win at Oregon State. The Cardinal won-loss record was now 17-0.

A Saturday afternoon road game was next up—at always-tough, always-loud McArthur Court in Eugene, OR. Nearly eighty years old, "Mac" Court had earned a reputation as a place where Oregon teams knocked off heavily favored opponents. Duck fans on January 31, 2004, were eager to add undefeated Stanford to the list.

There was adversity for Stanford prior to, and early in, the game in Eugene. The Cardinal was without starting forward Justin Davis, who had suffered a knee injury in the prior Stanford game and would miss the next six weeks. Whether because of that injury, or because of the Ducks' inspired play, or because of the loud Mac Court crowd, Stanford fell behind early and trailed, 39-24, at halftime. The Cardinal fell behind even further, 45-26, three minutes into the second half. Chris Hernandez had not scored a point in the game.

The score was 55-44 Ducks midway through the second half, but then the game turned in Stanford's favor. Chris Hernandez began to score, and sophomore Matt Haryasz—playing in place of the injured Davis—contributed some key baskets as well. At one point Hernandez scored twelve consecutive points for Stanford, and it was Hernandez's three-point play with just over four minutes remaining that tied the game at 67. Josh Childress' three-point basket a minute later gave Stanford a 70-69 lead.

The teams then twice traded scoring plays, after which the Cardinal still held a one-point advantage on the scoreboard. Hernandez then hit two pressure free throws in the final seconds to put the Cardinal up by three points. In part because of effective Stanford defense in the final seconds, Oregon misfired on a potential game-tying three-point basket at the buzzer. Final score: Stanford 83 – Oregon 80.

Stanford was now 18-0. Five nights later came a 30-point blowout home win over Arizona State, setting up an epic rematch at Maples Pavilion: #12-ranked Arizona versus #2-ranked Stanford. A national television broadcast, including famed announcers Brent Musburger and Dick Vitale, and a cast of luminary fans including alumni Jim Plunkett and Tiger Woods were on hand to witness what was expected to be another great Arizona-Stanford game at Maples. Seven times in the past thirteen meetings at Maples the UA-Stanford game had come down to a final shot in the final seconds. This game would be no exception.

Stanford led 44-35 at halftime, and seemed in command with a 67-58 lead midway through the second half. But then the Cardinal went cold. Stanford went scoreless over a seven-minute period, and when Arizona's Salim Stoudamire hit a long three-point basket with 58 seconds remaining, the Wildcats had put together a 19-4 scoring run that had Stanford trailing by four points, 77-73.

Josh Childress then hit one of two free throws with 43 seconds left to bring Stanford to within three points. Matt Lottich then stole the ball on Arizona's next possession, dribbled quickly up the court toward the right corner of the frontcourt and, upon terminating his dribble, passed the ball to Nick Robinson on the right wing. Robinson in turn passed to Chris Hernandez who, catching the ball at the top of the key, almost in one motion whipped the ball to Josh Childress, who was positioned in the left corner. Childress didn't hesitate upon catching the pass, launching and swishing a three-point shot attempt which tied the game at 77. Twenty-four seconds remained in the game.

Arizona coach Lute Olson called timeout. Following the timeout, the ball was inbounded to Salim Stoudamire, who dribbled the ball to chew up the clock in an effort to set up a final Wildcat shot in the final seconds. But with five seconds remaining in the game, Matt Lottich was able to slip a hand in and poke away the ball from the dribbling Stoudamire. Nick Robinson scooped up the loose ball in the backcourt with three seconds remaining, took a few dribbles which carried him three steps past the mid-court line and—just before the end-of-game buzzer sounded—heaved a 35-footer toward the north basket at Maples Pavilion.

It went in! Final score: 80-77 Stanford. Pandemonium. Jumping and screaming Cardinal fans streamed on to the floor, hurtling past the court-side seats of Tiger Woods and Jim and Gerry Plunkett, as well as the side-line broadcast table behind which sat Musberger and Vitale. The Stanford team and court-rushing fans engulfed Nick Robinson in celebration.

Said Nick Robinson after the game: "I knew we needed to get a shot off, so I just took it." Said coach Mike Montgomery after the game: "This is just another step in what's turning out to be a doggone good season." Both quotes, positive but with an accompanying tone of reserve, reflected the mood of the Stanford players and coaches, whose team was now 20-0. They knew some remarkable things were happening, but they also sensed that there would be challenges ahead in March and that the real mark of a college basketball team is made in March. And, to be sure, there would indeed be challenges—and accompanying drama—for the 2003-04 Stanford Basketball team in March.

Before the 2003-04 season reached the month of March, Stanford accomplished another milestone. #1-ranked Duke lost a game in mid-February, which elevated the Cardinal to the #1 national ranking in the ensuing weekly AP Poll released on February 17, 2004. Five days later, following two victories in Los Angeles over USC and UCLA—with Childress scoring a career-high 34 in the win at USC—the Cardinal returned for the final two home games at Maples. Stanford was 23-0 and remained the #1-ranked team in the nation.

On Thursday, February 26, 2004, Stanford dispatched Oregon State 73-47 at Maples. Stanford was now 24-0, 15-0 in the Pac-10. With a win in the home finale on February 28 over Oregon, Stanford would clinch its fourth Pac-10 regular season conference championship in six seasons. It was

Senior Day for Mattt Lottich, Justin Davis, and Joe Kirchofer, and it also would be the last home game for the junior Josh Childress, who would enter the NBA Draft three months later. The final score wasn't close: Stanford 76 – Oregon 55. Childress exited with a flourish, recording 29 points, 12 rebounds, five assists, and three blocks. Kirchofer also finished strong at Maples, ringing up career highs in points (13) and rebounds (10) in the win.

The February 28, 2004, Senior Day win meant that 2003-04 would mark the first season in Stanford Basketball history that a Stanford team entered March with an undefeated won-loss record. Two days later, the calendar turned to March and the pivotal basketball games to come, postseason and otherwise. Besides being pivotal, most of the March 2004 Stanford Basketball games would be nationally televised and have emotionally charged endings—both good and bad—for the Cardinal.

In all, seven Stanford games were played in March of 2004. Two were regular season Pac-10 games, three were Pac-10 Tournament games, and the remaining games were NCAA Tournament games. In four of those games, Stanford entered the game as either the nation's #1-ranked team or the NCAA Tournament #1 seed. Stanford, as one of the nation's two remaining unbeaten teams (with St. Joseph's), was in the center of the national college basketball spotlight.

What follows is a real-time diary of that momentous 17-day period for Stanford Basketball—the games of March 2004.

Thursday, March 4, Pullman, Washington

Stanford brings an undefeated 25-0 record and a national #1 ranking to Washington State's Friel Court. The arena is fuller than usual. WSU and its home-court fans are eager for the opportunity to knock off the top-ranked Cardinal.

Despite its 12-14 record, WSU rises up on this night, playing Stanford tough and taking a lead late in the game. With 25 seconds remaining, the Cougars are ahead by five points, 61-56. Stanford's 25-game, four-month run of perfection appears to be over.

Then, with 17 seconds remaining, Stanford reserve guard Dan Grunfeld hits a right-corner three-point basket and is fouled on the play. Grunfeld makes the free throw. WSU then cannot successfully inbound the ball from the back court baseline within the five seconds allotted. With still 17 seconds remaining, Stanford gets the ball back trailing by one point, 61-60. Stanford inbounds the ball and sets up for one final shot.

On the final play, Chris Hernandez loses control of the ball on a dribble-drive and the ball starts rolling toward the left sideline and away from the basket. With the ball rolling on the floor, Matt Lottich sprints over, picks up the loose ball 25 feet from the basket and has time only to fling it toward the basket. As the final buzzer goes off, Lottich's heave goes in! Three-point basket! Stanford wins 63-61!

A wild on-court celebration ensues, particularly Josh Childress, who runs from one end line to the other, arms flailing with joy. Disbelieving Cougar fans are standing motionless, except for the several who are throwing plastic beverage cups and other debris onto the floor in disgust.

Stanford's perfect record (26-0) remains intact, the courtside radio announcers exclaim into their microphones. And in Seattle, University of Washington guard Nate Robinson, watching on a locker room television, smiles broadly as he witnesses the miracle Stanford comeback. His hope—that Stanford will come to Seattle undefeated and ripe for a takedown—is realized.

Saturday, March 6, Bank of America Arena, Seattle

Ten thousand standing-room-only fans are present, as are the ABC television network and announcer Brent Musburger. Also present is a full UW student section, with many of the kids wearing plastic, purple-snouted Husky headgear items.

Stanford is off its game early, falling behind and missing shots so frequently and unusually that at one point a Stanford field-goal attempt from the left corner goes off the side of the backboard. UW is inspired, leads wire-to-wire, and sends Stanford to its first defeat of the 2003-04 season, 77-63, ruining the Cardinal's bid to become the first Pac-10 team ever to win all 18 regular season conference games.

Husky students flood the court at the sound of the final buzzer, and a few Husky players are briefly hoisted in celebration on student fans' shoulders. Stanford's #1 ranking is gone. Its record is now 26-1, 17-1 in the Pac-10. The regular season is over. The postseason is about to begin.

Thursday-Saturday, March 11-13, Staples Center, Los Angeles

The big news going into the Pac-10 Tournament is that Stanford's Justin Davis is returning to the court after a six-week absence due to a knee injury. As the regular season Pac-10 champion, the Cardinal is the top seed in the tournament.

In the quarterfinal game, Stanford defeats Washington State by 21 points. The next night, Stanford knocks off Oregon 70-63 in the semi-final game. In the tournament final—with announcer Dick Enberg and a CBS national television audience on hand—Stanford gets a revenge matchup with Washington and defeats the Huskies by the score of 77-66. Following the win, the victorious Stanford team is honored at a midcourt trophy-award and team-photo ceremony. Josh Childress is named Pac-10 Conference Tournament MVP, just as he had been named the Pac-10's regular season Player of the Year a few days earlier.

On Sunday, March 15, Stanford is selected as the #1 seed in the 2004 NCAA Tournament's West Region. NCAA rounds one and two for the Cardinal will be played in Seattle. Seattle holds some unhappy memories for the Cardinal program. Five years earlier, in 1999, Stanford as the West Region's #2 seed lost to #10-seed Gonzaga in Seattle's Key Arena. And of course, also in Seattle eight days earlier on March 6, #1-ranked Stanford had suffered its first loss of the 2003-04 season at Washington.

Spirits are high among Stanford fans, though perhaps dampened a bit with the awareness that powerful Connecticut has also been placed in the West Region as the #2 seed, just behind the Cardinal. Players pack their books and computers and board the charter flight for Seattle on Tuesday, March 16. For them, the first week of the NCAA Tournament will coincide with winter quarter final examinations, which will be completed by several of the players remotely from Seattle.

Wednesday-Thursday, March 17-18, Key Arena, Seattle

Stanford draws UT San Antonio, the West Region's #16 and worst-seeded team, in the first round. On Wednesday, the coaching staff puts the team through a vigorous practice. On Wednesday night, many of the players are up much of the night handling quarter-end finals and related academic matters.

On Thursday, March 18, the Cardinal plays a bit lethargically; early in the second half, Stanford is ahead by only four points. The national upset alert is quickly quelled, however. The #1-seed Cardinal regroups and wins by 26 points. For an eighth consecutive season, Stanford advances to the second round of the NCAA Tournament.

Saturday, March 20, Key Arena, Seattle

On Saturday, March 20, Stanford gets #8-seed Alabama in Round Two. Two days earlier, the Crimson Tide had squeaked past #9-seed Southern Illinois by a mere one point in its first-round game.

Stanford opens the Alabama game with a lead, leads at halftime, and with seven minutes remaining is comfortably ahead by 13 points. And then the Cardinal hits the wall—hard. Stanford suddenly cannot score, either inside or outside. Josh Childress fouls out. Calls go against the Cardinal. In the space of seven minutes, Stanford's 13-point lead has somehow become, incredibly, an *eight-point deficit*. Only 29 seconds remain in the game.

The Cardinal then stages a furious comeback. Matt Lottich hits two three-point baskets and Justin Davis hits two free throws, sandwiched around three free throws by Alabama. The Cardinal trails by only three points with six seconds remaining and Alabama guard Earnest Shelton at the free-throw line for two free-throw opportunities. Does Stanford have another miracle left in game #32, having won games #20 (Nick Robinson last-second shot against Arizona at Maples) and #26 (Matt Lottich last-second shot at Washington State) with miraculous game-winning shots?

Incredibly, Earnest Shelton *misses both* free throws! Stanford, out of timeouts, has a chance to tie but must act quickly. Nick Robinson dribbles the ball hurriedly upcourt and finds Dan Grunfeld open on the right wing. Grunfeld has time to catch and launch a 25-foot jump shot toward the basket with one second remaining. It rims off, no good.

Stanford falls, 70-67. The CBS network desk in New York is ready to roll the dramatic highlights throughout the remaining afternoon and evening of televised NCAA second-round games. Another huge March Madness upset has occurred. It is all over for #1-seed Stanford.

There is mass despondency in the Stanford locker room. There are tearful comments on the radio postgame show from Matt Haraysz, who despite the glistening eyes manages to verbalize to listeners his deep respect for departing Stanford seniors Matt Lottich, Justin Davis, and Joe Kirchofer, who have had their Cardinal careers abruptly ended.

Two hours later, in Stanford's Seattle hotel lobby, Nevada coach Trent Johnson—whose team had upset Michigan State in an NCAA second-round game earlier in the day in the same arena—shows up unexpectedly and is seen consoling Justin Davis. Five years earlier as a Stanford assistant, Johnson had participated in the recruitment of the 2003-04 Stanford seniors including Justin Davis. The fact that Davis was still rusty in the Alabama game—having returned from the six-week injury layoff just one week before—arguably was a dispositive factor in Stanford not having been able to get by Alabama and having its season end earlier than expected.

So ends the painful Stanford Basketball diary of March 2004.

Looking back, however, the 2003-04 Stanford team's accomplishments were historic. The Cardinal posted a 30-2 record, the highest season winning percentage in Stanford Basketball history. The Cardinal had become one of the few NCAA Division 1 teams in the most recent three decades of college basketball to enter March with an undefeated record—26 wins without a loss to start the 2003-04 season. Appropriately, an elaborate video chronicle of the 2003-04 Stanford Basketball season currently resides online on YouTube.

Yes, the video tribute also contains the two painful losses—two games, two opportunities lost, two suffering Saturdays in Seattle—that are among the most painful defeats in Stanford Basketball history. But these losses are painful only because of the lofty record, the #1 national ranking and the #1 NCAA-Tournament seeding that the great 2003-04 Stanford Basketball team had achieved—undeniably the greatest regular season résumé put together in the program's history.

A month after season's end, the most successful run of Stanford Basketball head coaching also came to an end. After 18 seasons, 393 wins, four Pac-10 championships, and thirteen NCAA Tournament appearances, head coach Mike Montgomery was offered, and accepted, the head coaching position with the NBA's Golden State Warriors.

Although the 2003-04 campaign will be remembered more for the team's achievement than for any individual's accomplishment, significant individual milestones nevertheless were achieved. Both Chris Hernandez and Josh Childress were named to the All-Pac-10 team, and Childress became the first-ever Stanford player to be named Pac-10 Player of the Year.

The Stanford Basketball coaching search in the spring of 2004 did not take long. Athletic Director Ted Leland looked to the Mike Montgomery coaching tree for a successor. Forty-eight-year-old Trent Johnson, the head coach of the Nevada Wolfpack since 1999 and an assistant under Montgomery for five seasons from 1994-95 through 1998-99, became the 17th head coach in Stanford Basketball history on May 25, 2004.

OPPOSITE: *Mike Montgomery, whose 18-year tenure as Stanford's head coach produced 393 wins and a .702 winning percentage—both program highs.*

Josh Childress, a consensus first-team All-American (2004), became the first and remains the only Stanford player to be selected conference Player of the Year (POY) since the Pac-8/Pac-10/Pac-12 POY award came into being in 1975.

Chris Hernandez was a three-time All-Pac-10 honoree (2004-06) as a Stanford point guard and was known for his late-game "winning play" heroics.

XI. The Trent Johnson Era

More Twins, More Big Wins, and a Painful Ending

Starters Chris Hernandez and Rob Little, along with part-time starter Nick Robinson, returned for the 2004-05 Stanford Basketball campaign—the first for Stanford under new head coach Trent Johnson. All were upperclassmen. Forward Matt Haryasz and guard Dan Grunfeld, both juniors, would round out the 2004-05 starting lineup. Robinson had even been recruited by Trent Johnson in the late 1990s, when Johnson was a Stanford assistant under Mike Montgomery. So the new Stanford coach had an experienced, and somewhat familiar, core with whom to work.

Two things would work against Johnson in his inaugural Stanford season. The first was a difficult non-conference schedule that, in part, had been inherited from former coach Mike Montgomery. The second difficulty was the loss of two of his top six players at the midway point of the season. There was one huge positive for the Stanford team going into the 2004-05 campaign: a newly renovated Maples Pavilion. The $26 million Maples facelift, financed entirely through private donations, featured a new playing surface that no longer exhibited the trampoline-like springiness that the former floor did. The re-done arena also featured upgraded locker rooms, student-athlete lounges, state-of-the art strength-and-conditioning and trainer's rooms, and a multicourt practice facility. Also new and stunning was the four-sided, hung-from-the-ceiling, video-enabled, state-of-the-art scoreboard.

One thing was clear as the 2004-05 season commenced: Chris Hernandez would be asked to be a big-time scorer from his point guard position. In the very first game of the season, against USF at the Oakland Coliseum Arena in the Pete Newell Challenge, Hernandez demonstrated that he would be capable of fulfilling that challenge. The junior point guard scored 30 points, a career high, in a 93-83 Stanford win.

But that 2004-05 non-conference schedule—which had seven of the ten games played away from Maples, including the first seven games to open the season—quickly became a negative factor in Stanford's quest for wins. At the Maui Invitational, the Cardinal had to play Tennessee, BYU, and Louisville, winning only the middle game against BYU in that three-game stretch.

Just two days after returning from Maui, the Cardinal visited Santa Clara and fell to the Broncos by ten points, 86-76. Then it was on to the Palace at Auburn Hills for a mid-December game against #13-ranked Michigan State. The Spartans dominated Stanford and easily prevailed, 78-53. On December 18, a month after the season began, Stanford finally played its first home game, a 72-62 victory over UC Davis. Its won-loss record following the victory over the Aggies was 4-4.

Stanford won its remaining four non-conference games but then dropped its first three Pac-10 games prior to facing #13-ranked Arizona at Maples Pavilion on January 8, 2005. What came next was the first of Stanford's two great "game" performances of the 2004-05 season. The Cardinal overwhelmed Arizona, 87-76, behind a career-high 29 points from Dan Grunfeld, 23 points from Chris Hernandez, and 16 points and 12 rebounds from Rob Little.

The Cardinal continued winning, reeling off five consecutive Pac-10 wins following the victory over Arizona. The winning streak owed much to Trent Johnson's coaching philosophy: win with tenacious defense and rebounding. In each of the five consecutive Pac-10 wins—including three on the road against each of Stanford's in-state conference foes Cal, UCLA, and USC—no opponent scored more than 70 points. And the Cardinal did this without one of its two best defensive players, reserve guard Tim Morris, who in early January was lost to the team for the remainder of the season.

Stanford's Pac-10 record was 6-3 at the halfway point of the 2004-05 Pac-10 schedule. The Cardinal split the next eight games, putting its conference won-loss record at 10-7 and its overall record at 16-11 going into the regular season finale against another highly ranked and tough Pac-10 foe, #10-ranked Washington. An extremely negative occurrence during that stretch of games was a season-ending knee injury to Dan Grunfeld, who had been averaging a team-high 18 points in a breakout junior season.

With just 16 wins and a berth in the 2005 NCAA Tournament a very uncertain issue, the Cardinal desperately needed a win in its home finale against the high-flying Husky team led by 5′ 9″ dynamo Nate Robinson.

In that March 5, 2005, game, without Grunfeld's scoring or Morris's ability to help defend the guard-centric Husky offense, Stanford somehow found a way to prevail. Behind one of the great unexpected off-the-bench performances in Cardinal Basketball history—a career-best 18-point scoring performance from junior reserve guard Jason Haas—Stanford upset Washington, 77-67, virtually assuring Stanford an 11th consecutive NCAA appearance, assuming at least one additional win could be gained at the Pac-10 Tournament the following week in Los Angeles.

Stanford got that one win at the Pac-10 Tournament—a two-point squeaker over Washington State in the quarterfinal round—and received its 11th straight NCAA bid on Selection Sunday two days later. The Cardinal was sent to Charlotte, NC, with a #8 seed in the Austin Region and was matched against #9-seed Mississippi State in a first-round NCAA Tournament game. The game tipped at 9:57 P.M. local time on March 18, 2005, and at approximately midnight the game and the Cardinal season ended with a 93-70 loss to the Bulldogs.

Dan Grunfeld was named to the All-Pac-10 team, as was Chris Hernandez for a second consecutive season. Stanford's won-loss record for 2004-05 ended up at 18-13. It was the Cardinal's first sub-20-win season in eleven years, in large part due to the difficult non-conference schedule.

Three of five Stanford starters returned for the 2005-06 season. All seniors, the returnees Chris Hernandez, Dan Grunfeld, and Matt Haryasz would need to play even better than in past seasons to make up for the losses of Nick Robinson and Rob Little, who had graduated. The new starters, at the beginning of the season, were sophomore guard Tim Morris and sophomore forward Taj Finger, both of whose skill sets in 2005-06 offered more on the defensive end than on the offensive end. Despite the significant experience and talent of Hernandez, Grunfeld, and Haryasz, 2005-06 would prove to be the toughest on-court season for a Stanford Basketball team since Brevin Knight's freshman year back in 1993-94.

The Cardinal struggled through a 4-4 non-conference schedule of games, which included losses at UC Davis and Montana and a home loss to UC Irvine. It was clear that occasional lack of offense would be an issue for this Cardinal team—only three players would average more than five points per game in 2005-06. With that narrow roster-scoring profile, one would have expected that Stanford would have not finished above .500 in Pac-10 play, but that is not what occurred. The Cardinal finished the 18-game conference schedule with an 11-7 record. How, despite the lack of offense, did the 2005-06 Cardinal do it? It did it largely due to the remarkable senior seasons turned in by Matt Haryasz, Chris Hernandez, and Dan Grunfeld.

For three consecutive weeks from mid-January through early February of 2006, one or the other of Matt Haryasz or Chris Hernandez was the Pac-10 Player of the Week. Haryasz was the Pac-10 Player of the Week for back-to-back weeks, averaging 26 points and 8 rebounds in a split of the two-game Arizona road trip, then averaging 23 points and 9 rebounds in a home sweep of the Washington schools the ensuing week, which included a win over #9-ranked Washington. Haryasz shot nearly 60% from the field during those two weeks.

The January 29, 2006, win over Washington in Maples reflected both the late-game excellence of Chris Hernandez and Matt Haryasz as well as a dose of the Cardinal's Trent Johnson–inspired, never-say-die attitude. Stanford was down 63-60 to the Huskies with just two seconds remaining in regulation. Stanford had the ball on a backcourt inbounds after a time-out, during which Trent Johnson attempted to diagram something on the clipboard that might get Stanford a chance at a game-tying score.

Johnson succeeded. Freshman forward Lawrence Hill, inbounding the ball from the backcourt baseline, threw an overhand strike to Matt Haryasz who had sprinted from the frontcourt free-throw line to the mid-court center circle to catch the pass. In one seamless motion, Haryasz simultaneously caught the ball chest high, pivoted to his left and whipped a 20-foot chest pass forward to Chris Hernandez, who was situated outside the arc on the right wing with Husky defender Justin Dentmon hovering near the Cardinal guard.

Hernandez caught the ball, momentarily eluded the closely defending Dentmon and fired a three-point shot attempt toward the basket. It missed, but Dentmon had made contact with Hernandez as the buzzer sounded. With no time on the clock, and no players on the free-throw line (by rule), Hernandez's challenge was to make all three pressure-filled free-throw attempts to tie the game. Amazingly, Hernandez did just that, sending the game to overtime.

The overtime was all Cardinal. With Hernandez hitting four more free throws, Stanford outscored Washington 13-4 in the extra period to prevail over the #9-ranked Huskies by the score of 76-67. It was the second consecutive season that Stanford had knocked off a top ten-ranked UW squad at Maples Pavilion.

What did Chris Hernandez do for an encore the next weekend at the Oregon schools? He merely hit the go-ahead basket with 11 seconds remaining to give Stanford a one-point victory at Oregon, then—with Haryasz out of the game due to a finger-poke in the eye—scored 22 of his game-high 28 points in the second half in to lead the Cardinal to a seven-point win at Oregon State. Little wonder Hernandez was named Pac-10 Player of the Week that week.

Stanford's record in 2005-06 in Pac-10 play, in games with game margins of seven points or fewer, was a remarkable 5-2. The final two of those five wins came late in the conference schedule. Freshman guard Anthony Goods's tip-in basket with three seconds remaining gave the Cardinal a two-point win at Washington State on February 25. Five nights later, Chris Hernandez hit two free throws in the final four seconds to give the Cardinal a 58-56 home win over USC.

Hernandez's toughness, along with Hernandez's, Haryasz's and Grunfeld's frequent big-scoring games in 2005-06, did a lot to help this low-scoring Stanford team achieve eleven conference wins. It was not enough, it turned out, to get the Cardinal a 12th consecutive NCAA bid, but it was good enough to get Stanford to the postseason for a record 13th consecutive season. Stanford received a bid to the 2006 NIT.

After a decisive home victory over Virginia, 65-49, in the first-round NIT game, the Cardinal faced a difficult travel trip in its second-round game, to Springfield, MO, to face Missouri State. There the Stanford season—and the careers of the three great seniors Chris Hernandez, Matt Haryasz, and Dan Grunfeld—ended in a nine-point loss to the Bears, 76-67. The final Stanford won-loss record in 2005-06 was 16-14.

Chris Hernandez was named to the All-Pac-10 team for a third consecutive season. He averaged 14 points, made over 90% of his free throws, and over 47% of this three-point field-goal attempts. Matt Haryasz was named to the All-Pac-10 team for the first time, having averaged 16 points and nearly nine rebounds per game in 2005-06.

One thing was abundantly clear as the 2006-07 campaign began: It would be an underclassmen-dominated team—in fact the most underclassman-dominated Stanford Basketball team since the freshman seasons of Todd Lichti, Howard Wright, Terry Taylor, and Bryan McSweeney back in 1985-86.

Headlining the underclassmen were two seven-foot twins, freshmen Brook and Robin Lopez. The sons of a Stanford graduate and former member of the women's swim team, Deborah Ledford, Brook and Robin Lopez drew immediate comparisons to Jason and Jarron Collins. As with the Collins twins, the Lopez twins seemed destined for long NBA careers whenever their Stanford time was over, and likewise both seemed capable—for as long as they wore Cardinal uniforms—to take Stanford to rare heights of team achievement.

The Lopez twins were the fifth and sixth McDonalds High School All-America honorees to matriculate to the Farm—in the footsteps of prior honorees Casey Jacobsen, Jarron Collins, Jason Collins, and Josh Childress. Individually, each Lopez was independent, artistic, and once-in-a-while prone to test the authority of the head coach. And each would find out that Trent Johnson was not one to back down.

The tough love and discipline began almost right away. Despite his all-around talent, Brook Lopez was not a starter in November and December, despite the fact that his brother Robin—from the start an intimidating defensive force in the paint—had become a starter. With Brook disappointed and perhaps not coincidentally not greatly productive as a reserve player for the first time in his young life, the 2006-07 Stanford team suffered two embarrassing non-conference losses in the November-December period, 79-45 at home to an Air Force team that ran the mystifying Princeton offense, and 62-46 at home to Santa Clara in the first game back following Stanford Basketball's traditional two-week layoff for Dead Week and Finals Week.

Despite these non-conference losses, Trent Johnson was nonetheless generally pleased with his team's progress. Despite the fact the Cardinal had won every other non-conference game that had been played in 2006-07, practices got tougher. There were challenging conversations between Johnson and individual players off the court. The head coach needed more scoring from the bench. And Johnson was looking for leadership—something hard to find in a team with no scholarship seniors on the roster.

In early January, he would find it. Having begun the Pac-10 schedule with a win at Arizona State followed by losses at Arizona and Cal, Stanford faced a cross-country trip to Charlottesville, VA, and a Sunday, January 7, 2007, matchup with the Virginia Cavaliers. Johnson made a change in the starting lineup prior to the Virginia game. Brook Lopez became a starter for the first time, replacing point guard Mitch Johnson in the lineup. Anthony Goods became the starting point guard—not his natural position—with junior Fred Washington and sophomore Lawrence Hill starting at the wing positions and the Lopez twins starting at the power forward and center spots.

Virginia—historically an extremely tough team at home no matter what the season—was 8-0 in its new, state-of-the-art John Paul Jones

Arena, which had opened just three months earlier. With its new starting lineup, Stanford led by two points at the half, but Virginia took its first lead, 45-44, with 14 minutes remaining. In a game notable for its many second-half lead changes, the margin of advantage, predictably, was very small for both teams during the remainder of the game.

Virginia retook the lead, 55-54 with ten minutes remaining. The Cavaliers extended the lead to four, 63-59, with seven minutes remaining—about the same time in the game that Brook Lopez fouled out, which compounded Stanford's problems. The Cardinal, however, came back to take the lead, 67-66, on two free throws by sophomore Lawrence Hill with five minutes left.

Down the wire the game went. With 9.4 seconds left, Virginia guard J.R. Reynolds hit two free throws to put the Cavaliers ahead, 75-74. In years past, Trent Johnson could rely on the ever-clutch Chris Hernandez in a situation like this, but, of course, the graduated Hernandez was no longer around. Did the 2006-07 team have a "clutch" component, even as it was clear that Johnson's roster as a whole had more talent than any of his prior Hernandez-captained teams?

The answer came on the final play of the game. The ball was inbounded to Fred Washington in the backcourt. Washington weaved his way upcourt with the dribble. He did not look to pass off. He kept dribbling forward, got into the paint, got near the rim—and then was cut off. Rather than force a shot in traffic, Washington deftly dished the ball to Lawrence Hill, who was eight feet from the basket to the left of Washington. There were three seconds left on the scoreboard clock.

Hill caught the pass, knifed toward the rim with the dribble and—amid contesting Cavalier defenders—laid the ball in the basket with 0.9 seconds remaining, giving the Cardinal a one-point lead! Virginia could not answer following a timeout, giving the Cardinal the win, 76-75.

The win at Virginia revealed the 2006-07 team's great balance on the offensive end, as compared to the prior year's Cardinal team. All five Stanford starters scored in double figures, something that had been done only rarely the prior season. In addition, the Stanford bench in the Virginia game contributed 14 points, substantially more bench points than were typically provided in a 2005-06 Stanford game. And the Cardinal had proved that someone other than the graduated Chris Hernandez could make a game-winning play in a tough road venue against a high-level opponent.

Virginia would beat Duke and North Carolina at home later that 2006-07 season. It had already decisively defeated Gonzaga in the new building. In fact, Virginia's only loss at home, in 2006-07 in the maiden John Paul Jones Arena season, was its loss to Stanford.

Stanford's won-loss record was 9-4 overall following the win at Virginia. Fifteen Pac-10 regular season games still remained on the 2006-07 schedule. With its new starting lineup of the Lopez twins, Lawrence Hill, Fred Washington, and Anthony Goods, Stanford began to roll, winning several big games as the Pac-10 schedule progressed—sometimes in dramatic fashion. Stanford came from behind to beat Washington by one point in its next game, which was played at Maples Pavilion. Two days later, Goods scored a career-high 30 points, played all 45 minutes, had no turnovers, and hit the game-winning three-point basket with four seconds remaining as the Cardinal edged #22-ranked WSU, 71-68, in overtime at Maples.

After a split at the Oregon schools, including a seven-point loss at #9-ranked Oregon, Stanford returned home to face #25-ranked USC and #2-ranked UCLA the following weekend. The USC game was a coming-out party for Brook Lopez. The Cardinal freshman recorded a school-record 12 blocks, to go along with a game-high 18 points and a game-high 11 rebounds—the first-ever "triple double" stat line in Stanford Basketball history—as the Cardinal dominated USC, 63-50. The Trojans were not an easy team to hold to 50-or-fewer points. Two USC players who played in the game, Taj Gibson and Nick Young, would be good enough after college to play several years in the NBA.

Trent Johnson's tough love approach with Brook Lopez was beginning to bear fruit. "He is going to be a lottery pick after tonight," said Trent Johnson after the USC victory. "He was exceptional on the defensive end."

The momentum continued on Saturday afternoon against #2-ranked UCLA. Although trailing by 12 points at halftime, Stanford exploded in the second half, scoring 50 points after the halftime break. At one stretch during the second half, Stanford outscored UCLA 15-0, with Lawrence Hill scoring seven consecutive points during that run. Anthony Goods scored 17 of his 20 points in the second half, and Stanford's defense held the Bruins to just 35% field-goal shooting.

The final score was Stanford 75 – UCLA 64. It was the highest-ranked UCLA team Stanford had beaten at Maples Pavilion since the 1975 upset of John Wooden's #2-ranked Bruins in the memorable Miracle at Maples game. It was also only the third time a Stanford Basketball team had beaten a #1-ranked or an #2-ranked team at Maples Pavilion.

Lawrence Hill's 22 points led the Cardinal in the win over UCLA. The next day, Stanford learned that it had been ranked #23 in the weekly

AP Poll. It was the first time Stanford had been ranked since the 2003-04 season. The Cardinal's won-loss record was now 14-5, including 6-3 in the Pac-10 games. By this point in the 2006-07 season Stanford had notched three wins over Top 25 teams—a good résumé builder for a team seeking an at-large bid to the upcoming NCAA Tournament.

Stanford would notch a fourth Top 25 win three weeks later, at #15-ranked Oregon as Brook Lopez scored a career-high 26 points. But the remainder of the Pac-10 schedule was problematic for the 2006-07 Cardinal. The team was swept in the state of Washington. The team was also swept in Los Angeles, losing by 4 points at USC and by 14 points at UCLA. Going into the regular season finale, Stanford was 18-10, 10-7 in the Pac-10. The regular season finale was a home date with Arizona.

Stanford played a horrible first half, trailing by 19 points at the break. Anthony Goods, who had missed the past five games with a sprained ankle, was out for the Arizona game as well, and backup point guard Mitch Johnson was unavailable due to a bout with food poisoning. The prospect of a comeback looked bleak for Stanford, being so thin at the guard position.

Enter walk-on guard Kenny Brown. Brown, a sophomore who had scored less than 60 points in his two-year Cardinal career, scored 17 of his team-high 22 points in the second half—including a game-tying three-point basket with six seconds remaining in regulation—to send the game into overtime. Unfortunately, Arizona outscored Stanford 14-9 in the overtime period and won the game, 85-80.

At the Pac-10 Tournament, Stanford faced USC and again suffered an overtime loss, 83-79, after leading by as many as eleven points at one point during the second half. Anthony Goods returned to action and led the Cardinal with 19 points and five assists, but his bid for a game-winning basket in the final seconds of regulation was thwarted when his jump shot was blocked by USC's Taj Gibson. Freshman reserve forward Landry Fields had a career-high 15 points in the loss.

There was no doubt that, with an overall 18-12 record—including four Top 25 wins and a road win at Virginia—Stanford would receive a bid to the 2007 NCAA Tournament. However, having lost four of its past five games and with a 10-8 conference record, Stanford's seeding wasn't likely to be a particularly good one.

Stanford was the last team announced on the CBS Selection Show. None of the seeding slot, first-round opponent, game location or starting time was good for the Cardinal: an #11 seed, the opponent to be Rick Pitino–coached Louisville, the game to be played in the close-to-

Louisville city of Lexington, KY, and the tip time to be 12:30 P.M. EST, which would mean 9:30 A.M. Stanford player "body time." Additionally, the Cardinal hoopsters had to travel 2,400 miles to the game site. These negative factors did not prompt many to predict a Cardinal victory.

Prediction proved reality. Louisville's pressure defense forced Anthony Goods—who had just come back from the ankle injury and was still relatively new to the point guard position—and his Stanford teammates into committing 21 turnovers, many of which resulted in easy first-half baskets for Louisville. With five minutes left in the first half, the score was 41-13 in Louisville's favor, and the game—and season—was effectively over for Stanford.

Stanford's won-loss record in 2006-07 ended up being 18-13. Lawrence Hill, who led Stanford in scoring in 2006-07 with a 15.7 points-per-game average, was the lone member of the Cardinal selected to the All-Pac-10 team.

Whereas the 2006-07 Stanford team—though talented—skewed toward inexperience, the following year's roster would be experienced and unusually deep. Not only would all five starters return in 2007-08, the top twelve scholarship players from the 2006-07 roster would be back. As things would turn out, not only did the 2007-08 season not want for experienced players, it did not want for drama.

The first source of drama was the academic ineligibility of Brook Lopez for the first nine games of 2007-08, an announcement made prior to the beginning of the season. Brook Lopez would have no problem becoming reeligible by the conclusion of the 2007 Fall Quarter, but most observers assumed that his absence would cost the Cardinal a game or two during the November-through-mid-December portion of the schedule. Even knowing Brook Lopez would be unavailable to Stanford until mid-December, the AP Poll voters still felt good enough about Stanford's overall talent and prospects to give the Cardinal a #23 preseason ranking.

Stanford won its first three games of the season at home on successive nights in early November. Sophomore reserve guard Drew Shiller—a transfer from USF—scored 18 points in his Cardinal debut to lead Stanford past Harvard, 111-56, a game in which Harvard's starting guard, Palo Alto High alum and future NBA player Jeremy Lin, was held scoreless in 21 minutes of play. Two Cardinal wins followed, over Northwestern State and UC Santa Barbara, in which Stanford's average margin of victory was 29 points.

Heading off on the road, the Cardinal ran its record to 4-0 with an 11-point win at Northwestern on Thursday, November 15, 2007, with Goods scoring 19 points and each of Robin Lopez and Landry Fields contributing 16 points. For the sophomore forward Fields, the 16 points represented a career high and came from, among other sources, four three-point baskets.

The next morning, the team boarded a bus in Evanston, IL for O'Hare Airport and an 8:00 A.M. flight from Chicago to Albany, NY. Due to Friday morning traffic and other snafus, the team barely made it to the airport in time to board its flight. Some of its equipment—most notably team members' basketball shoes—did not, however, make it onto the plane, meaning the team could not practice in Albany that day in advance of its 1:00 P.M. Saturday matchup against Siena at Knickerbocker Arena.

Not only would rustiness and the absence of Brook Lopez be negatives going into the Siena game, the home Siena fans would be a problem as well—possessing as they did a couple of extra incentives to cheer loudly against the Cardinal. For one thing, the 2007-08 Cardinal was the type of Top 25-ranked, big-conference Goliath that any mid-major program such as Siena hungered to play and beat. And there was, of course, the well-known history of Siena having secured an upset over a previous highly ranked Stanford Basketball team—the shocking upset of the #3-seeded Cardinal in the first round of the 1989 NCAA Tournament.

Siena played to the script early, leading by two points at halftime. Stanford then retook the lead, 46-45, with ten minutes remaining in the game. The Saints then went on an 11-0 scoring run to grab a 56-46 lead with seven minutes remaining, and the Cardinal could never come close to regaining the lead. As the final buzzer sounded, the Knickerbocker Arena fans streamed onto the court in celebration. The 79-67 victory was Siena's first win over a ranked opponent in 18 years—since, in fact, that upset of Stanford in 1989. So bottled up had been Stanford's starters that the Cardinal's leading scorer in the game was reserve guard Kenny Brown, who finished with 12 points.

Although it had lost its Top 25 ranking in the polls, Stanford bounced back following the Siena loss with four consecutive victories. The first three wins came at home—over Yale, Colorado State, and Sacramento State—and the fourth win was gained in Boulder, CO, over Colorado. The 2007-08 Cardinal was 8-1 heading into the two-week hiatus for the "Dead Week" study week period and the ensuing "Finals Week" of examinations.

The first game following the Fall Quarter examination period was a home game against Santa Clara. One year earlier, the same cast of Stanford players lost at home to the Broncos by 16 points. This game flipped that outcome, as the Cardinal won by 24 points. Headlining the win was Brook Lopez's return to action for the first time in 2007-08. The sophomore scored 20 points and had six rebounds to lead the Cardinal in the win.

Next up was a road game three days later at the American Airlines Arena in Dallas against the Bobby Knight–coached Texas Tech Red Raiders. Both Brook and Robin Lopez drew two first half fouls, and each spent a moderate portion of the first half on the bench as the Red Raiders built a seven-point halftime lead. In the second half, after having scored just two points in the first half, Brook Lopez began asserting himself on the offensive end of the court. With Brook scoring 14 of Stanford's 32 points during the first 18 minutes of the second half, the Cardinal found itself tied with Texas Tech with two minutes remaining in the game.

Brook Lopez then hit two free throws to put Stanford up 60-58, then hit another free throw with 27 seconds remaining to give the Cardinal a 61-58 advantage. A bit later, Mitch Johnson's single free throw with two seconds to go in the game—with his team ahead by three points—clinched the win for Stanford.

Said Trent Johnson, after the game, of his budding sophomore star Brook Lopez: "The thing I was most proud of was that he played through adversity on the floor. There's no secret. Brook Lopez is one of the best players in the country."

A post-Christmas win, at home over Fresno State, ended the non-conference portion of the 2007-08 Cardinal schedule. As the calendar turned to 2008 and a daunting Pac-10 schedule loomed, Stanford had an 11-1 record and a #24 national ranking. Not since the 1990s—and perhaps ever—were there more good teams, and more outstanding players, than were in the Pac-10 in 2007-08. In the December 31, 2007, AP Poll, five Pac-10 teams were included in the Top 25: Washington State at #4, UCLA at #5, Arizona at #21, USC at #22, and Stanford at #24. In addition to these teams, Oregon also was a worthy conference foe that season, as evidenced by its having been ranked #11 in the 2007-08 preseason AP Poll just two months earlier.

As to future NBA players, Stanford had the Lopez twins. UCLA had Kevin Love, Darren Collison, and Russell Westbrook. USC had O.J. Mayo and Taj Gibson. Arizona had Chase Budinger and Jerryd Bayless. Arizona State had James Harden. Cal had Ryan Anderson. All but one would be first-round NBA Draft selections, and most would be draft lottery picks. The Pac-10 was crazy-good in 2007-08.

The conference slate began at Maples Pavilion on January 3rd against #5-ranked UCLA. Another Maples sellout crowd saw the Lopez twins and Lawrence Hill battle the physical and efficient Bruin frontline of Kevin

Love, Luc Richard Mbah a Moute, and Alfred Aboya to what essentially was a draw as far as scoring and rebounding were concerned. Lamented the frosh phenom Love later of his struggle to get shots off, "I could go up and get past one Lopez, but then there would be the other one."

Stanford trailed by just one point at halftime, 35-34. Stanford hung close for the first 11 minutes of the second half, trailing by just two points, 51-49, following a Mitch Johnson layup. But over the next five minutes, the Bruins went on a 13-4 run—the last six points coming on consecutive three-point baskets by wing Josh Shipp—to take a 64-53 lead with 3:59 to play.

From that point, the Cardinal could get no closer than six points and would ultimately lose the game by the score of 76-67. Shipp—who was animated throughout the game as if to visibly demonstrate his team's intent to avenge the Cardinal's upset of the then #2-ranked Bruins one year earlier in Maples—finished with a game-high 21 points that included five three-point baskets. Russell Westbrook chipped in with 15 points for UCLA on 6-of-7 field-goal shooting. Each of the Lopez twins fouled out late in the game, having made only 9 of 25 shots combined against the solid UCLA front line. Anthony Goods led Stanford with 17 points.

Two nights later, Stanford's defense got the job done against #22-ranked USC, 52-46. Stanford shot only 27% from the field—its worst shooting performance in nine seasons—and yet somehow still managed to win the game. The reason was Stanford's team defense. As but one example, with Fred Washington harassing O.J. Mayo outside and the Lopez twins providing help in the paint on Mayo drives, the Trojan star was held to 5-of-14 shooting. Acknowledged Mayo ruefully after the game, "We have some good bigs in the Pac-10, don't we?"

And the Cardinal defense would get better and better as Pac-10 play continued. Stanford won eight of its next nine conference games, allowing more than 65 points just once during that stretch of games. Included in that streak was a 65-51 win at Washington in which Brook Lopez scored a career-high 31 points and pulled down 13 rebounds, as well as a 67-65 overtime win at #9-ranked Washington State two days later in which Robin Lopez scored the decisive layup in the final half-minute of the game.

Following that winning streak, Stanford's won-loss record was 17-3 overall, including a 9-2 mark in the Pac-10. The Cardinal's national ranking stood at #9 in the February 4, 2008, AP Poll. A 72-68 overtime loss at ASU followed in the next Cardinal game, despite Brook Lopez's 30 points. Two days later, at Arizona's McKale Center, Robin Lopez's fingertip block of a Chase Budinger baseline layup attempt in the final second of the game preserved a 67-66 Cardinal win in Tucson. Three more home wins, over Cal and the Washington schools, followed over the next two weeks.

Senior Day, 2008, at Maples Pavilion was a particularly memorable one. Coach Trent Johnson started each of his seniors—Taj Finger, Fred Washington, Kenny Brown, and Peter Prowitt—along with sophomore Brook Lopez in the home finale against #22-ranked Washington State. It was the first time in memory that a Stanford coach had given starts to all of his graduating seniors, in a situation in which most of them were not regular starters.

Given that unusual starting lineup, it wasn't surprising that the Cardinal fell behind, 11-1, in the opening minutes. Johnson then brought his regulars into the game, and predictably the Cardinal began its comeback. It took over 25 minutes of game time, but eventually the Cardinal ceased trailing on the scoreboard. With four minutes remaining in the game, a Taj Finger basket—just the fifth three-pointer of his career—tied the game and triggered a thunderous Maples Pavilion roar. Stanford never trailed after that, closing the game with a 9-2 scoring run to win the Senior Day game, 60-53.

Going into the final regular season weekend of the season, Stanford had a chance at the conference title. Stanford's record was 24-4 overall and 13-3 in the Pac-10, just one game behind first place UCLA which was 14-2 in conference play. Stanford's ranking in the AP Poll was #7; UCLA's was #3. Conveniently for both teams, the next game of each team's schedule was Cardinal versus Bruins in Los Angeles. The Pac-10 schedule makers for 2007-08 had guessed that this matchup might decide the conference race, and they were right.

The stage was set: Thursday, March 6, 2008, Stanford versus UCLA in Los Angeles. A national television audience would be watching, and a sellout Pauley Pavilion crowd of more than 12,000 would be in attendance to cheer loudly for the Bruins, intimidate the Cardinal, and perhaps harass or influence the referees. First place in the Pac-10 was at stake.

The Cardinal got off to a great start in the game. Stanford raced out to early leads of 12-2 and 28-14. Then it was UCLA's turn to go on a scoring run. The Bruins closed the deficit to 12 points by halftime. The Cardinal scored the first four points of the second half, but then a 27-13 Bruin scoring surge reduced the Bruin deficit to just 45-43 with nine minutes remaining.

Stanford then went on an 11-2 scoring run, with the Lopez twins scoring nine of the points, to take a 56-45 lead with 5:37 remaining. Things were looking very good for the Cardinal at that point in the game. But behind Russell Westbrook and Kevin Love and the screaming Pauley

Pavilion crowd, UCLA stormed back. Eight straight Bruin points, four each by Westbrook and Love, pulled the Bruins to within three points with 3:17 left. Taj Finger then converted for two Stanford points, then Love answered for UCLA with a basket. Finger scored again, then so did Luc Richard Mbah a Moute and then Russell Westbrook as well. At this point the score was 60-59 in Stanford's favor. 50 seconds remained on the scoreboard clock.

Stanford worked time off the clock during its next possession, near the end of which Brook Lopez was fouled. Lopez made one of two free throws. Twenty-three seconds remained on the clock, with Stanford now ahead by two points. On its next possession, Finger fouled Westbrook. Westbrook made both free throws to tie the game at 61. Thirteen seconds remained in the game.

Against UCLA's full-court pressure, Stanford inbounded the ball to Hill. Seeing an open lane, the junior dribbled upcourt, weaved his way past each of the UCLA defenders and converted a go-ahead layup basket with seven seconds left. Stanford had the lead, 63-61, and needed just one stop to win the game.

UCLA had no timeouts left. The ball was immediately inbounded to Collison, who sped upcourt with the ball. Attacking the left wing, he pulled up for a ten-foot jump shot with three seconds remaining. Lawrence Hill was defending Collison as the Bruin guard released his shot. Hill's arms were extended vertically upward and clearly touched nothing but the orange leather ball. But referee Kevin Brill blew the whistle. A foul was called on Hill.

Trent Johnson winced with body language full of disbelief and frustration, as did the Cardinal players on the bench. Collison made both pressure free throws, sending the game into overtime. Deflated, Stanford could not muster much of anything in the overtime period, while UCLA scored 14 points in the extra session. Final score: UCLA 77 – Stanford 67.

Stanford had come within a whistle of sharing first place with the Bruins. And speaking of the referee's controversial whistle, here is what the Pac-10 coordinator of officials, Bill McCabe, said after the game: "There was body contact, but it's not a strong call, not a game appropriate call. It's not an incorrect call and that doesn't make it wrong. But I want solid calls."

The game—and particularly the referee's call on Hill—was the top topic on sports talk radio stations across the country the following day. It was no solace to Trent Johnson and his Stanford Basketball team. Still deflated by the controversial and painful loss, the Cardinal lost by 13 points to O.J. Mayo–led USC at the Galen Center in Los Angeles two days later.

Three games at the Pac-10 Tournament followed, also in Los Angeles. Stanford knocked off Arizona 75-64 in the quarterfinal, then dispatched #21-ranked WSU 75-68 in the semifinal, setting up a tournament championship game matchup with—who else?—UCLA on March 15, 2008. Despite not having forward Luc Richard Mbah a Moute due to an ankle injury, and despite Kevin Love playing with a lower leg injury, the Bruins prevailed one more time over the Cardinal, 67-64, before a Pac-10 Tournament record crowd of 17,534 at the Staples Center.

With 26 wins, including a second place finish in the brutally tough Pac-10, Stanford anticipated receiving—and received—a very favorable seed and opening weekend location in the 2008 NCAA Tournament. Stanford was seeded #3 in the South Region, with first and second-round games to be played at the Anaheim Pond arena on March 20 and 22, 2008.

The Cardinal easily defeated #14-seed Cornell in the first-round matchup, 77-53. Trent Johnson was able to clear his bench late in the game. Freshman reserve forward Josh Owens—who had received very little playing time behind the Lopez twins, Hill and Finger during the regular season portion of the schedule—scored seven points in the game, his first points scored since November.

Next up was a second-round matchup with #6-seed Marquette, which had defeated Kentucky in the first round. The date was Saturday, March 22, 2008—ten years to the day that Stanford pulled off its most memorable, last-minute, come-from-behind postseason performance to beat Rhode Island in the regional final in the 1998 NCAA Tournament in St. Louis.

The Marquette-Stanford game would equal the late-game drama of ten years earlier, on several fronts.

The Golden Eagles, coached by Tom Crean, had a roster of multiple future NBA players, including Wesley Matthews, Lazar Hayward, and Jerel McNeal. It would not be easy for Stanford, with or without in-game drama, to get past Marquette. The game was back-and-forth early, with Robin Lopez leading Stanford in scoring early with ten points during the first ten minutes of the game. With 3:36 remaining in the first half, Lawrence Hill fouled Lazar Hayward, leading to a mandatory television timeout. The score at the time was 25-24 in Marquette's favor.

What came next was the "first half" drama in the Stanford-Marquette game. As play stopped and the timeout began, Trent Johnson walked out to the free-throw line area, with his coaching staff behind him. It's a typical place where coaches gather, in the early seconds of a timeout, to confer among themselves as to what the head coach will tell the team in the huddle subsequently during the timeout period.

Referees David Hall and Curtis Shaw did not see things as being so benign. Even before the Stanford head coach had begun his stride on to the court as the timeout began, Hall whistled a technical foul on Johnson, apparently as the consequence of a just-concluded and heated in-game conversation between Johnson and the official. Then, as Johnson was walking out onto the floor, Shaw immediately hit the Stanford head coach with a second technical foul whistle, ostensibly because Johnson had walked too far onto the court. The second technical foul, of course, meant an immediate ejection of Trent Johnson from the game.

Johnson left the court glaring at the officials. He was thinking what everyone was thinking, "how can a coach who hasn't done much, if anything, against the rules or coaching etiquette be ejected from *an NCAA Tournament game*?" Assistant coach Doug Oliver had to get over the shock quickly; he would be the one taking over the head coaching duties for Stanford during the rest of the game.

It was hard to believe. At the CBS announcing table at midcourt, commentator Jay Bilas motioned referee Curtis Shaw to come over to the broadcast table to explain what happened. Shaw tried to explain, Bilas tried to understand. Wes Matthews made all four of the technical foul free throws to give Marquette a 29-24 lead. The lead grew to 36-25 before Stanford reeled off five consecutive points to end the first half, which left the Cardinal down at the break by only six points, 36-30.

Things were heated. In the stands, Stanford head football coach Jim Harbaugh reportedly was involved in an altercation. In the locker room, Stanford players were heated. Trent Johnson, already having been banished to the locker room for the rest of the game, tried to calm his players down. A television set in the locker room reportedly was knocked off its elevated stand.

The second half would produce even more drama. Stanford clawed back, finally tying the game at 49 with 13:47 remaining on a three-point basket by Anthony Goods. Stanford next was able to build a six-point lead, then lost the lead when the Golden Eagles immediately went on a 16-6 scoring run to take a 65-61 lead with 5:43 remaining in the game. With 5:18 left, Brook Lopez hit a free throw to cut the Cardinal deficit to three points. Neither team would lead by more than three points during the remainder of the game—it was that close a game in the final minutes and seconds.

With 19 seconds remaining in regulation, Stanford trailed 71-70 but got a rebound off a missed shot by Lazard Hayward. Mitch Johnson dribbled the ball into the frontcourt, drove the lane but missed the layup. However, both Fred Washington and Robin Lopez battled for the offensive rebound, with Lopez being fouled by a Marquette player in the process.

Two pressure free-throw attempts loomed for Robin Lopez. His missed the first, but made the second, tying the game at 71. Marquette had a last shot attempt to win the game, but Brook Lopez blocked Lazar Hayward's fall-away shot attempt, which sent the game to overtime.

Stanford was thus confronted with another overtime game in an NCAA Tournament—its third overtime game in an NCAA Tournament since 1997. The Cardinal had lost the prior two overtime games, losses which had ended Stanford Basketball's NCAA runs in each of 1997 and 1998.

The overtime, for Marquette, was all Jerel McNeal. Within the first three minutes of overtime, the Golden Eagle guard had made three three-point baskets. But Stanford managed to keep up Marquette's scoring pace, with Brook Lopez scoring six points and Mitch Johnson adding three points during that three-minute stretch. With 2:21 remaining in the overtime period, the score was 81-80 in favor of Marquette.

There would be no more scoring for the next 2:19 of elapsed time on the game clock. Brook Lopez missed three shots. Jerel McNeal likewise missed three shots, the last of which was missed with 19 seconds left. Fred Washington secured the rebound for the Cardinal. Acting Stanford coach Doug Oliver called timeout with eleven seconds remaining to set up a play. Stanford still trailed, 81-80.

Following the timeout, Stanford inbounded the ball from the sideline to Mitch Johnson, who dribbled toward the right wing side of the frontcourt, outside the arc. With five seconds left, he dumped a pass to a posting Brook Lopez on the block on the right side of the lane. Lopez's back was to the basket.

Lopez caught the ball, turned his body leftward toward the baseline, and lofted up a soft, eight-foot, half-hook-type shot toward the hoop. The ball hit the front of the rim, then bounced sideways toward the glass backboard, then bounced off the glass, and then fell through the hoop. The scoreboard clock read 1.3 seconds. Stanford now led 82-81!

Following a Golden Eagle timeout, Marquette's effort to pull off a last-second miracle play was foiled by Stanford. For the first time in seven seasons, Stanford had advanced to the Sweet 16 of an NCAA Tournament. Ten years to the calendar day—March 22nd—that Arthur

Lee had performed his last-minute magic in St. Louis in an NCAA regional final, Brook Lopez had produced last-second magic to send Stanford to the Sweet 16.

Ironically, both Arthur Lee and Brook Lopez wore uniform number 11 for Stanford. The parallel was amazing: two #11s for Stanford Basketball, doing their last-minute magic thing on a calendar date with the number 22. Two "elevens," together, making "twenty-two" a memorable date on the Stanford Basketball calendar!

The South Region Sweet 16 game for Stanford in 2008 would be played in the state of Texas. The Cardinal would face the South Region's #2-seeded team, Texas, in Houston's Reliant Stadium. The Longhorns, playing in front of a largely pro-Texas crowd in Houston, dominated the Cardinal 82-62, ending Stanford's Final Four dream as well as its drama-filled season. The 2007-08 team's final record ended up being 28-8, tied for the third-most Stanford wins in a single season, eclipsed previously only by the Final Four team in 1998, the Final Eight team in 2001, and the 30-2 team in 2003-04.

The end of the games did not, however, end the drama. In early April 2008, reportedly as a result of the inability of both sides to come to terms on a contract extension, Trent Johnson resigned his position as the Anne & Tony Joseph Director of Basketball at Stanford University, having accepted an offer to become the head coach at LSU.

Privately, with tears, Trent Johnson immediately following his departure shared with a few supporters how much he loved coaching at Stanford and how painful the events of the recent days had been. The timing of Johnson's departure was not ideal. Several months earlier, Johnson had signed prep star and future NBA player Miles Plumlee to a Stanford letter of intent, and just a month prior to his departure Johnson had nearly succeeded in securing a commitment from Miles's brother Mason Plumlee to come to Stanford as well. Johnson loved pitching a Stanford education and the Stanford Basketball experience to all of his recruiting targets, and had especially enjoyed the process of recruiting the Plumlees.

Now, a month later, Trent Johnson was no longer the Cardinal head coach. Publicly, he praised his players, wishing them, and the eventual new hire, good fortune in the future. Stanford Athletic Director Bob Bowlsby immediately commenced a nationwide search for a new coach. Stanford Basketball was losing four of its top seven players, including the Lopez twins who had opted to leave school and enter the NBA Draft. It was also losing Miles Plumlee, who due to the coaching change was released from his Stanford letter-of-intent obligations and ended up signing with Duke.

The coach search process for Stanford wasn't an easy one. Johnson was—and remains—very popular in the college basketball coaching community, making it difficult or impossible for some coaches to pursue the job. Also problematic to some candidates, though a huge attraction to others, was Stanford's longtime and strongly maintained emphasis on balance between athletic and academic prominence.

Despite these hurdles, Bowlsby finally was able to secure a big name in the college basketball world, one with considerable NCAA Division 1 coaching experience as an assistant as well as considerable NBA playing experience. Johnny Dawkins—the National Player of the Year in 1986 as part of Duke coach Mike Kryzsewski's first Final Four team—was the choice to become Stanford Basketball's 18th head coach.

Trent Johnson, who averaged 20 wins per season in his four years as head coach, is one of three coaches to have taken a Stanford team to the NCAA Tournament Sweet 16.

Twin big men, Brook and Robin Lopez, were both all-conference selections and helped lead Stanford to NCAA Tournaments during each of their years as Cardinal players.

Brook Lopez, celebrating with teammate Fred Washington after Lopez's game-winning basket in the final two seconds against Marquette in the second round of the 2008 NCAA Tournament.

XII. From the Coach "K" Tree

A New Leader with a Disciplined Pedigree and a Winning Personality

Johnny Dawkins had never been a head coach. But Dawkins had received, in his 11 years as a Duke assistant coach, great mentoring from Coach K, and Dawkins was someone virtually everyone in the basketball world liked and respected. His NBA and Duke playing résumé would guarantee instant respect in the locker room and in recruit's homes, and he was a gentleman away from the court.

Besides the new coaching staff, the big change in Stanford Basketball going into the 2008-09 season was that the Lopez twins would no longer be anchoring the Cardinal front line. Both Brook and Robin Lopez had opted to enter the NBA Draft following their sophomore seasons in 2007-08. Each was a first-round selection in the 2008 NBA Draft, with Brook Lopez selected #10 overall by the New Jersey Nets and Robin Lopez selected #15 overall by the Phoenix Suns.

The result of the Lopezes' early departure for the NBA meant Stanford's 2008-09 squad would have a fewer number of, as well as a less experienced stable of, frontcourt players than any Stanford team since the early 1990s. Stanford's tallest starter in 2008-09 was 6′ 8″ sophomore Josh Owens, who had to play the center position in the smallish Cardinal starting lineup. Owens had played in just 18 games in 2007-08, for a total of only 105 minutes, and scored just 30 points.

The first game for Stanford was a road game at Yale. Though misfiring on its first six shots, Stanford eventually found its rhythm and took a 30-29 halftime lead. With returning veterans Lawrence Hill, Anthony Goods, and Mitch Johnson—all seniors, all with starting experience—providing the scoring punch, the Cardinal prevailed 75-67. Hill led the way with 22 points and 12 rebounds, with Goods hitting for 19 points and Johnson contributing 11 points and six assists. It was the first time each of Hill, Goods, and Johnson had scored in double figures in the same game. The Cardinal won despite being outrebounded by ten.

Stanford was 1-0 in the Johnny Dawkins era. And for a while, it looked like his team would never lose. Three more November 2008 games followed, each of which resulted in a Stanford win: 103-55 over Cal State Northridge, 76-57 over Air Force, and 76-62 over Colorado. The two-week break for Dead Week and Finals Week followed, with no games played. Immediately following the break, Stanford traveled to Colorado State and, with Goods scoring 23 points, the Cardinal overcame the Rams by the score of 74-63. Coach Dawkins's team was 5-0.

During the next two weeks, the Cardinal won five more games—pushing its record to an impressive 10-0. The wins came at home over Northern Arizona and Northwestern, on the road at Santa Clara, and at home over Texas Tech and Hartford. The win at Maples over Texas Tech was a stunner, 111-66, with the Cardinal shooting 56% for the game. Each of Anthony Goods (21 points), Landry Fields (19 points), Lawrence Hill (17 points), and Josh Owens (12 points) scored in double figures in the unexpectedly lopsided Cardinal win.

With the turn of the calendar to 2009 came the beginning of the Pac-10 conference games. Prior to the season, the Cardinal was picked in a poll of media members to finish ninth out of the ten conference teams. The departure of the Lopez twins was the primary reason for the low predicted finish for Stanford.

As it turned out, the prediction proved correct. The Cardinal finished 6-12 in the conference standings. But each of the six wins was by 10 points or more, including two over Pac-10 teams that at the time were ranked in the national Top 25.

The opening weekend featured home games against Arizona State and Arizona. The Sun Devils, behind guard James Harden's and center Jeff Pendergraph's combined 48 points, throttled the Cardinal 90-60. But two days later the Cardinal bounced back with a 76-60 pasting of Arizona, as Landry Fields matched his career high of 19 points and grabbed a career-best 11 rebounds. Helpful to the Cardinal cause was a defensive effort that limited Arizona's star guard—and future NBA first-round pick—Chase Budinger to just 4 of 11 in field-goal shooting.

Stanford's first Pac-10 road trip in the Dawkins era was a frustrating one: two one-point losses at both Washington (84-83) and Washington State (55-54). In each game, Stanford had a chance to win with a last possession, but a Landry Fields stumble in the lane at Washington and

Anthony Goods's last-second miss at WSU in the final seconds kept Stanford from gaining victory.

Dawkins used those losses as teaching points the following week in practice, as the Cardinal prepared to host Cal the following Saturday. The game would mark new Cal coach Mike Montgomery's first coaching appearance in Maples Pavilion since his Stanford coaching days. Stanford responded in an appropriately inhospitable fashion by rocking the #22-ranked Golden Bears, 75-69. In the Cardinal win, Lawrence Hill matched his career high with 25 points.

Coach Dawkins praised his team for bouncing backagainst a Top 25 opponent, no less—following the bitter onepoint losses the prior weekend in the state of Washington: "We were in position to win two games and didn't win either. We learned from that, though. I said, 'Sometimes a tough lesson is the lesson we learn the best.' I don't think we would have responded had we not had that experience last weekend."

The quote, and the long week of practice, provided insights about the new Stanford head coach: a big aversion to losing, a determination to use setbacks as teaching vehicles, and a relentless work ethic.

Including the Cal win, Stanford would split three of its next six Pac-10 games, with one of the losses being a one-point loss at USC when Lawrence Hill's baseline jumper barely missed as time expired at the Galen Center. Stanford was now 4-6 in the conference standings, with three of its losses having been by one point.

Five consecutive conference losses followed—with three occurring on the road. The 2009 Valentine's Day loss at Cal was particularly frustrating. Stanford had built up a 22-point lead with 4:33 remaining in the first half, helped in part by a trio of three-point baskets from freshman reserve guard Jeremy Green. But the Golden Bears cut the deficit to 14 points by halftime, and in the second half Cal held the Cardinal to just 25 points while scoring 46 points themselves. Each of these factors contributed to an 82-75 victory for Mike Montgomery's team.

Challenging practices followed the Cal loss. Once again the Cardinal responded positively to Johnny Dawkins's teaching, winning two of its three final regular season Pac-10 games. One of the wins consisted of another win over a national Top 25 team.

On March 5, 2009, in Tempe, AZ, Stanford faced #21-ranked Arizona State, the team that had beaten the Cardinal by 30 points in the conference opener. From the opening tip, Stanford's defense was stifling. ASU did not score a field goal until James Harden scored a basket with 12 minutes remaining in the first half. Stanford pushed its lead to 14 points at two different junctures in the second half—the second of which came on senior reserve guard Kenny Brown's three-point basket with 3:49 to play. It was over for the home team at that point; the final score ended up being Stanford 74 – Arizona State 64. Landry Fields had 20 points to lead the Cardinal in scoring, with Anthony Goods, Lawrence Hill, and Kenny Brown contributing 15, 13, and 12 points, respectively.

With an overall won-loss record of 17-12, 6-12 in the Pac-10, Stanford traveled to Los Angeles for the Pac-10 Postseason Tournament as the #9 seed. In the first round against #8-seed Oregon State, the Cardinal avenged two regular season losses to the Beavers by winning 62-54. Again the key was defense—Stanford held OSU to 39% field-goal shooting for the game, including no field goals by Oregon State in the final 3:45 of the game. Anthony Goods's 23 points led the way for Stanford on offense.

The Cardinal next faced the tournament's top seed, #13-ranked Washington. The Huskies had been a Top 25 team virtually all season, but did not have an easy time with Stanford during the regular season, winning by margins of just one point and seven points in the two games between the two schools.

The first half was a battle. The lead changed eight different times in the first half, and at halftime the Huskies led by just three points, 38-35. Washington opened up double-digit leads at two different times in the second half, but twice in response the Cardinal closed the deficit to five points. In the end, however, the inside power of Husky forward Jon Brockman and the scoring-ability of diminutive guard Isaiah Thomas proved to be too much for the Cardinal to overcome. Final score: Washington 85 – Stanford 73.

Anthony Goods scored 26 points, while Landry Fields added 16 and a career-best 15 rebounds. Freshman guard Jeremy Green, who had been named to the Pac-10 All-Freshman team earlier in the week, contributed 13 points off the bench. Green's scoring contributions had discernibly accelerated during the latter portion of the season, aided in no small measure by many repetitions of individual shooting drills conducted at the direction of Cardinal assistant coach Mike Schrage.

With a record of 18-14 overall, Stanford missed out on NCAA and NIT bids, but accepted a bid to the College Basketball Invitational (CBI) postseason tournament. A sixteen-team tournament in its second year of existence in 2008-09, Stanford was matched up against a 19-win Boise State team in a first-round game at Maples Pavilion on March 18, 2009. Stanford took control from the start and led by 20 points at halftime,

51-31. The Cardinal offensive surge remained relentless in the second half and the Cardinal won going away, 96-76.

Jeremy Green scored 19 points in just 16 minutes off the bench, hitting 7 of 11 shots to lead Stanford in scoring. Lawrence Hill added 18 points and Landry Fields contributed 16 points for a Stanford team that shot 53% for the game and also recorded a remarkable 20 assists.

Next up was a much tougher test—a road game at Wichita State. The Shockers, under second-year head coach Gregg Marshall, had won six games more than it had won the prior season and were a very tough team to beat on its home floor. The 8,800-seat Charles Koch Arena was low-roofed, circular, and very loud, and the 2008-09 Shockers had won 11 of 16 games in that building. Yet despite the ominousness of the opponent and venue, Stanford would keep the building unusually quiet virtually the entire night.

The Cardinal busted out to a 30-10 lead fourteen minutes into the first half, helped by three Jeremy Green three-point baskets. At halftime, the score was 42-26 in favor of Stanford, with the Cardinal having made a sizzling 61% of its first-half field-goal attempts and the Cardinal defense having limited Wichita State to just 32% field-goal shooting in the first half.

At halftime, Coach Dawkins exhorted his team to maintain its concentration and aggressiveness, to not let up, to not let the crowd become a factor. The halftime speech worked beautifully. Stanford kept Wichita State well under 40% shooting in the second half as well, which allowed the Cardinal to comfortably survive its own second-half downtick in shooting. The final margin of Stanford advantage was nearly the same as the halftime margin: sixteen points. The final score was Stanford 70 – Wichita State 56.

It was Stanford's 20th win of 2008-09, a higher-than-expected win total for the Cardinal. Conference observers at the beginning of the season had predicted a lower win total, given the Lopez twins' departure following the 2007-08 campaign and the impossibility of Stanford's replacing two players of such size and talent. In winning his 20th game, Dawkins surpassed Bob Burnett as the Stanford coach with the most wins in his first season as head coach.

It was on to the CBI semifinals, against a familiar opponent. For the fourth time in 2008-09, Stanford would face Oregon State. It would be the first time since the early 1960s that the Cardinal had faced the same team as many as four times in the same season.

Predictably, given the familiarity of each team with the other, the game in Corvallis was a dogfight. Oregon State led by two points at halftime, 28-26. Stanford then rallied and led by five points, 35-30, with fourteen minutes remaining in the second half. OSU then took command via a 21-10 scoring run over the next twelve minutes and led 51-45, with 2:30 remaining in regulation.

But the Stanford seniors would not go quietly. An 8-3 Cardinal scoring run in the final 2:30 was capped by a Lawrence Hill 15-foot jump shot at the buzzer that sent the game into overtime. Stanford seized the early momentum in the overtime period, going up by five points on an Anthony Goods three-point basket with 2:30 left. But there the Cardinal hit the wall, scoring just one more point as OSU—thanks in large part to the play of its 6′ 11″ center and multifaceted scoring threat Roeland Schaftenaar—who went on a 9-1 scoring run in the final 2:30 to win the game, 62-56.

In their final Stanford appearance, Anthony Goods and Lawrence Hill notched 20 points and 14 points, respectively. Senior point guard Mitch Johnson, also playing in his final Cardinal game, had five assists to push his career total to 534, second on the all-time career assist list behind only Brevin Knight. Also closing out his career in Corvallis, with Baylor Dental School awaiting, was senior guard Kenny Brown—one of the most statistically productive walk-ons in Stanford Basketball history.

Stanford finished the season with a won-loss record of 20-14. Stanford had won all thirteen non-conference games it played in 2008-09. Although its record against conference foes was just 7-14, including postseason contests, the Cardinal had beaten each of the other Pac-10 teams except Washington and UCLA at least once during the season. And of the losses against Washington and UCLA—the two conference teams Stanford did not defeat at least once in 2008-09—one or more of the two losses that season against each team had been by five or fewer points. The 2008-09 season had yielded another conclusion about the new Stanford coaching staff: Johnny Dawkins, along with his assistants Dick Davey, Mike Schrage, and Rodney Tention, could maximize the concentration and competitive traits of a given set of talent.

Year two of the Johnny Dawkins coaching era figured, on paper at least, to be a down year for Stanford Basketball. Three of the five 2008-09 starters—Anthony Goods, Lawrence Hill, and Mitch Johnson—had graduated, and a fourth starter, Josh Owens, would be lost to the team for the entire 2009-10 season due to medical reasons. Landry Fields, now a senior, was the only returning starter.

More often than not, the starters alongside Fields in 2009-10 consisted of a frontline of sophomore Jack Trotter, and sophomore transfer Andrew Zimmerman, and a backcourt of sophomore guards Jeremy Green and

Jarrett Mann. Except for Fields and Green, it was neither an experienced group nor a high-scoring group. But it was a tough, hustling, and reasonably solid defensive group. The sixth man in 2009-10, senior guard Drew Shiller, provided Johnny Dawkins with both a scoring weapon and a hustle component from the bench.

As expected, the Cardinal struggled a bit out of the gate in 2009-10. The team went 2-2 in its first four games, with home wins over Cal Poly and Florida A&M, a home loss to Oral Roberts, and a road loss at San Diego. The squad then headed to Cancun, Mexico, for a four-team Thanksgiving tournament, to be joined there by Cleveland State, Virginia, and Kentucky.

In what many considered a mild upset, Stanford got by Virginia in the first-round game on November 24, 2009, by the score of 57-52. Next up was a monster opponent—the preseason's #1-ranked team, Kentucky. The Wildcats had a roster full of future NBA players, albeit most of them freshmen. The marquee names were John Wall, DeMarcus Cousins, Eric Bledsoe, and Patrick Patterson.

It was, metaphorically and literally, a David and Goliath matchup. But the Cardinal, as the figurative David, brought more than a few slingshots to the Moon Palace resort ballroom, which served as the makeshift, 1,000-seat basketball arena for the tournament. Thanks to Landry Fields's consistent free-throw shooting and some big first half three-point baskets from Jeremy Green and Drew Shiller, Stanford found itself in the lead at halftime, 38-32.

The Cardinal maintained its advantage, holding a four-point lead with 7:38 remaining in the game. Kentucky clawed back, however, and tied the score, 61-61, on John Wall's 12-foot jump shot with 33 seconds left to play. Five seconds later, in an on-court scrum, Landry Fields was fouled and made both free throws. Stanford now led, 63-61. Kentucky did not call timeout. Wildcat guard John Wall quickly dribbled the ball upcourt, got the ball to DeMarcus Cousins on the block, and Cousins was able to get a shot off. The field-goal attempt missed, but Cousins was fouled. Twelve seconds remained.

Cousins, the 6′ 11″ freshman, missed the first free throw. Trying to miss the second, he succeeded, but the ball was rebounded by Stanford's Jarrett Mann. Two free-throw opportunities lay ahead for Mann. Ten seconds remained. Stanford was on the cusp of an enormous upset.

Unfortunately for the Cardinal, however, Jarrett Mann missed both free throws. Receiving the ball via the inbound pass, Kentucky's John Wall weaved his way downcourt, drove the right side of the key and crashed into Andrew Zimmerman, who had set himself defensively in the lane. The whistle went against Zimmerman.

Coolly, Wall hit both pressure free throws, sending the game to overtime. In the extra period, the Wildcats completely stifled the Cardinal, holding Stanford without a field-goal and outscoring Stanford 10-2 to emerge with a 73-65 win. It had been a great effort by Stanford. Playing against a team with eight future NBA players, including the #1 overall NBA Draft pick seven months later in John Wall, the Cardinal had nearly pulled off an epic upset win.

The 2009-10 Cardinal finished the non-conference season with a 6-6 record. This, coupled with a preseason media poll that predicted a last-place finish for Stanford in the Pac-10 race, did not engender much optimism for Cardinal fans heading into the opening week of conference play. The Cardinal did lose the conference opener at Cal, 92-66. But once again a challenging week of Dawkins practices ensued, and Stanford bounced back at home the following weekend against both USC and UCLA.

Against a ten-win USC team that had won its eight most recent games, the Cardinal played its best defensive game of the season to date, holding the Trojans to 42% field-goal shooting. Stanford's offense wasn't great, however, and when USC's Leonard Washington hit a three-point basket with 32 seconds remaining in the second half, the game was tied at 53.

Jarrett Mann was intentionally fouled six seconds later—the same Jarrett Mann who had missed the two potentially game-clinching free throws against Kentucky in Cancun six weeks earlier. What happened next was redemption for Mann. He hit one of his two free-throw attempts, putting Stanford ahead by one point. USC held the ball for the last shot, but missed two field-goal attempts in the final five seconds, giving Stanford a 54-53 win.

The game two nights later against UCLA featured more excellent Cardinal defense and a whole lot of Jeremy Green offense. The result was a second consecutive upset win for Stanford. With Green exploding for 30 points and Stanford's defense—keyed by Jarrett Mann on the perimeter—forcing 22 Bruin turnovers, Stanford defeated UCLA, 70-59.

Although Stanford would struggle the remainder of the 2009-2010 campaign, it managed to improve its conference record by one game as compared to the 2008-09 season, achieving seven Pac-10 victories. Included among the wins were home and road sweeps of the Oregon schools, both weeks of which Landry Fields was named Pac-10 Player of the Week. In the home win over Oregon State, the Cardinal defense held the Beavers to just 35 points for the entire game.

At the conclusion of the 2009-10 season, Landry Fields was named first-team All-Pac-10. More than a few Pac-10 observers believed that Fields should have been selected Pac-10 Player of the Year instead of Jerome Randle from Cal, the conference's regular season champion. In 2009-10, Fields finished with a conference-best 22 points-per-game scoring average—Stanford's highest per-game scoring average since Adam Keefe's 25 points-per-game average eighteen years earlier. Fields also was second in the Pac-10 in rebounding with 8.8 rebounds per game. Fields was also first in the Pac-10 with 36.3 minutes played per game and fourth in steals per game with 1.6. He also made 49% of his field-goal attempts. By any measure, Landry Fields's 2009-10 senior season was one of the greatest individual seasons in Stanford Basketball history.

With its 7-11 regular season conference record, Stanford earned a #7 seed in the 2010 Pac-10 Tournament. In the first round of the tournament at Staples Center, Stanford faced #2-seed Arizona State. One more time, the 2009-10 Cardinal defied expectation, utilizing big doses of Jeremy Green's and Landry Fields's skills on offense—as well as the surprising scoring contribution of a little-used bench player—in the game against the Sun Devils.

Leading by just one point at halftime, Stanford increased the lead to seven points, 42-35, with 13:19 remaining. Landry Fields then scored the next eight points of the game—three field goals, including a three-point basket, plus a free throw—over a mere 70-second stretch of elapsed game-clock time to give Stanford a commanding 50-35 advantage.

After ASU scored the next five points to cut the Stanford lead to ten points, the Cardinal outscored the Sun Devils 10-4 to go back up by 16 points with just 4:53 left. Five of Stanford's points during this stretch were scored by guard Emmanuel Igbinosa, an unrecruited walk-on who had scored just 65 points in 2009-10 after having scored just six points in 2008-09.

Igbinosa finished the game with 12 points—a career high—to join Jeremy Green (18 points) and Landry Fields (17 points) in double figures as Stanford upset ASU, 70-61. It would be Stanford's final win of the season, as Stanford lost its Pac-10 Tournament semifinal game against Washington—with Emmanuel Igbinosa again scoring in double figures—and the Cardinal thereafter did not participate in any postseason tournament. Stanford finished the season with a 14-18 overall won-loss record.

In addition to Landry Fields earning first-team All-Pac-10 accolades, Jeremy Green earned All-Pac-10 second-team honors.

The bad news for Stanford going into the 2010-11 season was that it would be impossible to replace Landry Fields. The good news was that Jeremy Green, whose 16.6 points per game had been among the highest scoring averages in the Pac-10 in 2009-10, was back. Also back, after a one-year absence (for medical reasons) was Josh Owens. So too was the team's best defender, Jarrett Mann. All were juniors and, on a team with no seniors, each would be called upon to provide leadership for Stanford Basketball in 2010-11.

Another unique feature, besides the lack of even one senior team member, was the fact that *nine* freshmen were on the 15-man Cardinal roster in 2010-11—an all-time record number of frosh for a Stanford varsity basketball squad. Coach Dawkins had roamed far and wide in recruiting his first-year players: forward Dwight Powell prepped at the prestigious IMG Academy in Florida, center Stefan Nastic was from Canada, forward Josh Huestis arrived from Montana, forward John Gage and guard Aaron Bright each came from the Seattle area, and wing Anthony Brown was from Southern California.

Rounding out the frosh roster members were walk-on freshman Robbie Lemons, who had been California's leading prep scorer the prior year as a senior at Country Day High School in Sacramento, and fellow walk-ons Chris Barnum and Doug Mills. And there was technically a tenth freshman on the 2010-11 roster—forward Andy Brown. Brown, a star on (Santa Ana, CA) Mater Dei High School's state championship teams and an incoming freshman in the fall of 2009, had suffered a third ACL tear in August 2010 and would miss his second consecutive season in 2010-11.

One of the freshmen, Dwight Powell, was in the starting lineup as the season got underway against the University of San Diego on November 15, 2010, at Maples Pavilion. The five-star recruit scored seven points, grabbed four rebounds, recorded three assists and had a steal in his Cardinal debut. Powell started the USD game alongside four juniors: guards Jeremy Green and Jarrett Mann, center Josh Owens, and forward Jack Trotter.

Good defense was an early theme of the 2010-11 Stanford Basketball campaign. Stanford won six of its first eight games, allowing only one of those opponents to score more than 65 points. The two losses came during a three-day Thanksgiving weekend tournament in Anaheim, the 76 Classic. One was a three-point loss to a very good Murray State team in the opening round; the other was a 12-point loss to Tulsa. In neither game did the Cardinal have Jeremy Green, the team's most potent weapon on offense. Green had been laid up by a stomach virus throughout the weekend.

Stanford ventured on its first non-California road trip the week before Christmas, and the young team clearly suffered growing pains. The Cardinal lost by a double-digit margin at Butler—later to be a Final Four team that season as it had been the prior season—and at Oklahoma State. Returning home to Palo Alto, Stanford's final non-conference game before the start of Pac-10 play was another defensive gem—a 60-44 win over Yale. The Cardinal held the Bulldogs to just 31.7% shooting for the game.

Entering conference play in January 2011, Stanford's record stood at 7 wins and 4 losses. Stanford's Pac-10 journey got off to a promising start. With Cal visiting Maples Pavilion in the opener, the freshman Dwight Powell rose up for a career-high 20 points, supplementing Jeremy Green's team-high 21 points as Stanford outscored the Golden Bears, 82-68.

The next weekend, in which the Cardinal would be playing its first two Pac-10 road games, featured a "high" and a very low "low." On Thursday, January 6, 2011, the Cardinal summoned some good defensive play in a 55-41 win at Arizona State. Stanford held ASU to just 35% field-goal shooting, including just 1 of 14 from three-point range. As positive as the ASU road win was, the ensuing game—and weekend—in Tucson proved to be a negative experience on multiple fronts.

The first negative thing was a national tragedy. On Saturday, January 8, 2011, Congresswoman Gabrielle Giffords was critically wounded in a shooting at a Tucson storefront, which resulted in a postponement of the Stanford-Arizona basketball game scheduled for that day. The game was played 24 hours later, in a more somber-than-usual McKale Center. Although Josh Owens (18 points) and Jeremy Green (15 points) helped keep Stanford in the game—the Cardinal trailed by just five points with four minutes to play—Arizona ultimately prevailed, 67-57.

With its conference record 2-1, the Cardinal returned home to play the Pac-10's highest-ranked team, the #18-ranked Washington Huskies. Washington, the Pac-10's first-place team with a 4-0 record, was also the only conference team that Johnny Dawkins had not, in his three-year Stanford tenure, yet defeated. Once again, a week of focused, challenging practices would produce a mighty payoff.

Stanford played superbly in the first half and entered the locker room at halftime with a 29-28 lead. During the first nine minutes of the second half, however, Washington outscored the Cardinal 21-9 to open up a 49-38 advantage. But then it was Stanford's turn. Over the next eight minutes, behind Jarrett Mann's five points—which included a breakaway dunk—and Jeremy Green's four points, Stanford outscored the Huskies 15-2 to retake the lead, 53-51. Just over three minutes remained in the game.

Washington then tied the game. Dwight Powell's layup then untied it, 55-53, with 1:44 left. Following a Stanford free throw and a UW three-point basket, which tied the game at 56, Josh Owens hit a midrange jumper with 29 seconds to go to put the Cardinal up by two points. The Stanford defense dug in from there, as two last-second Husky field-goal attempts missed the mark. Final score: Stanford 58 – Washington 56.

For the third time in his Stanford tenure, Johnny Dawkins had coached the Cardinal to a victory over a Top 25 opponent. Following the win, Stanford's Pac-10 record was 3-1, and its overall mark was 10-4 to that point in the 2010-11 season. But there the winning momentum would stop. During the ensuing stretch of twelve conference games, Stanford twice suffered four-game losing streaks and went 3-9 over that stretch of twelve Pac-10 games.

The reason for the losses was not the defense—in seven of those nine losses, the Cardinal held its Pac-10 foe to less than 70 points. The problem for Stanford was finding a consistent supporting cast of *scorers* to help Jeremy Green. In the nine losses during that difficult 3-9 stretch, Stanford averaged just 62 points per game—with Green scoring nearly *40%* of the team's points in those games. In a four-game stretch in February, 2011, Green converted *twelve* consecutive three-point field-goal attempts, the second-highest number of consecutive "made" three-point baskets in NCAA Division 1 history.

In the latter weeks of the season, however, supplemental scoring sources for Stanford began to percolate. On February 26, 2011, Josh Owens had a brilliant 31-point, 11-rebound afternoon in the new Matthew Knight Arena in Eugene, OR, as the Cardinal blasted the Ducks, 88-71. Three nights later, freshman Anthony Brown pumped in a career-best 21 points in a 77-66 non-conference win over Seattle University at Maples Pavilion.

Stanford closed the 2010-11 regular season with a loss at Cal. Still, the Cardinal's 7-11 conference won-loss record was no worse than the prior season's mark. The Cardinal had virtually no chance at a postseason tournament invitation—absent a miracle run to win the Pac-10 Tournament—but it did have a chance to finish the year with a .500-or-better won-loss record.

Stanford traveled to Los Angeles and the 2011 Pac-10 Tournament with a 15-15 record. As the #8 seed, the Cardinal faced the #9-seed

Oregon State. The first half against the Beavers was Stanford's worst half of the season on the offensive end. The Cardinal missed 30 of 34 first-half field-goal attempts—including a missed breakaway dunk attempt by Mann. Still, because of its excellent defense, Stanford trailed OSU by only eight points at halftime, 26-18.

A 16-8 explosion by Stanford in the first four minutes of the second half tied the game at 34. Oregon State then rallied to retake the lead, 48-43, with eight minutes remaining. From that point forward until the final minute, OSU held tenuous leads ranging from five to two points. Twice within the final 20 seconds, Stanford pulled to within one point. But the Cardinal could get no closer. A desperation half-court shot by Jeremy Green at the buzzer missed its target, and Stanford's 2010-11 season ended at Staples Center with a 69-67 loss to the Beavers.

At season's end, Jeremy Green was named first-team All-Pac-10. Although only a junior, Green had played his final Stanford game. Green opted to leave the program to pursue professional basketball opportunities following the 2010-11 season. Despite having played only three years, Green at the time of his departure was second on the all-time Stanford Basketball list for career three-point baskets.

Stanford finished the 2010-11 campaign with a 15-16 record. Stanford's offensive rating, according to the basketball website *Basketball Reference*, was just 217th out of the 345 NCAA Division 1 teams. But the defensive rating had been in the upper third of Division 1 teams, and the progress of Johnny Dawkins's team on the defensive end of the court would form the foundation for significant program success that lay just around the corner.

Stanford welcomed back eleven lettermen at the start of the 2011-12 campaign—Jeremy Green having been the only roster loss from the prior season. And they welcomed one significant newcomer, freshman guard Chasson Randle. Randle, a 6′ 1″ graduate of Rock Island High School in Rock Island, IL, had been a first-team all-state selection in Illinois and in his senior prep season had led his team to the Illinois 3A basketball championship.

Chasson Randle earned a spot as a starting guard for Stanford in the 2011-12 opener at home against Central Arkansas. The freshman's presence in the lineup paid immediate dividends for the Cardinal. Randle scored 15 points and had four assists in 27 minutes of action in Stanford's 91-52 opening game triumph.

The win over Central Arkansas was the first of four consecutive double-digit wins for the Cardinal to open the 2011-12 season. Following the Central Arkansas win, Stanford notched home wins over Fresno State (75-59) and Colorado State (64-52), then snagged a road win at UC Davis (70-49). In the Colorado State win, junior reserve guard Gabriel Harris tied a career high with 12 points, which included a spectacular 70-foot backcourt-heave basket as the first-half buzzer sounded. It was reportedly just the second time that a basket from beyond the half-court line had been made in a Stanford Basketball game at Maples Pavilion.

Stanford put its 4-0 record to the test as it traveled to New York City for the semifinals and finals of the Preseason NIT, the earlier wins over Fresno State and Colorado State having constituted the preliminary rounds of the tournament. On Thanksgiving Eve 2011, Stanford faced Oklahoma State in the semifinal contest at Madison Square Garden.

With center Josh Owens hitting his first nine shots from the floor on the way to a game-high 21 points, and with each of starting guards Chasson Randle and Aaron Bright contributing 15 points, the Cardinal eased past the Cowboys, 82-67. An 18-0 Stanford scoring run beginning in the final minutes of the first half and continuing through the opening minutes of the second half—giving the Cardinal a commanding 17-point lead—was a key factor in the win. "In our huddle before the game I told the team it doesn't matter if we're at the Garden, back at Stanford or in a playground, we had to come out and try to win," said Owens after the game. "It was a great experience to win here."

Another notable item in the game was that redshirt sophomore Andy Brown, having endured three ACL tears and three grueling rehabilitation periods over the prior 34 months, made his Stanford debut. It was just one minute of action, but the joy of seeing Andy Brown in a Stanford Basketball game for the first time was felt by every Stanford player, coach, administrator, and likewise by many Stanford fans. The win was also notable in that it made Stanford's all-time won-loss record at Madison Square Garden a remarkable 11-3 dating back to the first game a Stanford Basketball team played at MSG: the Hank Luisetti–led Stanford upset of Long Island University in 1936.

Even better, the win earned the Cardinal a spot in the 2011 Preseason NIT championship game. The opponent in the championship game was a tough one on a number of fronts. The opponent was undefeated and #5-ranked Syracuse, for whom a game in New York City was a quasi-home game. It also would be the first-ever matchup in basketball between the two universities.

Stanford battled the Orange for forty tough minutes. The Cardinal led at halftime by one point, 25-24. The Cardinal managed to maintain a lead throughout the second half, and when sophomore reserve forward John Gage swished a three-point shot with 6:11 remaining—part of Gage's ten-point second half—Stanford's advantage was suddenly increased to seven points, 58-51.

With that seven-point advantage, Stanford had four opportunities to increase its lead on its next possession—and could not do so. Syracuse got the ball back, and forward Kris Joseph hit a lucky, 25-foot, three-point bank shot from the left wing with 4:42 remaining to keep the Orange in the game. From there, the Orange exploded, forcing multiple Stanford turnovers and scoring basket after basket. By the time the final buzzer sounded, an 18-5 end-of-game Syracuse scoring run had turned that earlier seven-point Stanford advantage into a 69-63 Syracuse victory and the 2011 Preseason NIT championship for the Orange.

Once again Aaron Bright and Chasson Randle scored in double figures for Stanford. The Stanford starting guards couldn't have known it at the time, but the Syracuse game wouldn't be the last time, that 2011-12 season, that Bright and Randle would have a joint double-figure scoring game at Madison Square Garden.

Stanford was 5-1, and had held all six opponents—including the nation's #5-ranked team Syracuse—to less than 70 points. And that trend of good defense would continue the remainder of the non-conference portion of the 2011-12 schedule. Stanford easily won its next two games, a home win over Pacific (79-37) and a road win at Seattle University (72-49), in large part because its defense held each opponent to sub-50 point scoring totals.

Back home at Maples Pavilion against an eventual 2011 NCAA Tournament Sweet 16 team, North Carolina State, Stanford overcame a nine-point deficit with six minutes remaining to edge the Wolfpack, 76-72. Although the Cardinal had finally allowed an opponent to score more than 70 points, a 45-point second-half on offense was the key factor in the Cardinal win. Josh Owens's 19 points and 7 rebounds led the way for Stanford.

Two home wins, over the University of San Diego (75-55) and Bethune-Cookman (75-56), came next. The final non-conference opponent, Butler, presented a formidable challenge—the Bulldogs had a program good enough to have reached the NCAA Tournament championship game in each of the prior two seasons. Despite 17 points from Josh Owens, 16 points from Chasson Randle and 11 points from Aaron Bright, the Cardinal suffered just its second loss of the season, 71-66, to the Bulldogs at Maples Pavilion on December 22, 2011.

Stanford's record stood at 10-2 entering the beginning of conference play. In 2011-12, the Pac-10 had expanded to become the Pac-12, with the addition of Utah and Colorado. The conference schedule began with a December 29, 2011 home game against UCLA. The Bruins were riding a five-game winning streak and had beaten Stanford in nine of the past ten meetings between the two schools dating back to 2007.

Stanford led by one point at halftime, 24-23, although it had led by as many as eleven points during the first half. A pressing zone defense had helped ignite UCLA's late first-half comeback, but in the second half Stanford found its rhythm on offense, particularly from beyond the three-point arc. During one flurry in the second half, Chasson Randle hit two threes and Anthony Brown another to give Stanford a 56-51 lead late in the game.

UCLA came back, however, cutting the Cardinal advantage to one point in the final minute. Down 60-59, the Bruins had a chance to win in the final seconds. With three seconds remaining, UCLA guard Lazeric Jones tried a floater in the lane. But sophomore reserve forward Josh Huestis swatted away Jones's shot attempt to give Stanford the one-point victory.

A 51-43 home win over USC followed, with Aaron Bright scoring 16 points. The New Year's Eve victory featured more outstanding Stanford defense, with the Cardinal holding the Trojans to just 34.5% field-goal shooting for the entire game.

A road trip to the Oregon schools was up next. The Cardinal dropped a 78-67 decision to the Ducks in the first game of the road trip. It was an unremarkable game. Two nights later in Corvallis, however, Stanford would play one of the most historic games in the program's history.

The Cardinal played a sloppy first half defensively and trailed 43-36 at halftime. But a strong second half on offense put Stanford in a position to win the game in the final seconds, and it appeared that Stanford had done exactly that when—with the game tied at 77—Josh Owens put a follow-shot through the hoop with the buzzer sounding. But the replay showed Owens's shot had left his hand a half-second after the clock hit 0:00. The referees disallowed the basket. The game would go extra time—with the phrase "extra time" being a severe understatement.

In the first overtime, Anthony Brown's potential game-winning shot missed its mark, sending the game into a second overtime. In the second overtime period, Chasson Randle had a chance to win the game with a short jumper, but the shot was blocked by Oregon State's 6′ 10″ forward Eric Moreland. In the third overtime, Anthony Brown's three-pointer tied the game at 95 with 15 seconds remaining. In its final possession of the third overtime, Oregon State had two opportunities—both long jump-shot attempts—to claim the game. Both field-goal attempts missed. So it was on to the fourth overtime. Only one Stanford Basketball game had ever gone four overtimes—a Stanford–USC game way back in 1922.

In the fourth overtime, Stanford initially went ahead by five points, 100-95. Oregon State then scored the next four points. With 18 seconds left and Stanford leading by one point, OSU stole the ball but missed two shots, the latter of which was rebounded by Josh Huestis who was fouled on the rebound. Huestis made one of two free throws, putting Stanford up by two points with five seconds left to play. Hurrying the ball upcourt, OSU's Roberto Nelson had an open three-point shot in the final second of the fourth overtime, which would have given the Beavers the win. Nelson's shot rimmed off. The final score in four overtimes: Stanford 103 – Oregon State 101.

The game's final numbers were mind-boggling: 171 field-goal attempts, 108 rebounds, 54 fouls, 48 three-point tries, 41 assists, 14 ties, and 13 lead changes. The game took three hours and eight minutes to play. An average 40-minute college basketball game typically requires less than two hours to complete.

Stanford was 3-1 in the Pac-12 standings following the historic OSU win, but the Cardinal would experience periodic turbulence as the conference schedule unfolded. A home sweep of the Pac-12's newest members, Utah (68-65) and Colorado (84-64), took place the following weekend, with Josh Huestis scoring 13 points in each game in his increasingly significant off-the-bench role. But Stanford lost both games the ensuing weekend in the state of Washington, dropping 81-69 and 76-63 decisions at Washington State and Washington, respectively.

The Cardinal continued its win-two, lose-two pattern the next two weeks. A split of a two-game home series against the Arizona schools was followed by a split of two road games in Los Angeles against UCLA (72-61 loss) and USC (59-47 win). The win at USC was Stanford's first in the Galen Center in the six years of the building's existence. Chasson Randle led the Cardinal in scoring against the Trojans with 16 points, including four second-half three-point baskets.

Stanford's final five games of the Pac-12 regular season schedule continued the pattern—win, loss, win, loss, win. The most impressive win was a 24-point win at Colorado, the only home conference loss in 2011-12 suffered by the Buffaloes, which a few weeks later would reach the second round of the NCAA Tournament. The most galling Stanford loss during those five final regular season games was a 58-57 stinker at Utah—a team that would finish the conference schedule with a 3-15 record.

Following the frustrating Utah loss, coach Johnny Dawkins—who had been tinkering with the starting lineup at various junctures during the year—decided on a new starting lineup of senior Josh Owens at center, senior Andrew Zimmerman and sophomore Anthony Brown at the forward positions, and freshman Chasson Randle and senior Jarrett Mann at the guard spots.

It would be the 12th different starting lineup used by Stanford in 2011-12. It would be, as things unfolded, the starting lineup used by Johnny Dawkins for the remainder of the 2011-12 season. And that lineup would produce magic by the end of March 2012.

Having finished the regular season portion of the schedule with an overall record of 20-10, including a 10-8 mark in the Pac-12, Stanford was the #7 seed in the 2012 Pac-12 Tournament at the Staples Center in Los Angeles. The Cardinal faced #10-seed Arizona State in the tournament opener. In one of the greatest performances ever by a Stanford freshman basketball player, Chasson Randle scored 27 points in the first half—helping Stanford build a 50-30 halftime lead—and the Cardinal went on to crush the Sun Devils, 85-65. Randle finished the game with a career-high 30 points. The freshman was 7 of 11 in field-goal shooting, including 6 of 8 from three-point range, and he was 10 for 12 from the free-throw line.

Stanford, however, could not maintain the momentum in the ensuing Pac-12 Tournament game at Staples. The Cardinal fell to a 24-win Cal team, 77-71, in the tournament quarterfinals. Despite its 21-11 record, Stanford was not forecast as one of the teams that would be extended an NCAA Tournament bid, and in fact the Cardinal did not receive one. For the second time in four seasons, however, coach Johnny Dawkins would be taking his team to postseason play. Stanford earned a bid to the 2012 NIT, receiving a #3 seed in the one of the NIT's four eight-team brackets.

Coach Johnny Dawkins became the first coach in Stanford history to win as many as 20 games in his first season (2009) and, as of 2015, had compiled a remarkable 13-2 record in postseason (NCAA/NIT) games.

XIII. Johnny Dawkins on the March

More Stanford Postseason Magic

Stanford entered the 2012 Postseason NIT as a team almost completely without postseason experience. Only Josh Owens, Jarrett Mann, and Jack Trotter had ever played in a postseason basketball game for Stanford, and only Owens had played meaningful minutes. The NIT began for Stanford on Tuesday, March 13, 2012, with a home game against a Cleveland State team that had won 22 games in 2011-12.

In part because of its rebounding prowess, the visitors essentially played even with Stanford in the first half, trailing the Cardinal by one point at halftime, 31-30. The second half was a completely different story. Getting solid scoring performances from both Josh Owens and Anthony Brown, as well as a huge scoring boost off the bench from Aaron Bright, Stanford exploded past the Vikings in the second half—at one point in the second half, the Cardinal advantage was as much as 20 points. The final margin of victory for Stanford was 11 points, 76-65.

Josh Owens finished with 15 points on 6 of 9 in field-goal shooting. Anthony Brown had 15 points and a career-high 12 rebounds. Aaron Bright scored all 17 of his points in the second half, including 8 of 10 from the free-throw line. Demoted from his starting spot in the Cardinal lineup in mid-February, Bright seemed to be thriving in his sixth-man role, providing consistent scoring production on offense when summoned from the bench by Johnny Dawkins.

And Aaron Bright's off-the-bench scoring contribution would be even greater in the next game—Stanford's second-round NIT matchup against Illinois State on Monday, March 19, 2012. The Illinois State game, also played at Maples Pavilion, featured one of the NCAA's most accurate long-range shooting guard tandems in Nic Moore and Tyler Brown.

Moore and Brown made five three-pointers, combined, in the first half as the Redbirds were within three points of Stanford at halftime, 41-38. In the first eight minutes of the second half, on the strength of four more three-point baskets, Illinois State outscored the Cardinal 23-11 to take a 61-52 lead. Three minutes later, it was 71-60 in favor of the Redbirds. Illinois State had made 14 three-point baskets, and all signs pointed to a second-round Stanford exit from the 2012 NIT.

But Stanford still had a run to put forth. Or, more specifically, an Aaron to put forth. As in Aaron Bright.

During the incredible three-and-a-half minutes that followed, Bright scored 11 of the 13 points that Stanford scored during a 13-2 Cardinal run, and he assisted on the other two points scored (a basket by Josh Owens). With 5:40 remaining in the second half, the Stanford deficit was suddenly just one point, 74-73. The final 5:40 was a jumble of offensive fouls, turnovers and missed opportunities. With the game tied at 78, Stanford had the ball last, but Chasson Randle missed a three-point attempt with two seconds remaining. For a third consecutive postseason, Stanford would be playing an overtime game.

In the overtime, the tense manner of play continued. Eight times the lead changed in the first 3:30 of the overtime. But the ninth and final lead change went Stanford's way. Chasson Randle's three-point basket with 1:18 remaining in overtime put the Cardinal up for good, and an Aaron Bright basket and two Anthony Brown free throws sealed the win for Stanford, 92-88.

Aaron Bright's final stat line was impressive: a career-high 29 points, an 11-of-13 field-goal shooting game—including 6 of 7 from beyond the three-point line—and six assists. "I thought it was Aaron's best game he's had here," said Johnny Dawkins after the game. "I have not seen many players who played better than Aaron did tonight." Stanford won despite Illinois State making 15 of 30 shots from three-point range and converting 19 of 21 free-throws attempts.

Stanford, on the other hand, was one win away from a second 2011-12 in-season trip to Madison Square Garden. Stanford had received an enormous break going into its NIT quarterfinal-round game. Arizona, the top seed in Stanford's eight-team NIT regional bracket, had been upset at home in an earlier round, and therefore—instead of Arizona—Stanford's quarterfinal opponent would be Nevada. Once again, due to the Cardinal's better seeding, the game would be played at Maples Pavilion.

The NIT quarterfinal game wasn't close. Invigorated by its sudden postseason success and hungry for a postseason tournament trip to Madison

Square Garden, the Cardinal burst out to a 42-27 halftime lead, and at one point in the second half led by 32 points. Stanford cruised to victory thereafter, winning by the lopsided final score of Stanford 84 – Nevada 56.

Four Stanford players scored in double figures: Josh Owens and Chasson Randle scored 15 points apiece, reserve forward Josh Huestis added 12 points, and Aaron Bright contributed 10 points in another solid off-the-bench performance. For the game, Stanford made a sizzling 57% of its field-goal attempts and was a very good 14 of 17 from the free-throw line.

So, indeed, it was back to the Big Apple for Stanford Basketball. The NIT semifinal opponent for Stanford at Madison Square Garden was a tough one: 25-win University of Massachusetts. But the Cardinal, already a postseason-toughened unit, received an additional "toughness" boost a few minutes prior to the game. Through the efforts of Cardinal assistant coach Charles Payne, 13-time Pro Bowl linebacker Ray Lewis of the Baltimore Ravens, perhaps even better known presently as a master of motivational pregame oratory, was invited to speak in the Cardinal locker room.

Lewis delivered a Super Bowl–worthy rallying speech. "Leave your legacy!" thundered Lewis, after slapping fives with each Stanford player.

Still, the UMass game was a battle. Stanford led by just three points at halftime, 36-33. Both teams were having difficulty making shots. In the second half, it was more of the same. The score was tied with nine minutes remaining, and one minute later UMass took a one-point lead.

But then Anthony Brown, whose outstanding defense was a contributing factor in UMass's shooting struggles, dialed up some offense. The redshirt sophomore hit a three-pointer to push the Cardinal back on top by two points, then later scored seven points during an 11-3 scoring run that put Stanford in control of the game. With Chasson Randle saddled with four fouls during the latter part of the second half, Anthony Brown's offense was indispensable. He finished with a season-best 18 points and was a primary reason Stanford prevailed over the Minutemen, 74-64.

Among the starters, Josh Owens and Chasson Randle supplemented Brown's efforts by contributing 15 and 12 points respectively. And once again Aaron Bright was an effective spark plug on offense from off the bench. Playing 28 of the 40 minutes, Bright finished with 13 points.

Stanford had made it to the NIT championship game. The other semifinal matchup had pitted Pac-12 foe Washington—which had been the conference's regular season champion—and Minnesota. The Golden Gophers got past the Huskies, meaning it would be the Cardinal and Golden Gophers for the NIT title on Thursday night, March 29, 2012.

For Stanford, besides the hunger for a postseason title, there was a bit of score-settling motivation. The Cardinal had lost the Preseason NIT championship game at Madison Square Garden four months earlier, having given up a late lead in that November loss to Syracuse. To a man, the Stanford Basketball team was determined not to leave New York City a loser for a second time in 2011-12.

The NIT title game was tightly contested in the first half. The Cardinal was down by four points with eight minutes to go in the first half, 21-17, but then went on a 12-0 run to take a 29-21 lead three minutes later. Meanwhile, the Cardinal defense had been operating on full throttle throughout the first half, forcing Minnesota to miss 16 of its last 19 shots of the first half. Stanford's lead was six points, 31-25, at the intermission.

In the second half, the Cardinal seized control. A 16-6 scoring run in the first eight minutes of the second half put Stanford on top by 16 points, 47-31. Stanford's defensive effort, not only from Josh Huestis and Anthony Brown but also from Andrew Zimmerman and Jarrett Mann—each of whom had three steals—continued to lock up Minnesota ball-handlers, passers, and shooters. The game was over long before the final buzzer sounded, as Stanford scored 44 points and shot 57% in the second half. The final score in the 2012 NIT championship game: Stanford 75 – Minnesota 51.

For the third time in school history, a Stanford Basketball team had claimed a postseason tournament championship. Joining Stanford's 1941-42 NCAA championship team and Stanford's 1990-91 NIT champion team in hoisting a postseason trophy was the 2011-12 NIT championship squad. For seniors Josh Owens, Jarrett Mann, Andrew Zimmerman, and Jack Trotter, as well as retiring assistant coach Dick Davey, it meant ending their college careers with a postseason tournament victory—something very few people in college basketball are able to do.

For the former-starter-turned-sixth-man Aaron Bright, it meant something extremely improbable: the 2012 NIT Most Outstanding Player Award. Bright had a team-high-tying 15 points in the title game, giving him 84 points for the five-game tournament. Bright's statistical achievements in the NIT were truly impressive: 64% field-goal shooting—including 67% from three-point range—together with 88% shooting from the free-throw line during the five-game NIT run.

Aaron Bright's 16.8 points-per-game average led Stanford in NIT scoring, while Josh Owens averaged 14 points and each of Chasson Randle and Anthony Brown averaged 12 points. Randle and Brown shot 50% and 48% from three-point distance, respectively, in the tournament.

Sophomore Dwight Powell also took a major step forward in the postseason, averaging 9 points and 6 rebounds in a reserve role and making 65% of his field-goal attempts during the NIT.

Stanford's defense was equally impressive: the opposition shot just 38% over the five games, Stanford committed 23 fewer turnovers than did its opponents, and the Cardinal had 20 more steals than its foes. And this interesting statistic was stamped forever on the 2011-12 team: In 20 of the 21 games in which Stanford scored at least 70 points during the season—including the five postseason NIT contests—Stanford had won the game.

"This season was a little bit of a roller coaster ride for us," said Coach Dawkins of the 2011-12 campaign. "We started off so strong, battled some adversity in the middle and ended as strong as we ever could have imagined. When we look back, I just think we have grown together. We have grown up."

Indeed—Stanford Basketball under Coach Dawkins had grown greatly, with a postseason legacy having been generated and the promise of future success very much in evidence. With at least two years of eligibility remaining for each of Dwight Powell, Josh Huestis, Anthony Brown, Aaron Bright, and Chasson Randle—and for several other players from the 2011-12 team as well—it very much seemed as though higher postseason goals could be reached by Stanford Basketball in the years ahead.

Nevertheless, going into the 2012-13 season, everyone knew the 26-11 NIT championship season would be a difficult act to follow. Gone were Josh Owens's all-around game in the paint, Andrew Zimmerman's exemplary work ethic and leadership, Jarrett Mann's perimeter defense and on-court toughness, and Jack Trotter's off-the-bench contributions.

Also absent in 2012-13 was another valuable Stanford Basketball contributor, as associate head coach Dick Davey had opted to retire. The former longtime Santa Clara head coach had been an invaluable aide to Johnny Dawkins as well as to Cardinal players during his four-year coaching tenure on the Farm. On road trips, one often would frequently see Dawkins and Davey in airports or on planes conversing privately together about personnel, strategy, recruiting or whatever else was pertinent to Stanford Basketball.

The 2012-13 season began with wins over San Francisco (74-62, at the Oracle Arena in Oakland), Cal State Fullerton (81-68) and Alcorn State (69-51), followed by a loss to Belmont (70-62) —the latter three games having been played at Maples Pavilion. In the Belmont game, the Cardinal shot just 31% for the game and just 2 of 19 from three-point range.

The early season starting lineup for Stanford in 2012-13 included juniors Dwight Powell and Josh Huestis at the forwards, and a three-guard alignment of Chasson Randle, Aaron Bright, and Anthony Brown. But the Belmont game would be Anthony Brown's last of 2012-13, as a chronic hip injury would sideline him for the remainder of the season.

Given the graduation losses of Josh Owens, Andrew Zimmerman, and Jarrett Mann, the additional loss of Anthony Brown was a blow the 2012-13 team could ill afford. Brown had started 21 of the 37 games in 2012-13—including all five postseason NIT games—and his shooting accuracy and defense were key components in Stanford's drive to the NIT title. Those skills would have greatly helped the 2012-13 team.

Three games in the Bahamas from November 22-24, at the Battle for Atlantis Tournament, produced one win and two losses. After playing solidly but ultimately falling to #13-ranked Missouri 78-70 in the opening game, and then a day later blasting Northern Iowa 66-50, Stanford in its third game found itself tied with Minnesota—its NIT title game opponent eight months earlier—in the final seconds. A crazy sequence followed.

Minnesota had a baseline frontcourt inbound with ten seconds remaining in the game and the score tied 63-63. Dwight Powell, defending for Stanford, got a hand on the inbound pass, then tried to corral the loose ball before it went out of bounds along the frontcourt sideline. In so doing, the only thing Powell could do was bat the ball into Minnesota's backcourt. As the final few seconds ticked off, Minnesota guard Andre Hollins sprinted back and retrieved the ball in the backcourt, all the while being harassed by Chasson Randle. Hollins dribbled a couple of times, got to the halfcourt line and flung the ball toward the basket a half-second before the final buzzer sounded. Randle, trying only to bother the shooter Hollins but not touch him, nevertheless made mild contact with the Golden Gopher guard and the referee blew the whistle.

No time was left on the scoreboard clock. It would be three free throws for Andre Hollins, one of the best free-throw shooters in the nation. He made all three, making Minnesota a winner, 66-63.

The Minnesota game began a trend for Stanford in 2012-13—a trend of playing close-margin games. Between Thanksgiving and New Year's Day, Stanford played six non-conference games, and in only one of the games was the margin of victory or defeat greater than 12 points. Stanford won five of those six games, the only loss coming at #25-ranked North Carolina State, 88-79, a game in which Dwight Powell had an outstanding game of 23 points, eight rebounds and four assists. Included among the six games was a two-point win at Northwestern, 70-68, a game in which junior walk-on guard Robbie Lemons was a surprise starter and scored a career-high 12 points on four baskets from beyond the three-point arc.

The game at Northwestern was another of Stanford's close-outcome 2012-13 games. The Wildcats had possession of the ball in the final seconds, down by two points. Northwestern guard Tre Demps missed a potential game-tying shot with six seconds remaining, and Stanford's Andy Brown outhustled everyone on the court for the loose-ball rebound to secure the victory for the Cardinal.

Andy Brown—he of the three ACL injuries and the three grueling rehabilitation periods—was back and was getting more and more minutes as the 2012-13 campaign proceeded. After making 17 of 27 shots during the November games in his reserve role, Brown averaged 21 minutes of playing time per game in the six post-Thanksgiving non-conference games and scored a career-high 17 points in the home win over Seattle. Once Pac-12 play began, Andy Brown's contributions to the 2012-13 team would become even more significant.

The Pac-12 season began at the Galen Center in Los Angeles against USC. Stanford led by nine points at halftime, but its poor free-throw shooting in the second half allowed USC to come back, and with seven seconds remaining in the game, two free throws by USC guard Jio Fontan put the Trojans ahead, 71-69.

By this point in the game, Andy Brown had scored 17 points—including three three-pointers—and on its final possession, Coach Dawkins made sure Andy Brown was in the game for a potential game-winning shot opportunity. Chasson Randle worked the ball upcourt for Stanford in the final seconds, looked toward his teammates—including Andy Brown—on the wings but ultimately decided to drive the lane and shoot a floater. The shot missed, and Dwight Powell's rebound-dunk effort also was unsuccessful as time ran out.

The USC game was the last time Andy Brown would be a reserve. He was in the starting lineup two days later at UCLA, and started every game thereafter in 2012-13. Andy Brown, Aaron Bright, Chasson Randle, Josh Huestis, and Dwight Powell would be the starters the remainder of the season.

Stanford split its next six Pac-12 games, the last of which was a surprisingly dominating 29-point road win at Utah, 87-56. The leading scorer for Stanford in the Utah win was not one of the starters. Instead, it was 6′ 9″ junior forward John Gage. Gage, a "stretch 4"—which in basketball parlance means a power forward who is able to operate effectively well away from the basket and make long jump shots—put his considerable distance-shooting skills on display that night in Salt Lake City. Gage made all four of his three-point shot attempts, made 6 of 8 field-goal attempts overall, and finished the game with a career-high 19 points.

Following the Utah game, Stanford returned to Maples Pavilion the following weekend for games against the Oregon schools. Oregon in particular presented a big challenge—the Ducks were the #10-ranked team in the country. It was to be the best home weekend yet for the Cardinal in 2012-13.

Against Oregon, Stanford showed it could compete successfully against a top-ten-ranked team. Shooting 52% for the game, the Cardinal built up a 25-point lead in the first half, was never seriously challenged thereafter, and cruised to a 24-point victory over the Ducks. Josh Huestis and Dwight Powell each recorded double-doubles, with Huestis recording 14 points and 13 rebounds and Powell ringing up 12 points and 13 rebounds. Said Johnny Dawkins after the win over a top-ten-ranked opponent: "This definitely ranks up there as one of the better moments for our program."

And the winning momentum continued two nights later against Oregon State. Josh Huestis led the way for Stanford with 16 points and 13 rebounds in an 81-73 Cardinal win over the Beavers. Huestis also had a key block in the final minute of the game—with OSU down by only two points—to preserve the lead and help secure the victory for Stanford.

Josh Huestis's defense and rebounding were being increasingly noticed around college basketball. Earlier in the year he had had a 10-block game against Seattle, and he would end the year with 111 offensive rebounds, the highest number of offensive rebounds by a Stanford player in a season since Adam Keefe in 1991-92. Little wonder Huestis was headed for a spot on the All-Pac-12 Defensive Team at season's end.

Stanford was 5-4 in Pac-12 play following the Oregon State win, but could not keep the three-game winning streak going. The Cardinal dropped five of its next seven Pac-12 games, although none by more than eight points. In one of the two wins—a three-point road win at Arizona State—an Andy Brown steal of an ASU pass in the final seconds of the game kept the Sun Devils from a potential game-tying three-point shot attempt.

With its won-loss record 7-8 in the Pac-12 and 16-12 overall, Stanford prepared for its final three conference games. A frustrating two-point loss at home to Colorado—with Andy Brown tying his career-high of 17 points—was followed by another feel-good story in the home finale against Utah. Senior reserve guard Gabriel Harris, on a Stanford Basketball Senior Day in which he was the lone senior, scored a career-high 14 points, missing only one of seven shots in Stanford's 84-66 win over the Utes.

The regular season finale in Berkeley, against a 20-win Cal team with a 12-5 Pac-12 record, proved surprisingly easy. Chasson Randle scored 20 points, Josh Huestis added 18 points, and Aaron Bright had 16 points in an 83-70 Cardinal victory. The toughest part of the game for Stanford—indeed, for both teams—was a late-game scuffle in which two players and three assistant coaches from both schools were ejected.

The Pac-12 postseason tournament in Las Vegas was next. Stanford's only path to an NCAA Tournament berth was if the Cardinal could win four games in four days. Stanford in fact was unable to win even one game, although its first-round exit occurred in a thrilling game. In an overtime contest against Arizona State—a game in which two players each shorter than six feet tall would score at least 27 points to lead their teams in scoring—the Cardinal fell to the Sun Devils, 89-88.

Arizona State's 5′ 10″ freshman Jahii Carson scored a game-high 34 points in the game, but Stanford's 5′ 11″ Aaron Bright was equally brilliant with 27 points and 5 assists. Also notable for Stanford in the loss were the performances of Dwight Powell, who had 23 points and 9 rebounds, and Josh Huestis, who contributed 17 points and 9 rebounds.

With an overall won-loss record of 18-14, Stanford accepted a bid to the 2013 NIT. Although the Cardinal won its NIT opener in Maples Pavilion—a stomach-churning one-point win over Stephen F. Austin University during which Dwight Powell had 12 points, 15 rebounds, and four blocked shots—it could not keep the winning going, falling in Tuscaloosa to Alabama, 66-54, four days later. The loss to the Crimson Tide ended the Cardinal's 2012-13 season.

Stanford finished the 2012-13 campaign with a 19-15 record, including a 9-9 mark in the Pac-12. Dwight Powell's 14.9 points per game led the squad in scoring, with Chasson Randle, Josh Huestis, and Aaron Bright contributing scoring averages of 13.6, 10.5, and 9.3 points per game, respectively. Huestis led the team with nine rebounds per game, and he also recorded a team-high 71 blocks for the season.

On a down year for the Cardinal as far as team shooting percentages were concerned, Andy Brown was the shining star, making 48.5% of his field-goal attempts. From three-point range, John Gage was not only exceptional for the Cardinal—making 44.6% of his three-point shot attempts to lead the team—he in fact also led the entire Pac-12 in that category.

Dwight Powell was named first-team All-Pac-12 for 2012-13, while

Chasson Randle was named second-team All-Pac-12. Josh Huestis was honored as a first-team selection on the Pac-12 All-Defensive team. But Stanford Basketball in 2012-13 clearly was missing a piece that kept it from achieving more success. That missing piece was Anthony Brown's scoring and defense, which was unavailable due to Brown having been sidelined with the season-long hip injury.

Anthony Brown would be fully recovered from his hip surgery and rehabilitation by the time the 2013-14 season began. He, along with Dwight Powell, Josh Huestis, Aaron Bright, John Gage, and Stefan Nastic would be returning as fourth-year players in 2013-14. Andy Brown, too, was coming back, as a fifth-year senior. Chasson Randle, too, would be an upperclassman in 2013-14. In other words, it would be a very experienced, stable, and hungry-for-achievement Stanford Basketball team in 2013-14. The sixth Johnny Dawkins team sought new and higher goals—and it was very well positioned to reach them.

In part because of the upperclassmen-laden roster and its potential, Johnny Dawkins and his staff put together a challenging pre-conference schedule for the 2013-14 campaign. The Stanford Basketball point person in crafting the November and December portion of the schedule, Director of Basketball Operations Jeff LaMere, sought to schedule teams that he believed would reach the NCAA Tournament—the better to increase Stanford's "RPI" number, a metric used by the NCAA Tournament Committee to select at-large teams. LaMere's scheduling also sought, at the same time, to secure opponents who could provide good competition for the Cardinal as preparation for both Pac-12 conference and, hopefully, postseason tournament play. LaMere's efforts proved to be a spectacular success with regard to both objectives, as would become obvious in March 2014.

The 2013-14 Stanford Basketball campaign began on November 8 with a 72-68 win at Maples over Bucknell, an NCAA Tournament team the previous season. Chasson Randle scored 18 points, Dwight Powell added 17 points and 12 rebounds, and new starting center Stefan Nastic chipped in with 11 points and 6 rebounds. To Maples Pavilion fans in attendance, the enthusiasm surrounding Stanford's opening-game win was tempered by the realization that Andy Brown—who had suffered yet another ACL injury, his fourth, during the summer—would be lost to the team for 2013-14 and had played his last Stanford Basketball game.

Andy Brown had been a starter the final 20 games on 2012-13. Without Andy Brown, and having decided to use Aaron Bright as a spark plug off the bench rather than as a starter, the 2013-14 starting lineup consisted of the following players: Randle and Anthony Brown at guards, Dwight Powell and Josh Huestis at forwards, and Stefan Nastic at center. It was a lineup capable of occasionally spectacular offense and, in time, effective defense.

Game #2 of 2012-13 at Maples Pavilion, against BYU, revealed both the prolific features of Stanford's offense and, unfortunately for the Cardinal, the work-in-progress aspect of its defense. BYU prevailed, 112-103, shooting 53% against a Stanford defense that, clearly, had an off night. But the Stanford offense was lights out: Chasson Randle poured in a career-high 33 points, Dwight Powell burst forth with 28 points, and Anthony Brown added 16 points.

Its record 1-1, the Cardinal bounced back with three consecutive mid-November wins, at home against Northwestern and Texas Southern and on the road at Denver University. Anthony Brown averaged 18 points in the three wins to lead the Cardinal. Thanksgiving Week brought the first of two trips to the New York City area—the two games on the trip being the semifinal and final of the Progressive Legends Classic held in the new Barclays Center in Brooklyn. On Monday, November 25, Stanford got past Houston 86-76, with Anthony Brown and Dwight Powell scoring 20 points apiece, Stefan Nastic tallying a career-high 14 points, and Josh Huestis contributing 13 points and 13 rebounds.

In the championship game the following night, against a Top 25-ranked University of Pittsburgh team, Stanford was no match for the Panthers, whose captain Lamar Patterson scored 24 points. Stanford outshot Pitt 50% to 45% in field-goal shooting, but the Panthers got the free-throw line 34 times, making 30, and made 8 of 17 three-point shots. The free-throw and the three-point shooting differential were the main reasons Pitt prevailed over the Cardinal, 88-67.

Stanford's final game prior to the two-week break for Fall Quarter final examinations, as well as its first game following the finals break, were both blowout wins: a 32-point victory over South Dakota State and a 27-point triumph over UC Davis, respectively. In each win, four of the five Stanford starters scored in double figures. The week prior to Christmas, with its record at 7-2, the Cardinal returned to the East Coast. Two more highly ranked and perennial NCAA Tournament teams awaited as Stanford's opponents.

On Wednesday night, December 18, 2013, the Cardinal faced #10-ranked Connecticut in Hartford, CT. Stanford was winless (0-4) in its basketball history against UConn, with each of the most recent three games in the series having been double-digit-point Husky victories. The 2013-14 Stanford-UConn meeting appeared headed for another of those lopsided UConn victories. Connecticut led by 10 points at halftime and was ahead 43-30 with sixteen minutes remaining in the game.

And then Stanford's defense came of age. UConn would score only eight more points over the final 16 minutes of game action. Meanwhile, the Cardinal offense scored 14 unanswered points between the 16:00 mark and the 10:00 mark of the second half, with Chasson Randle scoring eight of the points. The scoring run put the Cardinal into the lead, 44-43, with ten minutes remaining in the game.

Several missed shots and lead changes occurred in the final minutes. With his team trailing by one point, Chasson Randle hit a jump shot with 6:14 remaining to put the Cardinal up 50-49, and then—after a few more missed shots by both sides—Randle made a layup three minutes later to put Stanford ahead by three points, 52-49. Stanford scored just one more point after that.

But the Cardinal defense remained stout, forcing UConn to miss five of its final six shots including four misses by Shabazz Napier, who four months later would earn the 2014 NCAA Tournament's Most Outstanding Player award. UConn forward Omar Calhoun launched a potential game-winning three-point shot attempt with two seconds remaining in the game, but Stanford contested the shot and it missed its target. Final score: Stanford 53 – UConn 51.

Stanford had held UConn—which in April 2014 would win the NCAA championship—to just 32% shooting for the game. The nation's most accurate three-point shooting team coming into the game, UConn was held to just 6 of 22 from three-point distance, including 0 for 12 in the second half. Coach Johnny Dawkins elected to employ primarily a zone defense in the second half, and the Stanford zone—with Josh Huestis, Dwight Powell, Anthony Brown, and Chasson Randle active on the perimeter—had hands in faces of UConn shooters seemingly the entire second half and were the primary causes of the dismal UConn shooting performance.

Chasson Randle's 22 points led the Cardinal in scoring. Randle outscored his counterpart Shabazz Napier by ten points. Stanford's rebounding too was superb, with Powell's 15 and Huestis's 10 rebounds helping the Cardinal achieve a 43-41 advantage on the glass. Powell also recorded four blocked shots in the victory.

Three nights later, back in Brooklyn's Barclays Center, Stanford squared off against Michigan. Despite another solid defensive performance, with the Wolverines being held to just 40% shooting, Stanford could not quite pull off a second consecutive upset as Michigan prevailed, 68-65. Chasson Randle had a chance to tie the game, launching a three-point field-goal attempt with two seconds remaining in the game, but the shot rimmed off. Randle's 18 points—which included 10 of 11 from the free-throw line—paced the Cardinal in scoring, while Stefan Nastic tied his career high with 14 points, making 5 of 6 field goals and 4 of 5 free throws.

The UConn and Michigan games—close games, pressure-filled endings, NBA-style arenas, and high-level opponents—were meant to mimic what March might look like for Stanford Basketball in 2013-14. It was fairly accurate foreshadowing, as things would later turn out.

Following a final non-conference win over Cal Poly, at Maples Pavilion on December 29, Stanford's overall won-loss record stood at 9-3. The good news for the Cardinal in November and December of 2013 was also the bad news: The five starters were the whole story and the only story. Of the young men anticipated to be key reserves—Andy Brown, Aaron Bright, John Gage, sophomore forward Roscoe Allen, and sophomore guard Christian Sanders—four were effectively lost to Stanford for the remainder of the season due to injury. Of these, only Gage was available to coach Johnny Dawkins as an off-the-bench contributor in games.

Due to circumstances surrounding a balky shoulder, Bright's season had been shut down in late November. Rosco Allen's season-long foot injury was not healing as fast as anticipated—he would play only seven minutes all season. Christian Sanders had sustained a season-ending hip injury and Andy Brown had been forced to retire from competition due to the ACL issue. Besides John Gage, the bulk of the reserve minutes therefore necessarily would fall to senior guard Robbie Lemons and freshman guard Marcus Allen. What could have been a very strong Cardinal bench had been thinned out quite significantly.

In the Pac-12 opener on January 2 against Cal, the bench "thinness" indeed hurt the Cardinal significantly. None of the Stanford reserves that played in the game scored any points in the Cardinal's 69-62 loss to the Golden Bears—one of the few Stanford Basketball games in recent memory in which only the starters scored.

Stanford lost its next game—the first half of the ensuing week's Oregon road trip—to Oregon State by a score of 81-72. Johnny Dawkins, upset with his team's effort, conducted a long meeting and held a long practice in Eugene, OR, the day after the OSU loss. And it paid off two days later against #17-ranked Oregon as Stanford edged the Ducks

82-80—a second road win over a Top 25-ranked opponent in 2013-14, something a Stanford team had not done in 12 seasons. Chasson Randle scored 25 points and Anthony Brown added 23 points for Stanford, whose cause was also aided by several minutes of solid and inspired play, on both offense and defense, from reserve guard Robbie Lemons.

Following a sweep of the Washington schools at Maples Pavilion, with Chasson Randle equaling his career high with 33 points in the win over Washington, Stanford traveled to Los Angeles for games against UCLA and USC. Stanford fell to the Bruins 91-74, but—as at Oregon two weeks earlier—had three days to prepare for the ensuing USC game. Although the game with the Trojans went to overtime, behind Randle's seven points and a block and a steal from John Gage in the overtime period, Stanford outscored the Trojans 18-10 in the extra session and secured victory, 79-71.

Its overall record 13-6 and its Pac-12 record 4-3, Stanford returned to Maples Pavilion the following week to host the Arizona schools. The game with Arizona held national appeal—the Wildcats were undefeated (21-0) and the #1-ranked team in the country. It was the 30th time in Stanford Basketball history the Cardinal had squared off against the nation's #1 team, but just the first time since 2003.

The Cardinal gave coach Sean Miller's Wildcat team all it could handle, dialing up another defensive gem. Stanford held freshman sensation and former Bay Area prep star Aaron Gordon to just five points and held the Arizona team to just 36% field-goal shooting for the game—two big reasons Stanford led by one point at halftime and was in front for the vast majority of the second half.

Having trailed by as many as seven points in the second half, the Wildcats fought back and tied the game, 53-53, with 6:30 remaining. Like the UConn and Michigan games a month earlier, the final six minutes were a defensive tug of war, pockmarked by missed shots and missed free throws. For the next five-and-a-half minutes, each team could manage just two points on the scoreboard.

Arizona's Nick Johnson then broke the tie with a three-point basket—off an offensive rebound and a kick-out pass—to put the Wildcats ahead, 58-55, with 49 seconds remaining in the game. Chasson Randle answered with two free throws with seven seconds remaining the game, as did Nick Johnson two seconds later following an immediately ensuing Stanford foul in the backcourt. His squad down 60-57, Randle hoisted a long three-point shot attempt just ahead of the buzzer that would have sent the game to overtime, but the shot missed the mark. All but one of Stanford's starters had scored in double figures in the game, but Arizona's reserves outscored Stanford's reserves 13-2, and that superior bench support was the main reason Arizona was able to eke out a 60-57 victory.

The Cardinal bounced back with a win on Saturday, February 1, 2013, outlasting Arizona State 76-70 as Dwight Powell scored 28 points and Anthony Brown added 21 points. The Cardinal then won four days later in Berkeley, 80-69, behind another strong game from Powell, who exhibited the whole of his versatile skill set with 22 points, 11 rebounds, and 6 assists.

Next up was a road trip to the Washington schools, and for the third consecutive two-game road trip weekend, Stanford lost the first game of the trip but rebounded to win the second game. Behind a career-high 30 points from Anthony Brown, the Cardinal's win at WSU on February 15 at least partially made up for a four-point loss at Washington three nights earlier.

Stanford swept the Los Angeles schools the following weekend—which included a nine-point win over UCLA in which the Cardinal shot a sensational 62% for the game. The weekend after that, however, Stanford dropped two games in the state of Arizona—to Arizona State and Arizona.

With a 9-7 Pac-12 record and an 18-10 overall mark, the Stanford team knew that its performance in the final week of conference play and in the conference postseason tournament would decide whether the Cardinal would make the 2014 NCAA Tournament. Despite the relatively modest overall win total, and given the number of Cardinal wins (3) over Top 25-ranked teams, including two of those wins having been on the road, it was believed that Stanford needed perhaps just two more wins—or three more wins to be absolutely sure—to earn a spot in the 68-team 2014 NCAA field.

Though it was not easy, the Cardinal got its three wins. Following a 59-56 loss to Colorado at home on March 5, 2014, Stanford closed the conference regular season by nipping Utah at Maples, 61-60, on March 8. The Utes had the ball with a chance to win the game on its final possession, but a turnover in the final seconds of the game ensured the Cardinal victory. On an emotional Senior Day in which six Stanford seniors were honored, junior Chasson Randle shouldered the offensive load by scoring a team-high 22 points. His defense was also a factor in the pivotal end-of-game Utah turnover.

The two other wins came at the Pac-12 Tournament in Las Vegas, and they were convincing ones. Seeded #6, the Cardinal dispatched #11-seed Washington State, 74-63, and then breezed past #3-seed Arizona State, 79-58. The Cardinal thereby advanced to the Pac-12 Tournament semifinals, where it fell to #2-seed UCLA, 84-59.

The three early March wins, which improved Stanford's overall 2013-14 win total to 21 wins, were enough to get Stanford to its first NCAA Tournament in six seasons. Stanford was slotted as a #10-seed in the South Region and would play its first week of competition in St. Louis. The first opponent for the Cardinal was #7-seed New Mexico.

Coach Johnny Dawkins, himself a decorated player in NCAA Tournament play while at Duke in the mid-1980s, commented prior to the start of the tournament that defense would decide how far the Cardinal would progress. The Stanford coach would prove prescient on that point.

The Cardinal got off to a fast start against New Mexico in the NCAA Tournament first-round game, exploding to an early 20-4 lead behind nine early points from Chasson Randle. The Lobos, however, righted themselves and closed the deficit to five points by halftime, 32-27. The second half proved very reminiscent of the Stanford–Connecticut and Stanford–Michigan games in December—narrow leads, tough defense, many missed shots. New Mexico narrowed the deficit to one point seven minutes into the second half, then fell behind by five points, then went on a 5-0 run to tie the game at 45 with ten minutes remaining in the game.

And then Stanford turned up its defense. During the ensuing seven minutes, New Mexico would not score. Meanwhile, although Stanford was having shooting troubles of its own, it managed a three-point basket by Chasson Randle and two-point baskets by Stefan Nastic and Anthony Brown during that seven-minute span to take a 52-45 lead with just over three minutes remaining in the game.

It was 54-47 Stanford with two-and-a-half minutes left to play. Neither team could score for the next 1:40, as turnovers, offensive fouls, missed field goals, and missed free throws plagued both teams. With 1:06 left to play, the Lobos hit a three-point basket, and then with 30 seconds remaining—following an offensive foul by Dwight Powell—Lobo center Alex Kirk made two free throws to cut the Stanford lead to 54-52. Given the small amount of time left in the game, New Mexico had to foul quickly and hope Stanford missed free throws.

The first Cardinal player to be fouled was senior reserve guard Robbie Lemons, who had just been inserted into the game by Coach Dawkins. Faced with a pressure one-and-one free-throw situation, and having attempted just 11 free throws for the season and just 22 free throws in his Stanford career, the walk-on hit both free throws to give Stanford a four-point lead with 23 seconds remaining in the game. New Mexico guard Kendall Williams then missed a three-point field-goal attempt. Stanford rebounded the miss, and Chasson Randle was fouled with seven seconds remaining. Randle capped his game-high, 22-point scoring afternoon with two final free throws to ice the game for Stanford. The final score: Stanford 58 – New Mexico 53.

Stanford's defense had carried the day. Not only did the Cardinal defense contribute to the Lobos's seven-minute, second-half scoring drought, it also held New Mexico to just 37% shooting for the game. Two of the three Lobo scoring stars—Kendall Williams and center Alex Kirk, both first-team All-Mountain West Conference honorees—were held to a combined six points for the game.

For its efforts Stanford won the right to face one of the highest of high-profile opponents, #2-seed Kansas, in the NCAA Tournament second-round game on March 23, 2014. With the game to be played in St. Louis, everyone knew that the Jayhawk team would have the vast majority of the 19,000 Scottrade Center fans in its corner. As an upper classmen-dominated team, however, Stanford would not be intimidated by KU. Having played—and defeated—Top 25-ranked teams such as UConn and Oregon in hostile enviroments earlier in the 2013-14 campaign, the Cardinal was mentally ready for the challenge.

And Stanford got an additional assist from an unusual source: the Kansas player press conference held the day before the game. When asked by the assembled media about Chasson Randle's potential impact on the upcoming game, KU freshmen Andrew Wiggins and Wayne Selden said nothing, and instead began chuckling. Whether intended to be so or not, this disrespectful behavior toward Randle was apparent to all in attendance and to those later watching a video replay of the interview. A video clip of the Wiggins and Selden giggle-fest was, to be sure, viewed multiple times by the Stanford team in a private team meeting held later that day.

Thus prepared and incentivized, the Cardinal players were ready for the battle with coach Bill Self's Jayhawk team. Stanford jumped out to an 18-11 lead, after which Kansas began using a full-court press to slow the Cardinal momentum. When reserve KU guard Conner Frankamp hit a three-point shot at the halftime buzzer, the Jayhawks had gained their first lead of the game, 24-22.

Kansas opened up a five-point lead 90 seconds into the second half, behind two close-range baskets by center Tarik Black. But an ensuing 7-2 scoring run by the Cardinal, capped by a Chasson Randle layup, regained the lead for Stanford, 30-28. KU tied the game on its next possession, making the score 30-30 at the mandatory "under 16 minute deadball" time-out in the second half.

Stanford then went on a 10-3 run to take a 40-33 lead with 12:52 remaining—the last four points scored on consecutive baskets by Stefan Nastic. The Jayhawks answered with a 7-4 run to pull to within four points, 44-40. But the Cardinal immediately re-upped the lead to seven points on a coast-to-coast dribble-drive and dramatic layup finish by Anthony Brown with 6:54 remaining, with Brown converting the layup ahead of a hotly pursuing Andrew Wiggins who fouled Brown from behind on the layup attempt. Brown hit the free throw to put the Cardinal up 47-40.

Kansas roared back, outscoring Stanford 9-2 to tie the game at 49 with five minutes remaining. As the first and only NCAA Tournament game being played in the United States at that time of the day, the entire nation was watching the game on CBS Television and—given the closeness of the score—was eagerly anticipating another exciting finish in an NCAA Tournament game.

Dwight Powell hit a jumper on Stanford's next possession to make it 51-49 in favor of the Cardinal. A minute later, Powell drove and missed a layup, but Josh Huestis caught the rebound and—while still in midair—banked the ball off the glass and through the hoop. The Huestis putback made the score 53-49 in Stanford's favor. Three minutes remained in the game.

Jayhawk forward Perry Ellis next made two free throws for KU to make the score 53-51 in the Cardinal's favor with two minutes remaining, but over the next 90 seconds Kansas missed two field goals and suffered a turnover by Andrew Wiggins—all while Stanford was making 5 of 6 free throws on its possessions. With 33 seconds remaining in the game, Stanford's lead was seven points, 58-51.

Stanford wilted somewhat in those final 33 seconds, missing three of five free-throws attempts while KU's Conner Frankamp was drilling back-to-back three-point baskets. Down by three, the Jayhawks had the ball with a chance to tie in the final seconds, but Frankamp's three-point attempt at the buzzer was well off the mark. Stanford had upset the #2-seeded Jayhawks; the final score was Stanford 60 – Kansas 57.

It was Stanford Basketball's most significant postseason win since the Elite Eight win on the very same floor sixteen years earlier—the 1998 Arthur Lee–led comeback win over Rhode Island. Defense had been the difference for the Cardinal; Stanford's defense had held Kansas to just 32.8% shooting. And Stanford's effective alternating of zone and man-to-man defenses helped hold the frosh All-American phenom Andrew Wiggins to just 1 of 6 field-goal shooting for the game.

Stanford won despite missing all nine of its three-point field-goal attempts. Once again, however, the Cardinal was aided by balanced scoring from among its starters—Dwight Powell scored 15 points, Chasson Randle added 13 points, and both Anthony Brown and Stefan Nastic had 10 points. Nastic made 4 of his 5 shot attempts, and Powell and Randle each made 50% of his field-goal attempts. For Johnny Dawkins, it was a landmark win. Said the Cardinal coach, "I could not be more proud of my guys and how they played for 40 minutes tonight."

Stanford had a golden opportunity to advance even further in the 2014 NCAA Tournament. The opponent in the Sweet 16 game in Memphis, TN, the following week would be a low-seeded team, #11-seed Dayton, which had upset both Ohio State and Syracuse in its initial two rounds. The game was rough going for Stanford, right from the start. Dayton's attacking, dribble-penetrating halfcourt offense was effective against the Stanford defense, and Stanford's starters could not find easy shots against the aggressive Flyer defense. Particularly flummoxed were the Cardinal guards Chasson Randle and Anthony Brown, who were guarded very tightly near or within the three-point arc and forced to improvise on offense. This strategy prevented Randle and Brown from finding a rhythm on offense—the pair, combined, made just 6 of 26 field-goal attempts in the game.

Stanford's big men kept Stanford in the game. Dwight Powell, Stefan Nastic, and Josh Huestis were able to shoot over the undersized Flyers if and when the Cardinal guards were able to get them the ball within or near the free-throw lane area. Despite its overall shooting woes—Stanford shot just 38% for the game—the three Cardinal big men collectively made 16 of 27 field-goals attempts.

The Cardinal trailed by ten points at halftime, closed the deficit to four points five minutes into the second half, then promptly fell behind by 12 points. Again Stanford closed the deficit—this time to six points—on a Dwight Powell layup with eight minutes remaining. But Stanford could get no closer the remainder of the game, falling behind by as many as 13 points late in the game and ultimately losing by a double-digit margin, 82-72. Stanford's 2013-14 season was over.

A contributing factor to the Sweet 16 loss may have been that, metaphorically speaking, the "bill came due" for Stanford's reliance on its starters for the vast majority of the minutes played. Dayton's bench outscored the Cardinal bench 34 points to 2 points. Four of the five Stanford starters, Stefan Nastic excepted, played 35 or more minutes in the game.

In his final game as a Cardinal player, Dwight Powell led the team in scoring with 17 points on 6 of 9 field-goal shooting, and he added 9 rebounds, 2 blocks, and 2 steals. It was Powell's 136th game in a Stanford uniform, at the time the most games ever played in the history of Stanford Basketball. Powell was named first-team All-Pac-12 for a second consecutive year in 2013-14, joining Chasson Randle as a first-team All-Conference honoree.

Like Dwight Powell, Josh Huestis had a strong Sweet 16 game, contributing 13 points and 8 rebounds in his final Stanford appearance. Having become Stanford's career shot-block leader earlier in the season, Huestis had four blocks in the Dayton game to finish his Cardinal career with 190 blocked shots—23 more than Tim Young's second place total of 167. Powell and Huestis also concluded their Stanford careers seventh and eighth, respectively, on the Cardinal career rebounds list. So it was less surprising to Stanford fans, than to perhaps others, that immediately following their graduations in June Dwight Powell and Josh Huestis were among the 60 players from around the world selected in the 2014 NBA Draft.

Coach Johnny Dawkins and members of the 2012 team after winning the NIT championship at Madison Square Garden.

Anthony Brown, who started 106 games in his Stanford career, starts a memorable second-half fast break in which he scored a key basket in the 2014 NCAA Tournament win over Kansas.

Stefan Nastic, who averaged 12 points and made an impressive 78% of his field-goal attempts in the three 2014 NCAA Tournament games, plays defense in the second-round win over Kansas.

XIV. Crowning Achievements to Cap a Century

A New Scoring King and Another End-of-Season Championship

As the 2014-15 season approached—marking the 100th season of Stanford Basketball—there were multiple reasons to be excited about the upcoming Cardinal hoops year. Many celebratory events were planned: a former-player reunion weekend, the unfurling of a commemorative 100-year anniversary logo, a halftime ceremony at each home game honoring a former all-time-great player, and the making of a 100-year highlight video.

At the former-player reunion in October of 2014, dozens of former Stanford Basketball players returned to the Farm, including All-Americans Todd Lichti, Adam Keefe, Brevin Knight, and Casey Jacobsen. The members of the 2014-15 Stanford Basketball team were able to speak to these and other basketball alumni—and to hear stories of the great individual player and team achievements through the years. One of the former players in attendance was 95-year old Leon Lafaille, the teammate of Hank Luisetti, whose off-the-bench contribution in the 1937 Stanford-Temple game nearly produced a Stanford win that likely would have caused Stanford, instead of Temple, to have been the Helms Foundation–designated national champion for 1937-38.

Thus, even in October, the 2014-15 Stanford Basketball team received a whiff of championship motivation.

Named as tri-captains for Stanford Basketball's 100th season in 2014-15 were the three returning scholarship seniors: guard Anthony Brown, center Stefan Nastic, and guard Chasson Randle. Each had already stamped a solid legacy for himself in program history, both as a player and as a student. On the academic side, each was already pursuing a master's degree in addition to a bachelor's degree. Never before in Stanford Basketball history had as many as three players been master's degree candidates in a year in which they were on the team—let alone starters—competing for Stanford. And on the basketball court, each of the tri-captains was poised to add to an already-rich résumé of individual Stanford Basketball accomplishments.

Anthony Brown entered the season already in the top 50 all-time, in both career points (1,015) and rebounds (435), and he seemed a sure bet to be one of the rare Stanford Basketball players who, with another productive statistical year in 2014-15, would finish in the top 20—or even higher up—in *both* of these major statistical categories. Brown had been named the Pac-12's Most Improved Player in 2013-14, and it was clear that he had a chance to make the All-Conference team in 2014-15.

Stefan Nastic, entering his second season as a full-time starter in 2014-15, had been the statistical star of Stanford's NCAA run in March of 2014. In the three NCAA Tournament games in 2013-14, Nastic made 78% of his field-goals attempts and averaged 12 points per game. In the two Stanford Pac-12 Tournament wins plus the regular season home finale win against Utah which helped Stanford secure an NCAA bid, Nastic was even better—a perfect 12 for 12 in field-goal shooting in those three games. This strong ending to his junior season in 2013-14 gave Nastic a considerable amount of confidence heading into 2014-15.

Chasson Randle's junior season could hardly have gone better: an 18.8 points-per-game scoring average, a career-best 47.4% field-goal shooting achievement, and a first-team All-Pac-12 designation. Randle also averaged a team-high 19 points per game in the three NCAA Tournament games in 2013-14, and his career-high six steals in the second-round upset of #2-seed Kansas were pivotal in the Cardinal win. Randle had finished his junior season just 685 points behind Stanford's all-time leading scorer Todd Lichti, and one of the intriguing Stanford Basketball storylines at the beginning of the 2014-15 season was whether Randle would catch Lichti and become the Cardinal's career scoring leader.

In addition to the tri-captain returning starters Brown, Nastic, and Randle, the fourth and fifth starters in the opening night matchup with Wofford were both forwards. One was 6′ 9″ sophomore Rosco Allen, who missed virtually all of 2013-14 due to a foot injury. The other was 6′ 8″ and 240-pound freshman forward Reid Travis, a McDonalds All-American in high school and an extremely powerful inside presence on both ends of the court.

The primary reserves were slated to be sophomore guards Marcus Allen and Christian Sanders and junior center Grant Verhoeven, although

Verhoeven began the year inactive due to his still-continuing recovery from off-season hip surgery. Freshman forward Michael Humphrey and freshmen guards Robert Cartwright and Dorian Pickens were also in the mix for playing time at the outset of the 2014-15 campaign.

Once again Stanford Basketball Operations Director and Assistant Athletic Director Jeff LaMere was shrewd in crafting the Cardinal non-conference schedule. LaMere scheduled, as Cardinal opponents, schools expected to produce good or at least decent RPI numbers during the 2014-15 season—once again, toward the goal of maximizing Stanford's chances of earning a bid to either the NCAA or the NIT in March, or to improving seeding for Stanford, if and upon Stanford's being invited to either of those postseason tournaments.

The season opened with a home game against Wofford, a team that had played in the NCAA Tournament in 2013-14 and—as things would unfold—would reach the NCAA Tournament in 2014-15 as well. Stefan Nastic was the dominant Cardinal player in the game, scoring a career-high 26 points on 11-of-14 field-goal shooting and a perfect 4-of-4 from the free-throw line. Anthony Brown and Chasson Randle added 16 and 12 points, respectively. Stanford won easily, 74-59. Collectively, the Cardinal tri-captains scored 50 of the 74 Stanford points in the win.

The Cardinal won its next game, at home over South Dakota, then traveled back to the Barclays Center in Brooklyn for a semifinal game against UNLV in the Coaches vs. Cancer Tournament. The Runnin' Rebels were no match for the Cardinal as Stanford won in dominant fashion, 89-60. The Cardinal three-point shooting was exquisite in the game—Stanford made 14 of 20 three-point attempts, and overall for the game made 50% of the field goals that it attempted.

The UNLV win secured a spot for Stanford in the tournament final against Duke, which meant a first-ever coaching matchup between Duke's legendary coach Mike Krzyzewski and his former All-American player and current Stanford head coach Johnny Dawkins. Duke and Stanford were meeting for just the third time ever; the Cardinal had won the previous two meetings—in 1999-2000 and in 2000-2001—each by a single point.

The Duke–Stanford game was a defensive battle. Both teams shot under 40% for the game, with each team making just 22 baskets in the contest. The Blue Devils, however, were a bit better in making threes and in getting to the free-throw line in the game, making six more three-point baskets and five more free throws than the Cardinal. The final score was Duke 70 – Stanford 59. The two head coaches, mentor Kryzyzewski, and pupil Dawkins, shared a warm embrace in the handshake line immediately following the game.

Stanford won three of its next four games. The wins consisted of victories at Maples Pavilion over Delaware, Denver, and Loyola Marymount. Those three wins were sandwiched around a disappointing road loss at DePaul, 87-72, a game in which Stanford committed a season-high 21 turnovers and allowed the Blue Demons to shoot 54% from the field.

With its won-loss record at 6-2, Stanford embarked on a challenging two-game, late-December road trip to BYU and Texas. These two games were the first two of twelve Stanford games during the remainder of the season that would be decided either in overtime or by a final margin of three points or less—or both. And in more than half of those eleven games, a Chasson Randle field-goal or free-throw attempt would decide the outcome in the final seconds.

The first of the seven "Randle final shot" games in 2014-15 was the December 20, 2014, contest against BYU. Stanford was behind by 13 points, 74-61, with 4:20 remaining in the second half when the Cardinal tri-captains suddenly took matters into their own hands. With Randle, Nastic, and Brown scoring 7, 6, and 4 points over the next 4:20—all 17 of Stanford's points during that stretch—the Cardinal outscored the Cougars 17-5 and found itself down by only two points, 79-77, with ten seconds remaining in the game.

At that point, with ten seconds left to play, BYU's Anson Winder went to the free-throw line for two free-throw opportunities. Winder missed both, and Stanford secured the rebound after the second of the missed free throws. However, Randle's 25-foot shot attempt from the right wing with four seconds remaining missed its target, and 79-77 turned out to be the game's final score, with the outcome in BYU's favor.

Three nights later, against #9-ranked Texas in Austin, Stanford again found itself facing late-game drama. With 30 seconds remaining and Stanford ahead by two points, 64-62, Anthony Brown was whistled for a foul—a very controversial call as Brown was simply pivoting while holding the ball near the sideline in the backcourt. Texas tied the game four seconds later, and when Stanford freshman Robert Cartwright missed a potential game-winning runner with one second left in the second half, the game went to overtime.

The overtime was tense. Stanford fell behind by four points 90 seconds into the overtime period, then tied the score 45 seconds later. Texas shortly thereafter briefly regained the lead, 71-70, but an ensuing layup by

Anthony Brown—his 24th and 25th points of the game—gave the Cardinal its first advantage in the overtime period, 72-71, with 1:08 remaining.

Stanford next withstood two missed shots on the next Texas possession, got the ball back, and worked the shot clock down to four seconds. At that point, Chasson Randle fired an elbow-area jump shot—and nailed it! Ten seconds remained in the game, and the Cardinal was suddenly ahead by three points. The Longhorns could not score in the final seconds, and the victory was Stanford's by the final score of 74-71.

Stanford had secured itself a road victory over a top-ten-ranked team—the kind of win that typically greatly helps a team's efforts to land a bid to the NCAA Tournament. The tri-captains had played a huge role in the win: Anthony Brown scored 25 points, Chasson Randle added 22 points and Stefan Nastic chipped in with 9 points. Freshman power forward Reid Travis helped considerably in the win as well, producing 7 points and a career-high 14 rebounds.

With his 25-point performance in the Texas win, Anthony Brown became the third of the senior tri-captains to have produced a 25 points-or-more scoring game in 2014-15. Only one other Stanford Basketball team in the program's 99 previous seasons had had as many as three seniors produce 25-or-higher scoring games in their senior seasons: the 2005-06 team, in which seniors Dan Grunfeld, Chris Hernandez, and Matt Haryasz each accomplished the feat.

For Chasson Randle, the Texas win provided a bit of redemption. Although his jump shot technically had not *decided* the outcome against Texas—the Cardinal having been ahead by one point at the time—it helped Randle get past the memories of having missed potential last-second game-winning or game-tying shots in prior Stanford games. In addition to his last-second miss in the BYU game, six times in his prior two seasons Randle had an opportunity to win or tie a Stanford game in the final seconds with a jump shot, and had missed each time. It happened three times during his sophomore season in 2012-13, twice against USC and once in the NIT against Illinois State. And it happened three times also in his junior season in 2013-14—against Michigan, Arizona, and Colorado.

Now Chasson Randle had converted an important late-game field goal to help Stanford get a win in a big game. And it would not be the only such important late-game shot the senior guard would make for Stanford Basketball in 2014-15. Not by a longshot.

Chasson Randle—bachelor's *and* master's degree candidate, first-team Academic All-American, community volunteer, and peer mentor—was not one who felt a lot of pressure when playing basketball. Strong psychologically and extremely even-keeled on the court, Randle played heavy minutes every game, and he had no reluctance being the player to take the final shot in close games. Situational drama in the final seconds simply was not a mental burden for him.

Yet it was an undeniable fact that a lot of drama would surround Chasson Randle beginning as the 2014-15 season calendar turned to January 2015. In addition to several more last-second shot situations that would confront him in future games, Randle also was moving within range of Stanford Basketball's two highest all-time career scorers, Todd Lichti and Adam Keefe. On January 1, 2015, with 19 regular season games plus the Pac-12 Tournament games plus whatever postseason games lay ahead of him, Randle's career scoring total stood at 1,854 points—482 points behind Lichti's 2,336-point total and 465 points behind Keefe's 2,319-point mark.

It seemed like a longshot for Chasson Randle to catch one or both of those former Cardinal greats. Almost certainly some postseason games, NCAA or NIT, would be necessary for Randle to break the career points record, given Randle's 2014-15 season scoring average of 18.4 points per game as of games through January 1, 2015. But would Stanford play in enough postseason games in 2014-15 to give Randle a chance?

Randle's next dance with late-game drama happened just three days into the new calendar year—at the back end of the first weekend of Pac-12 play. Following a win in the conference opener versus Washington State, the Cardinal hosted Washington on Sunday evening, January 4. The Huskies came into the game ranked #21 nationally in the AP Poll, with an overall won-loss record of 11-2.

The game was tied at halftime, 28-28. Stanford opened up a seven-point lead five minutes into the second half, but the Huskies answered with a 9-0 scoring run to retake the lead, 39-37, with 12 minutes remaining in the second half. The lead changed hands twice during the next nine minutes, with Washington taking a 56-52 lead with 1:18 remaining in the game on guard Andrew Andrews's jump shot. Anthony Brown's two free throws brought Stanford to within two points with 14 seconds remaining.

Chasson Randle immediately fouled UW's Nigel Williams-Goss on the Husky inbound pass following the second of Brown's made free throws. Williams-Goss missed the front end of the one-and-one free-throw opportunity, Stanford rebounded and the ball was soon in Randle's hands. Chasson dribbled the ball upcourt, and with six seconds remaining—instead of settling for a jump shot attempt—attacked the paint with a dribble-drive. As he neared the basket from the right side of the lane, he saw UW's seven-foot center Robert Upshaw sliding over toward him. Randle nevertheless rose for a three-foot shot attempt, twisted his body while in midair to avoid Upshaw's shot block attempt, and scored!

Tie game, 56-56, with two seconds remaining. The Huskies were unable to score in the remaining two seconds, and in the overtime period—propelled by five points from Anthony Brown—Stanford outscored Washington 12-4 to win the game by the score of 68-60. Chasson Randle finished with a team-high 24 points. The Cardinal was now 10-3, and was on the cusp of being ranked among the nation's Top-25 teams.

Stanford's next game, at UCLA four nights later, would provide the opportunity for the Cardinal to win its way into the AP Top-25 poll. It would also, yet again, test Randle's late-game "clutch-ness" quotient—not just one time, but in fact multiple times in the same game on the hostile Pauley Pavilion court.

Stanford led UCLA by fourteen points with ten minutes left in the second half. But the Bruins stormed back, outscoring Stanford 19-4 over the next six minutes to take a 66-65 lead with four minutes left to play in the second half. Only one more point would be scored in the second half—by Chasson Randle on a free throw with 1:52 remaining in the half. Although Randle and Anthony Brown each had a jump shot opportunity within the final ten seconds to win the game for the Cardinal, neither could make his field-goal attempt and the game moved to overtime.

Stanford took a 68-67 lead in the first minute of overtime on a Chasson Randle three-pointer, and Stanford was leading by two points, 75-73, when UCLA forward Kevin Looney attempted a layup with nine seconds left. Looney's shot missed. A Cardinal and a Bruin battled for the rebound, the ball went out of bounds, and—despite a television replay that seemed to show the ball last touching a UCLA player—the officials awarded the ball to the Bruins.

Immediately upon receiving the inbound pass, UCLA guard Bryce Alford hit a three-point basket from the right corner to give the Bruins the lead, 76-75, with eight seconds remaining. But Stanford, on the ensuing inbound, quickly got the ball to Chasson Randle, and the senior bolted down the left side of the court and directly toward the basket. To the delight of the Cardinal players, bench, and fans, Randle was fouled with two seconds remaining! Randle would have two free-throw attempts—two "makes" would give the Cardinal the win!

With the Bruin partisans in Pauley Pavilion screaming, Randle made the first free throw, although it bounced on the front rim and then the backboard before rolling through the rim. Tie game, 76-76. The second free throw had the same trajectory—but this one fell off the rim. The Bruins rebounded, and instead of a Stanford victory the game went to a second overtime.

The second extra session, unfortunately for the Cardinal, was no contest. Stanford led for only 27 seconds in the five-minute second overtime period, and when the Bruins opened up a five-point advantage with 15 seconds remaining the second overtime, the game was effectively over. The final score was UCLA 86 – Stanford 81. Chasson Randle had played brilliantly in the double-overtime thriller—he scored a game-high 32 points, including 7-of-13 from three-point range, and he had played 49 of the game's 50 minutes. But he and his teammates left the floor disconsolate.

Frustrated and exhausted, Chasson Randle nevertheless dutifully and politely answered questions in the postgame media session. "It's very disappointing that we weren't able to close out the game," said Randle. He and his teammates, whose collective team goal was a return trip to the NCAA Tournament, knew that a win over UCLA would have been a significantly positive résumé-item for Stanford when March rolled around and NCAA at-large bids were being decided upon. But the opportunity for a big win at Pauley had slipped through their hands.

Chasson Randle, who was now up to 1,910 career points, felt responsible for the UCLA loss. Despite Coach Dawkins's efforts to tell him that it was not his fault, that losses never happen solely due to one missed field goal or free throw, Randle was aching inside. He saw himself as a clutch late-game scorer in addition to being a premier point producer. But he was aching even more for Stanford victories—victories that would get the Cardinal back into the NCAA postseason picture.

The Cardinal regrouped, winning its next three games over USC, Cal, and Connecticut—the non-conference UConn win being aided in part by a fiery pregame motivational speech from assistant coach Tim O'Toole. A seven-point loss at Maples Pavilion to Pac-12 first-place-team and #7-ranked Arizona followed the three-game mid-January winning streak. However, two nights later, behind Chasson Randle's 21 points, Anthony Brown's 21 points, and Stefan Nastic's 20 points—the first time in eight seasons that as many as three Stanford players had scored at least twenty points in the same game—the Cardinal thrashed Arizona State, 89-70.

Four nights later, in Seattle on January 28, 2015, the Cardinal's winning trajectory continued. The tri-captains combined for 60 points and recently installed starting guard Marcus Allen added a career-high

12 points as Stanford handled Washington, 84-74. A new member of the starting lineup as of the Cal game three weeks earlier, the 6′ 3″ sophomore Allen scored on a variety of explosive, slashing drives to the basket. His scoring in the game relieved some of the defensive pressure being applied on Randle, Brown, and Nastic. Marcus Allen had become, and would remain through the rest of the season, the Cardinal's most-capable, most-consistent, and most sorely needed "fourth" scoring option in games.

Following the win over Washington, the Cardinal won-loss record in 2014-15 stood at 15-5 overall, and it was an even more impressive 6-2 in the Pac-12. A bid to the NCAA Tournament seemed a certainty, if the Cardinal could sustain its current winning pace. As things would play out, however, the Cardinal could not—for a while, at least—sustain its winning ways.

On January 31, 2015, Stanford fell to lowly Washington State, 89-88, in Pullman, Washington. The Cardinal surrendered 47 points in the second half and lost despite a career high-tying 33 points from Chasson Randle. Stanford bounced back to win three of its next four games at Maples Pavilion, with wins over USC, Cal, and Oregon State. Very much a bright spot for Stanford in the latter two wins was the play of 6′ 9″ freshman Michael Humphrey, who had moved into the starting lineup in mid-February when starting forward Rosco Allen was sidelined by injury. Against Cal and Oregon State, Humphrey was a revelation, scoring 28 points and grabbing 26 rebounds collectively in the two Cardinal wins.

The lone home loss during that three-week stretch of games was to UCLA at Maples Pavilion, with Chasson Randle—yet again—in the spotlight in the final seconds. The Cardinal fell behind the Bruins by sixteen points in the first half and trailed at halftime by six points, 31-25. Stanford fell behind further in the second half—the deficit ballooning to 22 points with eleven minutes remaining—and the Cardinal seemed destined for a blowout loss at home. But then Stanford started to go crazy on the offensive end of the court, outscoring UCLA 31-10 during the following 10 minutes, capped by a three-point basket by Rosco Allen with seven seconds remaining that cut the Cardinal deficit to just one point, 68-67.

Marcus Allen fouled UCLA's Bryce Alford immediately as he received the inbound pass following the Rosco Allen three-point basket. Alford missed the first but made the second throw. The score was now 69-67 in favor of the Bruins. With three seconds left, Randle received the inbound pass and sped upcourt. With one second left, he fired a running 22-foot jump shot from behind the top of the key. It missed. Ballgame to UCLA, 69-67.

Stanford and Randle had come just short on the scoreboard once again—the fourth time in 2014-15 that a potential game-winning or game-tying shot attempt by the Cardinal in the final seconds had gone awry. And, unbelievably, there would be still *more* games, during the final three weeks of the Pac-12 regular season schedule, in which the same thing would take place—a missed Stanford shot attempt in the final seconds that would have tied the game or put Stanford in the lead, the consequence of which would be a Cardinal defeat.

On February 15, 2015, Stanford trailed Colorado in Boulder, CO, by three points, 61-58, with 21 seconds remaining in the game. At that point in the game Colorado had the ball in the backcourt, but Chasson Randle suddenly stole the ball. Unfortunately for Stanford, Randle was called for an offensive foul upon dribbling toward the basket two seconds after making the steal. The Cardinal could not mount a comeback thereafter and ended up losing to the Buffaloes by six points.

Two weeks later, on March 1, 2015—Senior Day at Maples Pavilion—Stanford trailed Oregon by six points at halftime. The Cardinal clawed back to tie the game at 44 with 14 minutes left to play and the game remained tight thereafter, with neither team enjoying more than a three-point lead going into the final minute of the game.

With the score tied at 70, Oregon's Dwayne Benjamin stole the ball from Chasson Randle with seventeen seconds remaining in the game and was fouled immediately by Randle. Benjamin made one of two free throws. Randle received the inbound pass, dribbled through tight defense into the frontcourt and created a good shot for himself, but his jumper missed. Oregon rebounded, made two free throws and the Ducks prevailed as the final buzzer sounded, 73-70.

Stanford's record following the Oregon loss was 18-10, 9-7 in Pac-12 play, and two losses at Arizona State and Arizona the next week caused those won-loss records to fall to 18-12 and 9-9, respectively. The Pac-12 regular season was over. For Stanford the Pac-12 Tournament lay immediately ahead, and thereafter either an NCAA bid or an NIT bid. It was clear that, unless the Cardinal won four games in four nights at the Pac-12 Tournament in Las Vegas, it would not go to the NCAA Tournament and would, instead, receive an NIT bid.

Stanford managed just one win in Las Vegas, but what a win it was. On Wednesday, March 11, 2015, Stanford as the tournament's #6 seed squared off against #11-seed Washington in a first-round game. Like the January 4 overtime game at Maples Pavilion, the game was tied at halftime, 32-32. In the second half, the Cardinal fell behind early and was still trailing on the scoreboard as the game entered its final four minutes.

With the score 69-64 in favor of the Huskies, Stefan Nastic tipped in a missed Stanford shot attempt for two points, then a minute later converted a layup to pull the Cardinal to within one point, 69-68. Each team missed two shots on its next two possessions, and following a missed Washington free throw with 28 seconds remaining, Stanford had one last chance, still trailing Washington by the score of 69-68.

The ball went to Chasson Randle, who looked for a driving lane. Finding none, and rather than force up a difficult shot attempt he passed the ball to a teammate. Eventually the ball came to Rosco Allen, who launched a long jump shot from the right side of the court with thirteen seconds remaining in the game. It missed, but Marcus Allen grabbed the offensive rebound and immediately passed the ball out to a wide-open Randle in the left-wing area outside the three-point arc. Randle caught the ball and, with seven seconds remaining in the game, did not hesitate to launch a three-point shot attempt. Bottom of the net! Washington could not get a shot off in the final seconds, and Stanford had claimed its 19th win of the season.

Chasson Randle's Stanford teammates mobbed him on the court immediately after the final buzzer sounded. Finally, Chasson Randle thought to himself, I did what I know I can do, make a clutch shot to win a big game for my team. Of Randle, Stanford coach Johnny Dawkins said, "he's going to take the big shots for us, and that's not changing." Little did Dawkins know how prescient that statement would prove to be, as far as Randle taking—and making—*still more* late-game shots for Stanford before the 2014-15 season ended.

Stanford's stay in Las Vegas ended soon enough. The Cardinal was eliminated from the Pac-12 Tournament the next night, March 12, in an 80-56 loss to Utah. Three days later, Stanford got the news it expected—no NCAA Tournament bid, but indeed a spot in the 32-team 2015 National Invitation Tournament. Stanford was seeded #2 in the "Colorado State" bracket of the NIT, with Colorado State seeded #1 in that bracket. The other six teams in the Colorado State bracket were #3-seed Rhode Island, #4-seed St. Mary's, #5-seed Vanderbilt, #6-seed Iona, #7-seed UC Davis, and #8-seed South Dakota State.

Stanford's eighth-ever NIT journey began on Tuesday, March 17, 2015, at Maples Pavilion against UC Davis, a 25-win team and the regular season champion of the Big West conference. The Aggies star player was 6′ 3″ senior guard Corey Hawkins, the 2014-15 Big West Player of the Year, who averaged 20.4 points per game and whose three-point shooting percentage, 49%, was the best of any NCAA Division 1 guard. Hawkins, the son of former NBA player Hersey Hawkins, also happened to be Johnny Dawkins godson, Dawkins having been a teammate of the elder Hawkins with the Philadelphia 76ers in the late 1980s.

Although the Cardinal opened up a 27-15 first-half lead, the Aggies roared back with a 21-10 scoring run to close the first half trailing by just one point, 37-36. Hawkins was the UC Davis catalyst, scoring 21 of his team's 36 first-half points. Inside the Stanford locker room, Coach Dawkins verbally challenged his players, emphasizing that a better performance was needed in the second half or Stanford's stay in the 2015 NIT wouldn't last beyond one game.

The Cardinal players listened and heeded the warning with better play in the second half. Although Corey Hawkins scored 13 more points in the second half, his teammates scored just 15 points collectively over the same span as Stanford held the Aggies to 32% second half shooting. Seven minutes into the second half, the Cardinal led by eleven points, and the Cardinal did not allow the lead to fall below a double-digit margin for the rest of the game, winning by a score of 77-64.

Marcus Allen scored a career-high 22 points—most of them on explosive drives and above-rim-level layups. Fourteen of Allen's 22 points came in the second half. Chasson Randle added 18 points, Anthony Brown 11 points, and Reid Travis 10 points. Travis also grabbed a team-high 10 rebounds.

Next up for Stanford was Rhode Island in a Sunday, March 22, 2015, second-round NIT matchup at Maples Pavilion. The date, March 22, was significant for both teams. The date marked the 17th anniversary of the historic Elite 8 game in St. Louis between Stanford and the Rhode Island—the Arthur Lee–led Stanford comeback win in the final minute that sent Stanford to the 1998 Final Four.

Coached by Danny Hurley, Rhode Island brought a 23-9 won-loss record to Palo Alto—a record built primarily on the strength of aggressive man-to-man defense. Because of the Rams' defensive effectiveness on the perimeter, the Cardinal had trouble getting good three-point shot attempts in the game. Stanford made just 1 of 9 three-point attempts in the first half and led by just four points in the intermission, 31-27. The one player who was very much "on," offensively, for the Cardinal was Chasson Randle, who scored Stanford's first seven points of the game and 18 of his team's 31 points in the first half.

Given its struggles shooting long-range jump shots in the first half, the Cardinal adjusted its approach on offense in the second half. The second half strategy was this: take less long-distance jump shots, and instead do more dribble-driving toward the rim to get layup attempts or at least shots within at least eight feet of the basket. The strategy did not result in a much higher shooting percentage for Stanford in the second half, but it did result in Cardinal players getting fouled—a lot—by Rhode Island players playing their characteristically aggressive brand of defense.

Because of all the Rhode Island fouling, the Cardinal went to the free-throw line a whopping 35 times in the second half, making 24 free throws. Although the Rams closed the deficit to one point early in the second half, it was never able to draw even on the scoreboard as the Cardinal held on for a 74-65 victory. Chasson Randle stayed hot with his scoring pace in the second half, tallying 17 more points in the second half and finishing with a career-high 35 points—the most points ever scored by a Stanford player in a postseason tournament game, NCAA or NIT.

Chasson Randle of course was the story in the Rhode Island win, and his assault on Stanford's all-time scoring record by now had become a parallel front-banner media story. Randle hit 9 of 16 shots against the Rams—his teammates, by contrast, collectively made just 9 of 37 shots—and Randle's 35 points pushed his career total to 2,310 points. Randle was now just 9 points behind second place Adam Keefe and just 26 points behind first place Todd Lichti, on the Stanford career point total list.

Because #1-seed Colorado State had lost its first-round game to #8-seed South Dakota State, Stanford knew that its quarterfinal NIT game would also be at Maples Pavilion. Vanderbilt's second-round home win over South Dakota meant that the Commodores would be traveling to Palo Alto for the quarterfinal matchup on Tuesday, March 24, with the winner earning the right to advance to New York for the NIT semifinals the following week.

In the first half of the Stanford-Vanderbilt contest, the Cardinal outshot the Commodores 53% to 37% yet led by just five points at halftime. Anthony Brown was Stanford's big gun on offense in the first twenty minutes, scoring 17 of Stanford's 36 first-half points. Vanderbilt had stayed close on the scoreboard, however, by converting 5 of 10 three-point field-goal attempts in the first half. Vandy's seven-footer Luke Kornet made three of those five three-point baskets.

In the second half, Luke Kornet was injured and had to leave the game after being fouled by Anthony Brown on Brown's driving shot attempt midway through the second half. The Kornet loss was a significant blow to the Commodore hopes—it removed a significant three-point shooting threat from the Vandy lineup. In part because of Kornet's absence, Vanderbilt fell behind further, and with two minutes remaining in the game the Cardinal advantage on the scoreboard was a seemingly secure eleven points, 73-62.

The Commodores did not quit, scoring 13 points in a furious comeback attempt over the final two minutes of the game, and had a chance to tie the game in the final seconds on a Matthew Fisher-Davis three-point field-goal attempt. The shot missed badly, however, and Vandy did not get another chance. Stanford had prevailed, 78-75, and for the third time in program history would be advancing to New York for the NIT semifinals and, hopefully thereafter, the finals.

Anthony Brown finished with a season-high 26 points in the Vanderbilt win, while Randle tallied 16 points to pass Keefe for second place on the all-time Stanford scoring list. The senior tri-captain was now at 2,326 points—one point better than UCLA's Kareem Abdul Jabbar for fourth place on the all-time Pac-12 list and just ten points behind Todd Lichti for tops on the all-time Stanford list. It seemed now a certainty that Randle, in the next Cardinal game, would become the new Stanford Basketball career scoring king.

Stanford players were aware of and supported Randle's chase for the scoring crown, yet the goal of continuing to advance toward, and ultimately winning, the NIT championship remained the foremost objective. Said Brown after the game: "Like Coach says, we have to keep playing. Seniors want to go out with a win in their last game."

The next stage for Stanford was a very familiar one—Madison Square Garden. Dating back to Hank Luisetti's one-handed shot debut in Stanford's historic upset win over Long Island University in 1936 at MSG, Stanford Basketball teams had compiled a 13-4 record in nine previous trips to the famed arena, including NIT championship-winning visits in 1991 and 2012.

That Cardinal comfort-level was evident in the opening minutes of the semifinal game against Old Dominion, a #1 seed in its bracket of the NIT. Stanford exploded to a 15-0 first-half lead, and a bit later in the half extended the advantage to 25-4. Old Dominion battled back, however, with a 21-7 scoring run to close the deficit to 33-25 with 45 seconds remaining in the first half following a free throw by Javonte Douglas.

Following the Javonte Douglas free throw, Stanford inbounded the ball to Randle, who by this point in the game had scored 10 points to tie Lichti's 2,336 career point total. Eleven seconds into the Stanford possession, Randle was fouled by Douglas. Stepping to the free-throw line, Chasson Randle bounced the ball and calmly shot the free throw perfectly through the hoop for his 2,337th career point.

There was no fanfare, no stoppage of play, no scoreboard recognition—just as the low-key Randle would have wanted it. The new Stanford scoring king had a larger mission, on this New York trip, than ending his Stanford career as the program's career scoring leader. He wanted to end his career with a win and a team trophy.

Stanford led Old Dominion by six points at halftime, and the second half was played to an even closer margin than that. Stanford saw its lead disappear four minutes into the second half, then regained the lead, then lost the lead again when ODU's Richard Ross made a layup to put the Monarchs up by one point with eleven minutes remaining in the game.

Stanford regained the lead shortly thereafter, but the Cardinal advantage was just two points when Anthony Brown rebounded an Old Dominion missed jump shot with 1:31 left to play in the game. On the ensuing Cardinal possession, with the shot clock down to one second, Chasson Randle hit a clutch jump shot to put Stanford up by four points. Then, following two missed Monarch shots, Randle was fouled and made two of two free throws to give the Cardinal a six-point lead with 45 seconds remaining. Old Dominion did not threaten after that, missing all four of its shot attempts in the final seconds, and Stanford had itself a hard-fought 67-60 NIT semifinal victory.

Stanford had advanced to the championship game of the 2015 NIT. Chasson Randle had made multiple late-game shots to help secure the victory. And of course, earlier in the game Randle had set the all-time Stanford scoring record, prompting this Todd Lichti tweet, sent from Lichti's home in Australia, shortly after the game: "Congratulations to Chasson Randle and the team, happy to see the record go to such a class act."

Chasson Randle's 24 points spearheaded the Cardinal scoring in the NIT semifinal victory, with Stefan Nastic contributing 17 points and Anthony Brown adding 14 points. The three tri-captains had truly led the way, scoring a collective 55 of Stanford's 67 points in the game. The Stanford win set up an NIT championship game matchup between the Cardinal and the Miami Hurricanes.

The NIT championship game was set for Thursday night, April 2, 2015. Another way to write that date is *4-2-15*. Tri-captain Stefan Nastic's uniform number? *4*. Tri-captain Anthony Brown's uniform number? *21*. Tri-captain Chasson Randle's uniform number? *5*. The date itself seemed to portend a triumphant evening for the Cardinal's three tri-captains.

For a third consecutive game at MSG dating back to 2012, Anthony Brown scored the first Stanford points of the game. He and his fellow tri-captains led the way in the first half, combining for 24 of the Cardinal's 32 points as Stanford built up an 11-point halftime advantage, 32-21, over the Hurricanes. As in the NIT semifinal game, however, the Cardinal opponent in the title game fought back in the second half.

After Stanford opened up a 13-point lead two minutes into the second half, the Hurricanes spent the next 15 minutes clawing back. While the Cardinal missed 6 of its next 20 shot attempts during that stretch, Miami got closer and closer and eventually drew even, 53-53, with three minutes left to play. The 2015 NIT championship game, it appeared, was heading for some sort of dramatic ending.

Stefan Nastic made a clutch six-foot jump shot with 2:29 remaining to put Stanford back on top by two points, 55-53. Miami's Omar Sherman answered with a layup twenty seconds later to tie the score again. Chasson Randle then made a layup with 1:10 remaining to make it 57-55 Cardinal, then two free throws by Miami's Sheldon McClellan with 0:48 remaining tied the score again.

Fourteen seconds later, Randle's layup with 0:34 left to play put Stanford back up by two points, 59-57. But again McClellan answered. Driving to the basket, McClellan was fouled on a layup attempt by Reid Travis and—with 16 seconds remaining—made two more clutch free throws to tie the game at 59.

Stanford had the ball for one final possession. Chasson Randle dribbled the ball outside the three-point arc until six seconds were left on the clock. He then drove toward the lane but was cut off by multiple Miami defenders. Randle quickly spotted—and immediately passed the ball to—a wide-open Marcus Allen on the left wing, and Allen had time to launch a potential game-winning jump shot with one second remaining. Allen's jump shot rimmed off, however, no good. The NIT title game would go to overtime.

Chasson Randle's two free throws put Stanford up by two points, 61-59, one minute into the overtime. During the next three minutes of overtime, however, Miami outscored the Cardinal 5-0. Stanford called timeout, down by three points, with 48 seconds remaining in the overtime. The Cardinal would now need some last-minute heroics to win the NIT championship. And it seemed very likely that Chasson Randle would be the one to succeed, or fail, to be the Stanford Basketball hero.

Upon catching the inbound pass, Randle was fouled by Miami's Davon Reed. With no margin for error, Randle made both free throws. The score was now Miami 64 – Stanford 63. On Miami's next possession, Deandre Bennett missed a three-point jump shot attempt. Anthony Brown got the rebound—his 12th of the game—and passed the ball to Randle in the backcourt. Stanford had one chance left. Sixteen seconds remained in the game.

Chasson Randle worked the ball into the frontcourt, crossed-over with the dribble at the top of the key to evade a Miami defender, only to encounter another one—Davon Reed—at the left corner of the free-throw lane area. Just four seconds remained in the game. At that moment, Randle pump-faked a shot, getting Reed into the air, and then jumped into the air to shoot just as Reed made contact. A foul was whistled on Reed, meaning that two free-throw opportunities would be awarded to Randle.

Amazingly, this was the same scenario that Stanford had faced in the UCLA game 13 weeks earlier—Chasson Randle at the line for two free throws, with his team down by one point, with less than five seconds to go in overtime. In that UCLA game, Randle made the first free throw, but missed the second, and the game moved to a second overtime and eventually Stanford lost the game. One would think the memory of that bad UCLA game experience might still be lodged somewhere in Randle's mind—a possible source of pressure on the Cardinal senior tri-captain as he contemplated these upcoming free throws.

Before Chasson Randle could shoot his free throws, Miami coach Jim Larranaga called timeout. It is a time-worn practice, the opponent's coach calling timeout to force a free-throw shooter to think about his upcoming free throws, to worry about them—in other words, to "ice" the free-throw shooter. The Miami timeout, one assumed, would lather still another layer of pressure on the Stanford free-throw shooter Chasson Randle.

The timeout was over. Chasson Randle stepped to the free-throw line with 3.4 seconds remaining on the scoreboard clock. Randle launched the first free throw. Good. Stanford 64 – Miami 64. Randle launched the second free throw. Good. Stanford 65 – Miami 64.

Miami threw the ball away on the ensuing inbound pass. Stanford inbounded the ball to Anthony Brown, whom Miami immediately fouled. Brown missed the first but made the second free throw. The score was now Stanford 66 – Miami 64, with 1.8 seconds remaining.

Following a Miami length-of-the-court pass, which went off of Brown's hand and out of bounds, the Hurricanes had one last chance. The ball was inbounded to Sheldon McClellan in the right corner of the frontcourt.

McClellan caught the ball cleanly and launched a potential game-winning three-point field-goal attempt, but in so doing was harassed by Brown's fly-by defense.

The final buzzer sounded as McClellan's 22-foot shot attempt glanced errantly off the rim.

Stanford was the 2015 NIT champion!

Ten minutes later, each Stanford Basketball team member and member of the coaching staff took turns—triumphantly, joyously, with huge smiles and wide-arcing fist pumps—cutting down the Madison Square Garden nets. Chasson Randle was named the 2015 NIT Most Outstanding Player, while fellow senior Stefan Nastic was named to the All-NIT team along with Randle.

Said victorious Stanford head coach Johnny Dawkins after the game: "We were going to put the ball in Chasson's hand, and he was going to decide it for us." And decide it Randle did—a decorated Stanford Basketball player triumphant once again on the Madison Square Garden court, like Hank Luisetti had been in 1936, like Adam Keefe had been in 1991. It was a fine ending to the 2014-15 Stanford Basketball script.

And it was also a perfect ending to Stanford Basketball's prominent century of playing the roundball sport. Stanford's most prolific scorer, in a century of Stanford Basketball, had scored the game-deciding point in the final seconds of a championship game. And Stanford had ended its 100th year of basketball just as it had begun its first year of basketball a century earlier—with a two-point victory.

Freshman forward Reid Travis, the seventh McDonalds High School All-American honoree to be recruited to Stanford, played a key role in the 2015 NIT championship game victory over Miami and is a foundational piece of the beginning of the program's second century.

In the 100th season, Chasson Randle was selected All Pac-12 for a second time, completed his Stanford career with a program-record 2,375 points, and won the 2015 NIT Most Outstanding Player Award.

XV. Pinnacles and Celebrations

Selected Stanford Basketball All-Time Lists

Top 20 All-Time Stanford Basketball Games

1. *March 28, 1942, Kansas City, MO: Stanford 53 – Dartmouth 38 (1942 NCAA Championship Game).* Playing without injured scoring leader Jim Pollard, and with its second leading scorer, Don Burness, limited to nine minutes of playing time due an ankle injury, 1942 NCAA Tournament Most Outstanding Player Howie Dallmar leads the way with a 15-point scoring game as Stanford pulls away from Dartmouth to win the NCAA championship at Municipal Auditorium, 53-38. Sixth-man Jack Dana contributes 14 points and center Ed Voss scores 13 points as Stanford wins its school-record 28th game.

2. *March 22, 1998, St. Louis, MO: Stanford 79 – Rhode Island 77 (NCAA Midwest Region Final).* Trailing 71-65 with just under one minute remaining in the game, Stanford storms back behind the incredible play of junior guard Arthur Lee and earns a berth in the 1998 Final Four. Lee scores 10 points in the final minute, and his steal with 26 seconds remaining leads directly to a Mark Madsen three-point play that gives the #3-seed Cardinal a lead it would never relinquish. Lee's 26 points lead the way for the Cardinal; Tim Young adds 15 points and Mark Madsen contributes 14 points.

3. *March 28, 1998, San Antonio, TX: Kentucky 86 – Stanford 85 (OT) (NCAA Final Four).* Playing before a Final Four crowd of 40,509 in the Alamodome, Stanford scores the first eight points of the game, endures a game of multiple lead changes, battles Kentucky into overtime, suffers a controversial out-of-bounds call during the OT period, and falls to the Wildcats 86-85. Lee scores 26 points, and for a fifth consecutive NCAA

Tournament game in 1998 does not miss any of his free-throw attempts, setting a record for free-throw proficiency in a single NCAA Tournament year—35 made free throws in 35 free-throw attempts.

4. *March 21, 2014, St. Louis, MO: Stanford 60 – Kansas 57 (NCAA South Region Second Round).* As the #10 seed in the South Region, Stanford's defense is the story, holding #2-seed Kansas to 32.5% field-goal shooting and recording 10 steals in a 60-57 Cardinal victory over the Jayhawks, the highest-seeded NCAA Tournament opponent a Stanford team has ever defeated. Four Stanford starters score in double figures—Dwight Powell (15), Chasson Randle (13), Anthony Brown (10), and Stefan Nastic (10)—while Kansas's freshman All-American Andrew Wiggins is held to just four points on 1-of-6 shooting.

5. *March 22, 2008, Anaheim, CA: Stanford 82 – Marquette 81 (NCAA South Region Second Round).* Brook Lopez's 8-foot leaner from the right baseline with two seconds remaining gives the Cardinal an 82-81 overtime victory against #6-seed Marquette, in a game marred by the double-technical foul ejection of Stanford head coach Trent Johnson in the first half. Lopez scores a game-high 30 points, and point guard Mitch Johnson records a Stanford single-game record 16 assists. Robin Lopez's free throw with 8 seconds remaining in regulation—with Stanford trailing by one point—gets the Cardinal into the overtime.

6. *March 16, 1997, Tucson, AZ: Stanford 72 – Wake Forest 66 (NCAA West Region Second-round).* Arthur Lee's tip-in of a missed Stanford jump shot in the final minute is the key basket as the #6-seeded Cardinal upsets #3 seed and Tim Duncan–led Wake Forest 72-66—the final college game of Duncan's decorated four-year college career. Coach Mike Montgomery has four of his big men, Tim Young, Mark Madsen, Mark Seaton, and Pete Van Elswyk, take turns playing physical defense on Tim Duncan and that strategy helps hold the 1997 National Player of the Year to 18 points.

7. *March 27, 1991, New York, NY: Stanford 78 – Oklahoma 72 (1991 NIT Championship Game).* Stanford caps a five-game, two-week-long, cross-country winning streak by overcoming Oklahoma 78-72 in the championship game of the 1991 NIT at Madison Square Garden. All five Stanford starters—junior Adam Keefe (12 points) and seniors Kenny Ammann (22 points), Andrew Vlahov (14 points), John Patrick (13 points), and Deshon Wingate (13 points)—score in double figures in the game. A double-technical foul on Oklahoma coach Billy Tubbs in the first half, which followed a foul call against an Oklahoma player, results in six consecutive made free throws by the Cardinal which helped propel Stanford to victory.

8. *March 27, 2012, New York, NY: Stanford 75 – Minnesota 51 (2012 NIT Championship Game).* Freshman Chasson Randle and sixth-man Aaron Bright each score 15 points in the game as Stanford—ahead by only six points at halftime—outscores Minnesota 44-26 in the second half and cruises to its second-ever NIT championship at MSG. The Cardinal makes 53% of its field-goal attempts in the game, including an even better 55% from three-point distance, while holding the Golden Gophers to just 37% shooting. Bright, who is named the Most Outstanding Player of the 2012 NIT, also has a team-high six assists in the title game and finishes the five-game tournament averaging a team-high 16.8 points per game.

9. *December 30, 1936, New York, NY: Stanford 45 – Long Island University 31.* In the most memorable basketball game of any kind during the first half of the 20th century, Hank Luisetti–led Stanford ends powerhouse Long Island University's 43-game winning streak with a 45-31 victory before 17,623 awestruck fans at Madison Square Garden. Besides upstart Stanford ending Clair Bee–coached LIU's long winning streak, the game is remembered as the national coming-out party for Luisetti's one-handed running shot, which in an era exclusively dominated by the two-handed set shot was hailed by the media as revolutionary and soon adopted by players all over the United States.

10. *February 7, 2004, Stanford, CA: Stanford 80 – Arizona 77.* Junior forward Nick Robinson's 35-footer heave at the buzzer, following a backcourt steal sequence engineered by teammate Matt Lottich, gives #2-ranked Stanford an 83-80 win over #12-ranked Arizona in front of a capacity crowd of 7,391 at Maples Pavilion. The shot caps a six-point Cardinal comeback in the final 25 seconds—the Robinson three-pointer having been preceded by a Stanford possession in which Josh Childress made a three-point basket following a Lottich steal—and improves Stanford's record to 20-0. Courtside attendees included Jim Plunkett, Tiger Woods, and ABC broadcasters Brent Musberger and Dick Vitale.

11. *April 2, 2015, New York, NY: Stanford 66 – Miami 64 (OT) (2015 NIT Championship Game).* Chasson Randle hits two free throws with 3.4 seconds remaining in overtime to lead Stanford to its third-ever NIT championship at MSG with a 66-64 victory over Miami. Randle, who in the NIT semifinal win became Stanford's career scoring leader, scores a game-high 25 points, tallies 118 points during the five-game tournament, and is named Most Outstanding Player of the 2015 NIT. Stefan Nastic—who joined Randle on the All-NIT team—adds 11 points, and Anthony Brown contributes 9 points, 12 rebounds, and a last-second defensive gem that thwarted a potential last-second game-winning three-point basket by Miami.

12. *December 21, 2000, Oakland, CA: Stanford 84 – Duke 83 (Pete Newell Challenge).* Casey Jacobsen's 10-foot fall-away jumper with 3.6 seconds remaining caps a late Cardinal comeback as #3-ranked Stanford takes out #1-ranked Duke, 84-83, before 19,804 fans—the most ever to attend a college basketball game in California—at the Oakland Coliseum Arena. The Cardinal, which trailed by as many as 16 points in the first half and by 11 points with just four minutes remaining in the game, is propelled by Jacobsen's career-high-tying 26-point scoring night.

13. *February 4, 1988, Stanford, CA: Stanford 82 – Arizona 74.* Junior starters Todd Lichti (23 points) and Howard Wright (21 points) lead the way as Stanford scores the final ten points of the game and earns its first-ever win over a #1-ranked team in an 82-74 victory over the Arizona Wildcats before a capacity crowd of 7,500 at Maples Pavilion. The Cardinal, which had been 0-20 previously in games against #1-ranked opponents, scores the last ten points of the game after trailing 74-72 with five minutes remaining in the game.

14. *January 17, 1975, Stanford, CA: Stanford 64 – UCLA 60.* In the first of the two famed Miracle at Maples games—in which Stanford defeated two top-five-ranked teams on successive nights—senior center Rich Kelley scores 22 points and grabs 13 rebounds, junior forward Ed Schweitzer contributes 22 and 8 rebounds, and senior guard Mark Gilberg adds nine points as Stanford upsets #2-ranked UCLA before a standing-room-only crowd at Maples Pavilion. The win comes over a UCLA team that two months later would claim its eighth NCAA championship in ten seasons—the final year of the John Wooden era at UCLA.

15. *January 18, 1975, Stanford, CA: Stanford 67 – USC 66.* Twenty-four hours later, in a similarly packed and boisterous Maples Pavilion, Rich Kelley caps the finest weekend of his Stanford career with his finest all-around single-game performance. Kelley pours in 30 points, collects 15 rebounds, and makes all ten of his free throws—including four of four in the final minute with Stanford clinging to a one-possession lead—as Stanford edges #5-ranked USC, 67-66. Ed Schweitzer adds 19 points and 7 rebounds—making 9 of 14 shots—and freshman Jay Carter makes all five of his field-goal attempts as the Maples Pavilion fans, for a second consecutive night, stream on to the court at game's end in raucous celebration.

16. *January 9, 1997, Stanford, CA: Stanford 109 – UCLA 61.* Stanford hands UCLA the worst loss, as measured by margin of defeat, in Bruin history in a 109-61 Cardinal win at Maples Pavilion. The Cardinal race out to a 17-1 lead—aided in part by a trio of three-point baskets by Brevin Knight—and lead by 31 points at halftime. Knight paces the Cardinal in the win with 25 points, making 6 of his 7 three-point shot attempts. Stanford makes a school-record 15 three-pointers (in just 32 attempts), makes 59.1 of its field-goal attempts and holds the Bruins—an eventual Sweet 16 team in the NCAA Tournament that season—to just 36.7% field-goal shooting.

17. *January 1, 1938, Cleveland, OH: Stanford 92 – Duquesne 27.* Hank Luisetti—by 1938 renowned as arguably the best-ever basketball player even as he was still a Stanford undergraduate—has the second of his two great single-game performances on the East Coast, scoring an incredible 50 points in Stanford's 65-point New Year's Day victory over Duquesne University in a game played in Cleveland. Luisetti, a senior in 1937-38, in what would be the second of his two national player-of-the-year seasons, makes 23 baskets and 4 free throws.

18. *January 5, 1989, Stanford, CA: Stanford 83 – Arizona 78.* In a rematch of the 1988 classic at Maples Pavilion in which the Cardinal took down the #1-ranked Wildcats, Stanford falls behind #7-ranked Arizona 21-4 in the opening minutes and trails by 10 at halftime. The second half features an epic individual scoring duel between Todd Lichti and UA's Sean Elliott, who would finish with 35 and 34 points respectively. In the second half, Stanford storms back to take the lead—aided by 11 consecutive points from Lichti—and staves off a last-minute Arizona comeback attempt as Brian McSweeney makes three free throws in the final three seconds to ensure victory for Stanford.

19. *December 27, 1978, Stanford, CA: Stanford 75 – UCLA 72.* Outmatched on paper by #3-ranked UCLA, Stanford reprises its Miracle at Maples–era magic with a win over the Bruins. Jeff Ryan hits a jump shot in the final seconds to give Stanford a one-point lead, was fouled on the play, and—following his intentionally missed "and one" free-throw attempt—teammate Orlando Ward rebounds the ball and dunks it through the basket as Stanford upsets the Bruins, 75-72. Senior guard Wolfe Perry has one of the greatest Maples Pavilion performances in history, scoring a game-high 34 points and making 15 of 20 field-goal attempts, including 7 of 9 in the decisive second half.

20. *February 21, 1981, Stanford, CA: Stanford 74 – UCLA 72.* In the most shocking game of the 1980-81 Pac-10 season, three Cardinal freshmen score 53 of Stanford's 74 points as Stanford holds on in the final seconds to upset #10-ranked and Larry Brown–coached UCLA at Maples Pavilion. Guard Keith Jones scores a game-high 23 points, making 9 of 10 field-goal attempts and overwhelming Bruin guards Rod Foster and Michael Holton, who are returning starters from the Bruin team that had appeared in the NCAA championship game eleven months earlier. Fellow freshmen John Revelli (16 points) and Hans Wichary (14 points) provide inside scoring help to complement Jones's electric offense.

66 Stanford Basketball Game-Winning/Game-Saving Last-Second Shots Since World War II

Criterion: a made field goal or made free throw in the final seconds of regulation or an overtime period in a Stanford Basketball victory

1. *Dick Berlin, February 15, 1946, Stanford Pavilion, Stanford, CA.*
Game-winning layup, 10 seconds remaining.
Final score: Stanford 50 – USC 48.

2. *Bill Stephenson, January 28, 1949, Stanford Pavilion, Stanford, CA.*
Game-winning follow shot, five seconds remaining.
Final score: Stanford 50 – San Jose State 49.

3. *Ed Tucker, December 18, 1950, Cow Palace, San Francisco, CA.*
Game-winning layup, three seconds remaining.
Final score: Stanford 62 – Colorado 60.

4. *Ed Tucker, February 23, 1951, Stanford Pavilion, Stanford, CA.*
Game-winning free throws, two seconds remaining.
Final score: Stanford 73 – USC 71.

5. *Ron Tomsic, December 28, 1951, Municipal Auditorium, Kansas City, MO (Big Seven Tournament).*
Game-tying basket, three seconds remaining in regulation.
Final score: Stanford 103 – Iowa State 102 (OT).

6. *George Zaninovich, December 1, 1952, Stanford Pavilion, Stanford, CA.*
Game-tying tip-in, ten seconds remaining in regulation.
Final score: Stanford 74 – USF 73 (OT).

7. *Dave Epperson, December 1, 1952, Stanford Pavilion, Stanford, CA.*
Game-winning tip-in in the final seconds of overtime.
Final score: Stanford 74 – USF 73 (OT).

8. *Russ Lawler, December 27, 1954, Walsh Gymnasium, South Orange, NJ.*
Game-winning jump shot at the buzzer.
Final score: Stanford 65 – Seton Hall 63.

9. *Ron Tomsic, January 14, 1955, Harmon Gym, Berkeley, CA.*
Game-winning jump shot, one second remaining.
Final score: Stanford 59 – California 57.

10. *Bill Bond, March 10, 1956, Stanford Pavilion, Stanford, CA.*
Game-winning basket at the buzzer in overtime.
Final score: Stanford 70 – California 68 (OT).

11. *John Arrillaga, December 17, 1957, Cow Palace, San Francisco, CA.* Game-winning jump shot, three seconds remaining.
Final score: Stanford 50 – USF 49.

12. *Dick Haga, February 27, 1959, Stanford Pavilion, Stanford, CA.* Game-winning free throw, no time remaining.
Final score: Stanford 59 – Washington State 58.

13. *Tom Dose, March 3, 1962, Stanford Pavilion, Stanford, CA.* Game-winning hook shot, seven seconds remaining.
Final score: Stanford 63 – USC 62.

14. *Darrell Sutherland, March 10, 1962, Stanford Pavilion, Stanford, CA.* Game-winning free throws, seven seconds remaining.
Final score: Stanford 68 – USC 66.

15. *Hollis Moore, December 29, 1962, Sports Arena, Los Angeles, CA.* Game-tying layup at the buzzer in regulation.
Final score: Stanford 63 – Washington 62 (2OT).

16. *Tom Dose, March 2, 1963, Los Angeles State University Gymnasium, Los Angeles, CA.*
Game–winning layup, three seconds remaining.
Final score: Stanford 60 – USC 58.

17. *Clayton Raaka, December 23, 1963, Stanford Pavilion, Stanford, CA.* Game-tying tip-in, two seconds remaining in regulation.
Final score: Stanford 69 – Kansas 64 (OT).

18. *Kent Hinckley, February 24, 1964, Sports Arena, Los Angeles, CA.* Game-winning free throw, four seconds remaining.
Final score: Stanford 64 – USC 63.

19. *Jack Gilbert, December 3, 1964, San Jose Civic Auditorium, San Jose, CA.* Game-winning jump shot, four seconds remaining.
Final score: Stanford 61 – San Jose State 59.

20. *Gary Loveridge, February 5, 1965, MacArthur Court, Eugene, OR.* Game-winning jump shot, three seconds remaining.
Final score: Stanford 77 – Oregon 75.

21. *Mal McElwain, February 23, 1968, Stanford Pavilion, Stanford, CA.* Game-tying layup, two seconds remaining in regulation.
Final score: Stanford 70 – Oregon State 67 (OT).

22. *Mal McElwain, March 7, 1969, Maples Pavilion, Stanford, CA.* Game-tying jump shot, one second remaining in regulation.
Final score: Stanford 83 – California 79 (OT).

23. *Dennis O'Neill, January 16, 1970, Maples Pavilion, Stanford, CA.*
Game-winning free throws, one second remaining.
Final score:Stanford 73 – California 71.

24. *Mike Michel, February 7, 1970, Maples Pavilion, Stanford, CA.*
Game-winning jump shot, one second remaining.
Final score: Stanford 71 – Oregon State 69.

25. *Claude Terry, February 4, 1972, Maples Pavilion, Stanford, CA.*
Game-tying free throw, five seconds remaining in the first overtime.
Final score: Stanford 93 – California 86 (3 OT).

26. *Scott Trobbe, December 3, 1973, Maples Pavilion, Stanford, CA.*
Game-winning tip-in, seven seconds remaining in overtime.
Final score: Stanford 63 – USF 61 (OT).

27. *Ed Schweitzer, February 22, 1975, Maples Pavilion, Stanford, CA.*
Game-winning layup, five seconds remaining.
Final score: Stanford 71 – Oregon 70.

28. *Tim Patterson, December 22, 1975, Maples Pavilion, Stanford, CA.*
Game-winning tip-in, one second remaining.
Final score: Stanford 63 – Cal Poly Pomona 61.

29. *Wolfe Perry, January 31, 1976, Stan Sheriff Center, Honolulu, HI.*
Game-winning shot, one second remaining.
Final score: Stanford 66 – Hawaii 65.

30. *Mark Pitchford, November 26, 1977, Maples Pavilion, Stanford, CA.*
Game-winning jump shot, six seconds remaining in overtime.
Final score: Stanford 81 – San Jose State 80 (OT).

31. *Jeff McHugh, November 30, 1977, Toso Pavilion, Santa Clara, CA.*
Game-winning tip-in, one second remaining.
Final score: Stanford 69 – Santa Clara 67.

32. *Jeff Ryan, December 27, 1978, Maples Pavilion, Stanford, CA.*
Game-winning jump shot, two seconds remaining.
Final score: Stanford 75 – UCLA 72.

33. *Jeff Ryan, December 29, 1978, San Diego Sports Arena, San Diego, CA.*
Game-winning tip-in, five seconds remaining.
Final score: Stanford 85 – San Diego State 84.

34. *Doug Marty, February 6, 1981, Maples Pavilion, Stanford, CA.*
Game-winning driving layup, two seconds remaining.
Final score: Stanford 80 – Oregon 79.

35. *John Revelli, February 5, 1982, McArthur Court, Eugene, OR.*
Game-winning free throw, four seconds remaining.
Final score: Stanford 79 – Oregon 76.

36. *Eric Reveno, December 20, 1986, Maples Pavilion, Stanford, CA.*
Game-winning bank shot, two seconds remaining.
Final score: Stanford 73 – Oregon State 71.

37. *Howard Wright, February 26, 1987, Maples Pavilion, Stanford, CA.*
Game-winning jump shot, one second remaining.
Final score: Stanford 55 – Arizona 53.

38. *Todd Lichti, December 23, 1987, Maples Pavilion, Stanford, CA.*
Game-tying three-point basket, three seconds remaining in the first overtime.
Final score: Stanford 116 – UCLA 110 (2 OT).

39. *Greg Butler, January 2, 1988, Maples Pavilion, Stanford, CA.*
Game-tying jump shot, 12 seconds remaining in regulation.
Final score: Stanford 83 – Seattle Pacific 78 (OT).

40. *Todd Lichti, January 12, 1989, Hec Edmundson Pavilion, Seattle, WA.*
Game-winning bank shot, two seconds remaining.
Final score: Stanford 71 – Washington 69.

41. *Kenny Ammann, January 7, 1990, Maples Pavilion, Stanford, CA.*
Game-winning baseline jump shot at the buzzer.
Final score: Stanford 58 – Oregon 56.

42. *Jim Morgan, December 28, 1992, Maples Pavilion, Stanford, CA.*
Game-winning bank shot at the buzzer.
Final score: Stanford 57 – American University 56.

43. *Brevin Knight, January 6, 1994, Maples Pavilion, Stanford, CA.*
Game-winning jump shot at the buzzer.
Final score: Stanford 67 – Washington 65.

44. *Brevin Knight, February 3, 1994, MacArthur Court, Eugene, OR.*
Game-winning driving bank shot, one second remaining.
Final score: Stanford 69 – Oregon 67.

45. *Brevin Knight, December 22, 1996, Continental Airlines Arena, East Rutherford, NJ.*
Game-winning free throws, three seconds remaining in overtime.
Final score: Stanford 83 – Seton Hall 81 (OT).

46. *Peter Sauer, March 6, 1997, Maples Pavilion, Stanford, CA.*
Game-winning baseline jump shot, six seconds remaining.
Final score: Stanford 81 – Arizona 80.

47. *Mark Madsen, December 6, 1997, the Pond Arena, Anaheim, CA (John Wooden Classic).*
Game-winning tip-in, nine seconds remaining.
Final score: Stanford 76 – Georgia 74.

48. *Kris Weems, January 24, 1998, Hec Edmundson Pavilion, Seattle, WA.*
Game-winning, top-of-the-key jump shot at the buzzer.
Final score: Stanford 74 – Washington 72.

49. *Jarron Collins, November 11, 1999, Madison Sqaure Garden, New York, NY (Coaches vs. Cancer Tournamant).*
Game-tying basket, three seconds remaining in regulation.
Final score: Stanford 80 – Duke 79 (OT).

50. *Casey Jacobsen, December 21, 2000, Oakland Coliseum Arena, Oakland, CA. (Pete Newell Challenge).*
Game-winning bank shot, three seconds remaining.
Final score: Stanford 84 – Duke 83.

51. *Tony Giovacchini, February 7, 2002, Maples Pavilion, Stanford, CA.*
Game-tying three-point basket, four seconds remaining in regulation.
Final score: Stanford 90 – Oregon 87 (OT).

52. *Josh Childress, January 8, 2004, Wells Fargo Arena, Tempe, AZ.*
Game-winning rebound basket, nine seconds remaining.
Final score: Stanford 63 – Arizona State 62.

53. *Nick Robinson, February 7, 2004, Maples Pavilion, Stanford, CA.*
Game-winning, 35-foot, three-point basket at the buzzer.
Final score: Stanford 80 – Arizona 77.

54. *Matt Lottich, March 4, 2004, Beasley Coliseum, Pullman, WA.*
Game-winning, 26-foot, three-point basket at the buzzer.
Final score: Stanford 63 – Washington State 61.

55. *Chris Hernandez, January 29, 2006, Maples Pavilion, Stanford, CA.*
Game-tying free throws, 0.2 seconds remaining in regulation:
Final score: Stanford 76 – Washington 67 (OT).

56. *Anthony Goods, February 25, 2006, Beasley Coliseum, Pullman, WA.*
Game-winning tip-in, four seconds remaining.
Final score: Stanford 39 – Washington State 37.

57. *Chris Hernandez, February 2, 2006, McArthur Court, Eugene, OR.*
Game-winning jump shot, 11 seconds remaining:
Final score: Stanford 58 – Oregon 57.

58. *Chris Hernandez, March 2, 2006, Maples Pavilion, Stanford, CA.*
Game-winning free throws, four seconds remaining:
Final score: Stanford 58 – USC 56.

59. *Lawrence Hill, January 7, 2007, John Paul Jones Arena, Charlottesville, VA.*
Game-winning floater, one second remaining.
Final score: Stanford 76 – Virginia 75.

60. *Anthony Goods, January 13, 2007, Maples Pavilion, Stanford, CA.*
Game-winning three-point basket, three seconds remaining in overtime.
Final score: Stanford 71– Washington State 68 (OT).

61. *Robin Lopez, March 22, 2008, Honda Center, Anaheim, CA (NCAA Tournament, South Region, Second-round).*
Game-tying free throw, nine seconds remaining in regulation:
Final score: Stanford 82 – Marquette 81 (OT).

62. *Brook Lopez, March 22, 2008, Honda Center, Anaheim, CA (NCAA Tournament, South Region, Second-round).*
Game-winning baseline leaner, two seconds remaining in overtime.
Final score: Stanford 82 – Marquette 81 (OT).

63. *Jeremy Green, February 11, 2010, Maples Pavilion, Stanford, CA.*
Game-winning jump shot, four seconds remaining.
Final score: Stanford 60 – Washington State 58.

64. *Chasson Randle, January 4, 2015, Maples Pavilion, Stanford, CA.*
Game-tying driving layup, two seconds remaining in regulation.
Final score: Stanford 68 – Washington 60 (OT).

65. *Chasson Randle, March 11, 2015, MGM Garden Arena, Las Vegas, NV (2015 Pac-12 Tournament).*
Game-winning three-point basket, 2.4 seconds remaining.
Final score: Stanford 71 – Washington 69.

66. *Chasson Randle, April 2, 2015, Madison Square Garden, New York, NY (2015 National Invitation Tournament, Championship Game).*
Game-tying and game-winning free throws, 3.4 seconds remaining in overtime.
Final score: Stanford 66 – Miami 64 (OT).

All-Time Defensive Team

Bill Cowden – G
John Hendry – F
Hollis Moore – G/F
Andrew Vlahov – F
Marcus Lollie – G
Darren Allaway – F
Brevin Knight – G
Arthur Lee – G
Kris Weems – G
Jason Collins – C
Curtis Borchardt – C
Justin Davis – F
Nick Robinson – F
Fred Washington – G
Taj Finger – F
Robin Lopez – C
Josh Huestis – F
Anthony Brown – G

Defensive Players of the Century

Guidelines for selection: one or more times selected as Stanford's Best Defensive Player at the end of a season, selection to the conference all-defensive team, repeated media references to the player's defensive skill, and/or author's direct observation of the player.

Josh Huestis
Robin Lopez
Brevin Knight

Best "Senior Day" (Home Finale) Games

1. *February 27, 1999.* Senior starters Arthur Lee, Kris Weems, Tim Young, and Peter Sauer, as well as key reserve Mark Seaton, make their last-ever Maples Pavilion appearance a memorable one as #6-ranked Stanford crushes #7-ranked Arizona, 98-83, clinching Stanford's first-ever Pac-10 title. Following the final buzzer, on the fan-filled and band-filled floor, Mike Montgomery and the team cut down the nets.

2. *February 28, 2004.* Stanford crushes Oregon 76-55, clinches the Pac-10 title for the fourth time in six seasons and exits February 2004 as the nation's #1-ranked team with a perfect 25-0 record. Seniors Matt Lottich, Justin Davis, and Joe Kirchofer, along with Pac-10 Player of the Year Josh Childress, make their final Maples Pavilion appearances.

3. *March 12, 1938.* Senior guard, captain and three-time All-American Hank Luisetti scores 26 points in his final college game, a 59-51 win over Oregon in the clinching game of the best-of-three series for the Pacific Coast Conference championship. Luisetti's Senior Day finale gives him a final career scoring total of 1,596 points (in only three years of varsity play), at the time the most points ever scored by a college player.

4. *March 2, 1989.* Completing the first-ever undefeated home season at Maples Pavilion by a Stanford Basketball team, the Cardinal defeats USC by the score of 74-65. All six graduating seniors score in the game: Todd Lichti (22 points), Howard Wright (19 points), Scott Meinert (11 points), Eric Reveno (8 points), Terry Taylor (4 points), and Bryan McSweeney (2 points). All told, the seniors tally 66 of the 74 Stanford points scored in the game.

5. *March 5, 2005.* Needing a win to solidify its uncertain hopes for an NCAA bid, Stanford shocks the #10-ranked, Brandon Roy and Nate Robinson–led Washington Huskies 77-67, denying the Huskies a share of the Pac-10 title. Junior center Matt Haryasz scores a career-high 24 points and junior Jason Haas scores a career-best 18 points—including 13 of 14 from the free-throw line—to enable Stanford seniors Nick Robinson and Rob Little to end their Maples Pavilion careers in style.

6. *March 8, 2014.* In a game Stanford needs to keep alive its NCAA Tournament hopes, the Cardinal—nursing a one-point lead—forces a Utah turnover in the final seconds to secure a 61-60 Stanford victory over the Utes. It is the final Maples Pavilion game for six seniors: Dwight Powell, Josh Huestis, Aaron Bright, John Gage, Andy Brown, and Robbie Lemons, whose collective career scoring total of 4,370 points is the fourth highest by a senior class in the first 100 years of Stanford Basketball.

7. *February 22, 1963.* Against a UCLA team that Stanford would end up tying for the conference championship, junior center Tom Dose has one of the greatest games in Stanford Basketball history, scoring 35 points in leading Stanford to a thrilling 73-69 overtime victory over coach John Wooden's Bruin team. All-conference guard and senior Don Clemetson makes two key free throws with 27 seconds remaining in overtime to ensure victory for Stanford, which had seniors Darryl Sutherland and Bob Sommers also conclude their Stanford Pavilion careers in the win.

8. *March 1, 1980.* Kim Belton explodes for a career-high 41 points in his final Maples Pavilion appearance, a 93-91 overtime win over USC. The game also marks the final home appearances of seniors Doug Barnes, Larry Harris, Daryle Morgan, and Tom Schmalzreid. Belton, a four-year starter and a multiyear All-Conference honoree, finishes his Stanford career as the Cardinal's all-time leading scorer (1,516 points) and rebounder (955 rebounds).

9. *March 10, 1956.* Senior captain and prolific-scoring guard George Selleck, together with fellow senior starters Barry Brown and Bill Flanders, pull out a 70-68 overtime win over California, giving Stanford a final record of 18-6—its best season winning percentage (.750) since the 1941-42 NCAA championship season. Brown scores 19 points and Selleck contributes 16 points, but it is a basket at the buzzer by junior Bill Bond—disputed by Cal but to no avail—that wins the game for Stanford.

10. *March 8, 1997.* In the final Maples Pavilion game of his glorious Stanford career, Brevin Knight scores 21 points as the #23-ranked Cardinal completes its first undefeated season at home in eight years, routing Arizona State 86-63. Stanford's home won-loss record during Knight's final three years, 38-3, is the best consecutive three-year won-loss mark at home in program history. The game also marks the final Maples Pavilion appearance of senior Rich Jackson, who also was voted the team's most inspirational player that season.

11. *March 14, 1992.* At a time when there was no Pac-10 Tournament, and needing a win to solidify its NCAA Tournament bid chances, Stanford senior Adam Keefe has a Senior Day to remember, scoring 34 points on 15-of-25 field-goal shooting and grabbing 14 rebounds to lead the Cardinal to a 76-56 win over Oregon State. After a three-year absence, Stanford does earn a bid to the 1992 NCAA Tournament and six days later comes within two possessions of upsetting Robert Horry and Latrell Sprewell-led Alabama.

12. *March 10, 1962.* In the final home game of senior forward and All-Pac-8 first-teamer John Windsor's Stanford career, junior guard Darrell Sutherland hits two free throws with seven seconds to play to break a 66-66 tie and give Stanford not only a two-point victory but also a perfect record at home and its highest conference finish (second) in seven seasons. Other seniors making their final Stanford Pavilion appearances that day: Phil Kelly, Mike Ledgerwood, Jim Bryan, Bill Elfving, and Fred Pegelow.

13. *March 6, 1959.* For the first time in 18 seasons dating back to 1940-41, Stanford completes an undefeated season (11-0) of home games at the Stanford Pavilion by defeating Oregon State 71-54, as senior co-captain and center Dick Haga scores a career-high 25 points, fellow senior Paul Neumann scores 21 points and junior John Arrillaga adds 10 points. Other seniors playing their final home game are Chris Burford and Doug Warren.

14. *March 1, 2008.* In a generous move, coach Trent Johnson does what no Stanford coach has ever done, starting as many as three seniors—Taj Finger, Peter Prowitt, and Kenny Brown—who were not regular starters. Stanford falls behind early, but behind the inspirational play of Finger—who hits a game-tying three-pointer with four minutes remaining, just his fifth-ever three-point basket—the #8-ranked Cardinal edges #22-ranked Washington State, 60-53, to improve its record to 24-4.

15. *March 3, 1984.* In the final Maples Pavilion game for a 1983-84 senior class that included Keith Jones, John Revelli, Hans Wichary, John Platz, and Rick Lewis, Stanford defeats Arizona State 74-66 for its 19th win of the 1983-84 season—the most wins by a Stanford team in 32 years. Revelli and Jones conclude their careers with the second and fourth highest career scoring totals in Stanford Basketball history.

16. *March 3, 1977.* In his final Maples Pavilion appearance, guard Mike Bratz scores a game-high 24 points—becoming only the second Stanford player to score 500-or-more points in a season—as the Cardinal blasts California 85-66. The game is memorable for another reason: Stanford freshman and future two-time tennis All-American Peter Rennert is selected as the halftime "one shot from midcourt to win $1,400" contestant, and—with an underhanded fling of the ball—swishes the 45-foot shot!

17. *February 25, 1955.* Senior co-captains and three-year starters Ron Tomsic and Russ Lawler, the two highest scorers on the team, lead Stanford to its 15th win and second-highest scoring game of the year in a 90-84 victory over California. Other seniors making their final Stanford Pavilion appearance are Leo Schwaiger and Bill Turner. Stanford's first-year head coach that game is Howie Dallmar, just thirteen years removed from being the Most Outstanding Player of the 1942 NCAA Tournament.

18. *March 6, 1964.* Having scored a Stanford Pavilion-record 42 points in the previous game, senior All-American Tom Dose and his senior teammates Hollis Moore and Lew Shupe end their Stanford careers as winners in a 61-59 overtime win over California. Dose hits two key free throws in the final minute of overtime to lead Stanford to victory. Supplementing Dose's 13 points were junior guard Kent Hinckley (16 points) and sophomore forward Bob Bedell (18 points).

19. *March 6, 1942.* Led by senior All-American Jim Pollard who scores a game-high 14 points, Stanford completes a 10-2 regular season home slate by winning its fourth game in four tries against rival California—Stanford's first-ever single-season sweep of the Golden Bears—by a score of 59-49. Within a month, Stanford would sweep through the NCAA Tournament and win the NCAA title, finishing with a 28-4 record.

20. *March 3, 2013.* Reserve guard Gabriel Harris—the first Cardinal player signed by coach Johnny Dawkins and Stanford's lone senior in 2013—goes for a career-high 14 points in his final Maples appearance in an 84-66 win over Utah. Coming off the bench and playing 23 minutes, Harris makes 6 of 7 shots, grabs a career-high seven rebounds, adds two steals, and contributes an assist in the win.

All "Pre-Television Era" Team (1914–1952)

Guidelines for inclusion on the list:
(A) An All-Conference selection two or more times, or
(B) An All-Conference selection one time, plus at least one of the following:
(i) selected 1st, 2nd, or 3rd team All-American one or more times, or
(ii) was a starter on the 1941-42 (or 1936-37) top-rated Stanford teams, or
(iii) was a member of the U.S. Olympic Basketball team, or
(C) Finished first or second in the conference in scoring at least once.

C.E. "Swede" Righter – C
Harlow Rothert – F
Bryan "Dinty" Moore – G
Hank Luisetti – F
Jack Calderwood – G
Art Stoefen – C
Don Burness – F
Bill Cowden – G
Howie Dallmar – G
Jim Pollard – F
Ed Voss – C
John "Babe" Higgins – G
Dave Davidson – F
George Yardley – C
Sebron "Ed" Tucker – F
Jim Ramstead – C
Jim Walsh – G/F

Player of the Era: Hank Luisetti

All "Vinyl Album Era" Team (1953–1984)

Guidelines for inclusion on the list:
(A) An All-Conference selection two or more times, or
(B) An All-Conference selection one time, plus at least one of the following:
(i) selected 1st, 2nd, 3rd team or honorable mention All-American at least once, or
(ii) was among the top 15 Stanford players in career "per-game" scoring average, rebounding average or assists average as of 2014-15, or
(C) Finished first or second in the conference in scoring at least once.

Ron Tomsic – G
Russ Lawler – C
George Selleck – G
Paul Neumann – G
John Arrillaga – F
John Windsor – F
Tom Dose – C
Bob Bedell – F
Art Harris – G/F
Don Griffin – G
Claude Terry – G
Rich Kelley – C
Ed Schweitzer – F
Mike Bratz – G
Kimberly Belton – F
Keith Jones – G
John Revelli – C

Player of the Era: Rich Kelley

All "Computer & Internet Era" Team (1985–2015)

Guidelines for inclusion on the list:
(A) An All-Conference selection two or more times, or
(B) An All-Conference selection one time, plus at least one of the following:
(i) selected 1st, 2nd, 3rd team or honorable mention All-American at least once, or
(ii) selected to an NCAA Tournament All-Regional or All-Final-Four team at least once, or
(iii) finished first or second in the conference in scoring at least once.

Todd Lichti – G
Howard Wright – F
Adam Keefe – F/C
Dion Cross – G
Brevin Knight – G
Arthur Lee – G
Mark Madsen – F
Jarron Collins – F
Jason Collins – C
Casey Jacobsen – G
Curtis Borchardt – C
Josh Childress – F
Chris Hernandez – G
Brook Lopez – C
Landry Fields – F
Dwight Powell – F
Chasson Randle – G

Player of the Era: Brevin Knight

End notes

[1] Don Liebendorfer, *The Color of Life Is Red: A History of Stanford Athletics, 1892–1972* (Palo Alto, CA: National Press, 1972), 157.

[2] Shelly N. Pierce, "The Basketball Season Success," *Stanford Illustrated Review* 22, no. 7 (April, 1921): 270.

[3] "California Loses Second Contest to Cardinal Quintet," *The Stanford Daily* 59, no. 10, (February 28, 1921): 3.

[4] Liebendorfer, 161.

[5] Ibid.

[6] Ibid., 162.

[7] Ibid.

[8] Ibid., 165.

[9] Ibid., 166.

[10] Ibid., 168.

[11] Ron Fimrite, "He Changed a Game Singlehandedly," *Sports Illustrated* (December 15, 1975).

[12] Liebendorfer, 168.

[13] Fimrite.

[14] Les Woodcock, "With One Hand Behind His Back," *Sports Illustrated* (December 9, 1957).

[15] Liebendorfer, 168-169.

[16] Tom FitzGerald, "The Same Game, A Different Time: Stanford's 1942 Champs Defined the Word 'Team,'" *San Francisco Chronicle* (March 27, 1998).

[17] Dwight Chapin, "Survivors Recall Stanford's Magical Title Run of 1942," *San Francisco Examiner* (March 27, 1998).

[18] FitzGerald.

[19] Liebendorfer, 171-172.

[20] Ibid., 176.

[21] Ibid., 176.

[22] Ibid., 182.

[23] Dave Robinson, "Shuffling the Cards: Changing Times," *The Stanford Daily* 166, no. 60: 5.

[24] Vlae Kershner, "Maples Miracle: Cards Down UCLA, USC," ibid.

[25] William F. Reed, "Cardinal Virtues," *Sports Illustrated* (January 16, 1989).